501
BENTO
BOX LUNCHES

Graffito Books
32 Great Sutton Street
Clerkenwell
London
EC1V 0NB
UK

www.graffitobooks.com

Printed in Portugal

ISBN: 978 0 9553398 5 1
British Library cataloguing-in-publication data
A catalogue record of this book is available at the British Library

GRAFFITO

501 UNIQUE RECIPES FOR BRILLIANT BENTO

CONTENTS

BENTO BASICS

by AMORETTE DYE

GETTING STARTED

Decide if you want your lunch to be cute, artistic, healthy or colourful. Don't worry about turning out aesthetically breathtaking bentos right away. You can hone presentation skills with time. Experiment with slicing hard-boiled eggs, wrapping rolls with lunch meat, and arranging vegetables. Don't forget to have fun.

A bento can be anything you want it to be; a strictly traditional Japanese-style lunch, a darling calorie-controlled selection, or a quick and easy arrangement of last night's leftovers. Be careful about food safety; if you won't be able to refrigerate your bento, make sure to only pack foods that will be safe at room temperature.
Try to pack cooked foods after they've cooled; hot-packed foods can spoil or steam other ingredients when sealed in a bento box. Make sure that any designs you make are firmly anchored in place, and that you transport them as flat as possible so that you don't have any 'abstract art' when you open your box at lunchtime.

FUNDAMENTALS

For authenticity, many purists advise the 3:2:1 ratio: three parts starches, two parts veggies, and one part protein. It's a practical guideline to follow, but not a rule. Bento can be beautiful, but don't lose sight of the fact that it's a boxed lunch. The majority of people who make bento don't go for big, intricate kyaraben every single day; the time and effort involved mean more when it's a special treat.

BENTO BOXES

Japanese bento boxes vary from traditional, ornate lacquerware, used in restaurants and taken on flower-viewing picnics, to disposable polystyrene ekiben boxes sold in train stations and convenience stores. Sizes can vary from large multi-serving boxes to small, cute character pieces intended for children. Pay attention to the size you're buying; boxes are often intended for either adult or child-sized portions.

Most bento boxes available today are inexpensive and made of different grades of plastic. Melamine tiffins and other stacked styles are widely available; the 'Mr. Bento' design is very popular. The 'Laptop Lunch', a sort of Westernized bento, is rapidly gaining popularity.

Not all boxes are microwave and dishwasher-safe, so be sure you know what you're buying. Many boxes will have easily-understood international symbols on the undersides, but some boxes only have instructions in Japanese or Chinese.

Bento boxes are widely available from online sellers, many of which offer their wares shipped directly from Japan. Websites like jlist.com and ichibankanusa.com offer a good selection. Discount stores often sell bento boxes without recognizing them for what they are.

Don't forget you can use ordinary food storage containers for bento. These are more readily available, usually less expensive, and nearly always microwave and dishwasher-safe.

EQUIPMENT

Far and above, the most essential bento item is your own imagination. Let it run wild.

A rice cooker is a good investment. You don't need a big one; a six-cup cooker works well, and most cookers come with measuring cups and rice paddles. You'll also need some good, sharp paring knives and a reliable cutting surface. Choose a cutting surface that won't become slippery with use. It is a good idea to keep an x-acto blade and a pair of manicure scissors exclusively for bento use; they're wonderful for precision cutting. Decorative paper-punches also work well.

Cookie cutters come in a wide variety of shapes and are very handy. Vegetable cutters can be found online or in gourmet cookery stores; they're typically longer than cookie cutters, with a cylindrical top that makes it easy to press into a thick, fibrous slice. For more intricate work, look for tiny gum-paste or aspic cutters, usually sold in shape-themed sets. You can also

improvise; a drinking straw can be used to cut small circles out of cheeses and hard-boiled egg slices.

Many bentos are subdivided with small paper cups or pieces of plastic 'sushi grass'. These are commonly available in Asian grocery stores, but you'll find a much wider variety online. Some paper cups have a plastic lining and are especially good for fruits and other moisture-rich foods. You can also use paper cupcake liners or washable silicone cupcake-cups, which are available in a rainbow of colours. The silicone cups are also handy for dyeing veggies and hard-boiled egg whites;

they can be pinched closed to allow rinsewater to drain, without losing the contents of the cup.

Search party supply stores and online vendors for cute and festive food picks. Toothpicks are useful both to spear foods and as tiny paintbrushes for intricate work; flexible plastic picks are especially good for painting with food colour. Liquid food colouring is now widely available in primary and neon colored sets; it's fun to experiment with a couple of drops in the rice-cooker water.

Other bento items include egg molds, which are used to form shelled hard-boiled eggs into shapes such as cars, hearts, stars, and bunnies. These eggs can then be added to the bento as-is or dyed any color you like. Tiny plastic bottles for sauce often come in round or fish shapes, and are normally used for soy sauce or lemon juice. They're available in many Asian grocery stores and can be found in fun shapes online. You can even find cutters to turn sausages into tulips, cute little shakers for seasonings, and little upside-down cups to hide special tidbits.

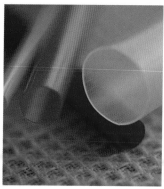

A lot of people have success with preparing batches of bento-friendly foods ahead of time and freezing them in single-serving portions; these can be popped into a bento box easily when you're in a hurry. Some wonderful techniques and recipes are available at lunchinabox.net.

A standard bento lunch shouldn't take more than half an hour to prepare. More elaborate kyaraben can take more time, so plan accordingly. If you have a design idea in your head, take time to develop it. You can print out photos or sketch out what you want to help solidify your plan; designs can be traced on wax paper and cut out with a sharp knife or x-acto blade.

Don't feel pressured to try and create beautiful kyaraben every single day, because it's not practical. Do it when the creative mood strikes, and think of it as a treat.

TRADITIONAL FOODS

Try out some traditional Japanese foods in your lunch, such as umeboshi (pickled plums) and onigiri (rice balls, pressed by hand or with a mold, with tasty fillings).

Kamaboko, pureed white fish sold in sliceable logs, is often made with a design running through it and can make a beautiful addition to your bento. Browse Asian grocery stores for items that appeal to you, and use bento-making as a learning experience.

TECHNIQUES

If you're just starting out, try hard-boiled egg-moulds to shape bunnies, stars, and hearts. Use cookie cutters to cut shapes from bread, cheese and vegetables. Print out or draw pictures and designs that appeal to you, and see if you can emulate them with food. Add a few drops of food-colouring to rice-cooker water to make pink rice-balls or a blue background for sky. You can also colour hard-boiled egg white by immersing cut pieces in food cups containing a few drops of color. This can produce really striking results.

Keep the size of your box in mind and make sure everything will fit. As you gain confidence, try your hand at cutting more intricate designs from nori or fruit-roll snacks. Try cutting designs freehand with a sharp paring knife or x-acto blade. Painting with food colours using a flexible plastic toothpick can also produce interesting and original designs.

Make sure items stay in place by using filler items (such as nuts, dried fruit, dry cereal or shelled edamame) to keep larger objects packed in tightly. If you're making a design on top of a rice background, anchor certain pieces in at an angle to hold the rest in place. Once you have your bento packed, give it a gentle experimental shake to see what happens. If the contents move around, you may need to add some filler. Keep in mind whether or not you're going to be able to refrigerate the bento, and fill accordingly. Some bento boxes are stacked with easy to use handles, others come in handy zippered cases. Standard bento boxes can be held together with elastic 'bento bands' and carried in lunchbags, special drawstring 'bento bags', purses, or backpacks. A convenient way to transport a bento is the furoshiki, a bandana-type cloth that wraps around the box in any number of pretty configurations. You can use any bandana or cloth of comparable size to do this. It doubles as a tablecloth when you're eating.

ART BENTO

GOOSE BENTO

1 cup long-grain white rice, cooked and tinted sky-blue (1 drop blue food color); 1 cup cooked and cooled couscous; 1 yellow 'pear cherry' tomato; 4 Baby Bella portabello mushrooms; 1/3 cup apple or pear sauce, non-chunky; blue food color; 1 generous handful green beans, ends trimmed; black decorating gel; 1 sheet of nori; 3 or 4 uncooked yam soba noodles; flexible plastic toothpicks. 1-tier bento box.

Using rice paddle, press blue rice into upper half of bento tier; fill in bottom half with cooked couscous. Tint apple or pear sauce with two drops of blue food color. Stir well and spread over most of couscous, leaving narrow shoreline. This is the pond. Split green beans lengthwise (French-cut) to form marsh grasses. Arrange around sides and bottom of the pond. Break soba noodles into short sticks; arrange them among green beans as reeds.

Work with contours and shading of mushrooms to carve bodies, wings and tails of geese. Assemble geese on cutting board then move onto rice. Wings of the flying goose are formed from cuts of mushroom, one draped over the goose's side and another stuck, in a perpendicular manner, into rice. Use nail scissors to cut necks and heads of geese from nori. Add to box. Use scraps of white mushroom-flesh as white feather-flashes on heads. With flexible plastic toothpicks, paint dabs of black gel over the nori to form eyes and beaks. Slice narrow end off the cherry tomato and position cut-side down over rice to serve as the sun.

GUITAR BENTO

1 cup cooked red rice; 1 slice fresh mozzarella cheese; 1 chunk peeled apple; 3 drops neon food color; lemon juice; black cake-decorating gel; 2 or 3 longish pieces canned bamboo shoots; 1 minneola or orange; 1 gel cup fruit snack; 1 small star-shaped aspic-cutter. 1-tier bento box.

Pack rice into bottom of box with rice paddle sprayed with non-stick cooking spray. Take apple and carve out body of guitar. Brush with lemon juice and dunk into blue-tinted water. Let sit for 5 mins. Blot dry with paper towels. Arrange on rice in the lower-left. Cut bamboo shoot pieces to make neck of guitar. Transfer onto rice. Cut piece of mozzarella for front of guitar, and three smaller pieces to sit on top. Arrange in proper places.

Using small amount of black decorating gel on tip of flexible toothpick, draw in frets and other details. Following a photo will help, and gel rather than coloring keeps tint from running on bamboo shoots.

Use aspic cutter to cut ten stars from remaining mozzarella and arrange around guitar. They help set off the brightness of the rice and the blue of the guitar-body. Serve with minneola and gel cup.

1 cup cooked rice, tinted green (1 drop green food color); 1/4 cup May Ploy green curry paste; 1 cup coconut milk; 1 lb diced chicken breast; 1 green bell pepper; 1/2 cup bamboo shoots; 1/2 onion; 1 cup pineapple chunks; 1/2 cup pineapple juice; 1 slice swiss cheese; 1 slice cheddar cheese; 6 mini carrot sticks; 4 mini frozen egg rolls; 1 tbsp corn starch; 1 sheet nori. 1-tier bento box with side-dish cup.

Cook Jungle Curry: Stir-fry May Ploy green curry paste in 1/2 cup coconut milk until fragrant. Add another 1/2 cup coconut milk and 1 lb diced chicken breast. Heat through until chicken is cooked. Cut green bell pepper into quarters and set 1 quarter aside. Dice remaining pepper. Add this, bamboo shoots, diced white onion, pineapple chunks and pineapple juice to the pan. Cook until bell pepper turns bright green. Thicken with corn starch.

Place the side-dish cup into your container. Fill the bottom of the main container with Jungle Curry. Wet your

PIRATE BENTO

1 cup cooked white rice; 3 mushrooms, 1 zucchini; 1 piece broccoli; 1 green bell pepper; 5 small carrots; 1 sheet nori; tilapia (or other white fish); serving angel-hair pasta; 1/2 lemon; 1 clove garlic; butter; lemon-pepper seasoning. 2-tier bento box.

Fill half of one tier with rice. Stir-fry sliced mushroom, sliced zucchini, one slivered carrot and slivered broccoli in a little oil and minced garlic. Season with salt and pepper. Place in the other half of first tier. Slice the green pepper into a hat shape; cut carrot slivers

to decorate the hat. With a pair of scissors, cut the nori into an eye, eye patch and mouth; arrange on rice.

Grill tilapia and place the fish to one side of the second tier. Cook angel hair pasta. Drain. In a large pan, melt butter over medium heat. Add fresh minced garlic, then pasta. Squeeze lemon and sprinkle pasta with the juice. Place in the remaining space in the box. Sprinkle the pasta with lemon-pepper seasoning. Cut the remaining carrots into bone shapes. Using a pairing knife, cut a skull out of the bell pepper. Place a piece of nori underneath to give the skull depth.

hands and form 2 monkey shaped heads with the cooked rice – arrange inside container on top of curry.

Cut remaining green bell pepper into slices. Place in gaps between monkey heads. Using a small star-shaped cookie cutter, cut small cheddar stars, scatter on peppers. Cut swiss cheese and nori into circles to form the monkey eyes and nori into nose and mouth shapes. Place on faces. Cook egg rolls according to instructions and arrange with carrot sticks in side-dish.

POTATO HEAD BENTO

Red chili tortilla; 2 slices swiss cheese; 3 slices salami; spicy mustard; bell pepper; sprig of cilantro; red bell pepper; 1/2 baked potato; 1/4 cup shredded white cheddar cheese; 1/4 cup shredded yellow cheddar cheese; 4 cherry tomatoes; 10 carrot sticks; 1 sirloin steak; pepper. 2-tier bento box.

Make a flat-shaped wrap with the tortilla, 1 slice swiss cheese, salami, mustard and sliced bell pepper. Place in the top tier. Fill remaining space with cilantro and red bell pepper. Cut cheese flowers from swiss cheese slice using mini cookie cutter, place on wrap. Cut holes into skin of baked potato to form eyes and a mouth. Place in other tier. Arrange nine carrot sticks, sliced steak and tomatoes next to the potato head. Use shredded cheese as hair for potato man. Slice swiss cheese for teeth and use a piece of tomato for tongue. Cut carrot into tear-drop for nose. Use black pepper to finish the eyes.

FISHIES BENTO

1/2 cup cooked rice; 1 carrot; 1 sheet nori; 1 ocean stick (imitation crab meat); onion leaves; 2 eggs; black sesame seeds. 1-tier bento box.

Whisk 2 eggs; make thin omelette. Cut strip from edge and set aside, place omelette on bottom of box. Layer rice on top. Steam carrot, cut into fish shapes. Add nori eyes. Slice imitation crab meat into strips; arrange in coral shape. Add onion leaves as seaweed. Cut air bubbles from omelette strip, sprinkle sesame seeds as sand.

MARIE ANTOINETTE BENTO

1 cup long-grain rice, tinted pink; 1 small Okinawan sweet potato, baked, contents scooped out, mashed; 2 or 3 cabbage leaves; 2 or 3 cauliflower florets; 1 small piece turkey lunch meat; black decorating gel; handful roasted almonds; handful dried fruit e.g. strawberries); 1 container mousse dessert; 1 zip-top food storage bag, end snipped off, fitted with a coupler and oval-shaped cake decorating tip. 2-tier bento box.

Using rice paddle sprayed with nonstick cooking spray, pack cooled rice into the undivided tier of bento box. Try to get a smooth, flat surface. Load the zip-top bag with half of the mashed sweet potato; set aside. Cut head, neck and shoulders from slice of turkey. Press firmly with the knife so that meat won't split and turn fibrous. Arrange on bed of rice. Conserve additional small pieces of turkey to use as hands. Use cauliflower to fashion a mountain of hair. Pinch off smaller pieces to use around face. If you run out of room, make hair bend off to one side, to mimic a toppling mound.

Using ruffled edges and texture of cabbage leaves, cut out pieces of dress and plumes for hair. Arrange on rice. When you have cabbage the way you like it, pipe in mashed sweet potato as contrast and fill-in for dress and hair. Use the decorating gel and flexible toothpick to draw a face. Arrange turkey hands on either side of head as if Marie is trying to hold up her hairstyle. In second tier, arrange remaining ingredients: almonds, mousse, sweet potato and dried fruit.

HEALTH SPA BENTO

2 slices of turkey luncheon meat; slice of white cheese; 1 cup cooked long-grain rice, tinted dark blue; 1 rolled-up string shape fruit snack; 1 can of squeeze cheese; 2 tsp mayonnaise, tinted light green; 1 slice corned beef; cucumber slices; 1 hard-boiled egg; 5 wheat crackers; 1 cup Green Goddess salad dressing; 1 clementine; 1 prepared and cooled portion stir-fry green peppers with peanut-butter sauce. 2-tier bento box.

Spread rice in bottom box. Cut neck and shoulder shapes from one slice of turkey. Cut large egg-shape from second piece of turkey for face. Place over neck to create face and chin.

Use small oblong scraps of turkey for ears. Cut two long half-crescents from cheese. Place with narrow point near ears. This forms turban. Cut more curves of cheese to fit over shoulders, and create collar. Cut lips and nostrils from corned beef. Spread thin layer of tinted mayo over face to create face pack. Squirt processed cheese to make earrings, add cucumber slices on eyes. Use fruit snack string to create trim for the robe and turban. Fill other tier with remaining food items as shown.

BENTO IN BENTO

1 cup long-grain white rice, cooked;
2 fruit leathers in dark colors (e.g.
grape or blackberry); 2 kumquats, one
halved; 3 slices red bell pepper; 3 pieces of raw green
bean, trimmed; 1 baby carrot, cut into
strips; 1 tube wasabi; 1 piece nori; 1 soy
sauce bottle; 4 mini chocolate biscuits;
6 unbroken yam soba noodles. 1-tier
adult bento box.

Pack rice into bottom of the bento box,
leaving space for inner box.
Unwrap fruit leathers; stack two-deep
on a cutting board.

Cut leathers lengthwise down middle
to form four equal rectangular pieces.
Use to make box shape in gap. Save a
little rice to pack around outside of
box.

Spread out half-sheet of nori and form
tiny sushi rolls with pinches of rice, thin
strips of carrot and a dab of wasabi.
Slice as you would a sushi roll. Set
aside all but two prettiest pieces. Place
against left wall of inner box.

Fill in rest of inner box with vegetables
and sliced kumquat. Arrange a table
top scene around inner box. Place
a kumquat as an orange, biscuits on
cupcake wrapper napkins, and soy

sauce bottle off to one side.

Group the uncooked yam soba noodles
into two batches of three or four. Wet
with warm water and bunch each batch
together tightly to form a chopstick.

Let dry briefly. The starch from the
noodles will keep the chopsticks stuck
together.

When dry, drape across the inner box
on the table top scene. If you're very
careful, the soba-chopsticks will even
work.

USED CAR LOT BENTO

1 cup cooked rice; 1 piece washed celery stalk (upper part with two 'branches' and main stalk); two different colors roll-up fruit snack; small piece narrow-lace red licorice; black food color in small plastic cup; 1 yellow Necco wafer; 1 handful veggie crisps; 1 serving leftovers (e.g. chicken casserole). 2-tier bento box.

Press rice into bottom tier of bento box.

Using one toothpick dipped in tiny bit of black food color, draw a "Used Cars" logo on Necco wafer and let dry briefly.

Use another toothpick as a signpost; place sign on right side of box.

Drape bits of red licorice from either side as strings on which to hang pennants.

Cut pennants from two colors of fruit snack and place along licorice runners. Rest celery stalk at an angle in front of pennants.

Use food-color toothpick to make small eye and mouth punches on celery; the aim is to represent an inflatable car-lot decoration.

Fill top tier with leftover vegetables and other leftovers, dividing the two using plastic 'grass'.

Sprinkle the main leftovers portion with veggie crisps.

TUX BENTO

Sliced cucumber; muenster cheese; deli sliced turkey; orange bell pepper; broccoli slaw (broccoli, cauliflower, carrot, dressing; refrigerate); cooked white rice; cubed leftover grilled chicken; yellow bell pepper; nori. 2-tier bento box.

Fill half of top tier with broccoli slaw. Spear cheese, turkey and bell pepper onto toothpick. Place on top of slaw.

In remaining space, place cucumber slices and any remaining cheese, turkey or sliced bell pepper.

Fill half bottom tier with rice. Shape to make penguin shape. Fill remaining space with chicken.

Take yellow bell pepper and cut out pieces for penguin feet and beak. Use scissors to cut nori into eye shapes, and to make black penguin tuxedo. Lay over rice to finish penguin as shown in image.

TWO FLOWERS BENTO

Smoked mushroom tofu; 6 mushrooms (4 whole, 2 chopped); 1 zucchini; 1/2 red pepper; 2 scallions; 4 green asparagus stems, steamed; 1/2 carrot; 1 clove of garlic; grated ginger; 3 tbsp soy sauce; handful roasted sesame seeds; olive oil; serving cooked basmati rice. 1-tier bento box.

Cook rice. Gently fry garlic, ginger and soy sauce in separate pan.

Add the chopped red pepper; cook for 4 mins.

Add the tofu, chopped mushrooms, chopped zucchini and scallions. Stir-fry for further 4 mins.

Cut the 4 remaining whole mushrooms with cookie cutter into flower shapes and fry in pan along with the zucchini 'leaves'.

Once rice is cooked, assemble bento as per the photo. Sprinkle with sesame seeds.

Pinsec frito/fried wontons; serving cooked rice; furikake; imitation crab stick; sweet and sour sauce; hard-boiled egg yolk, sliced; cooked diced vegetables; green tea-filled marshmallows. 2-tier bento box.

Spread rice evenly at bottom of bento box. Sprinkle furikake on upper right corner of the box to make night sky.

Shred crab stick into even strands to create white streaks.

Using kitchen shears cut nori into a tree-stump shape.

Add a few pieces of cooked diced vegetables to make houses on the horizon.

Add half egg yolk to make moon. Pour sweet and sour chili sauce into a small resealable sauce container.

Place pinsec frito and sauce container in second tier of bento.

PANDA BENTO

Tabbouleh; Swiss cheese; sliced salami; orange bell pepper; pineapple; cooked white rice; cucumber with skin; orange bell pepper; 1 sheet nori. 2-tier bento box.

In top tier, separate tabbouleh using small cup or muffin paper. Roll salami in a slice of swiss cheese. Cut into small pieces and pierce with food-pick. Arrange to one side. Add pineapple chunks and bell pepper slices. Tuck soy sauce bottle in.

Fill half bottom tier with rice. Shape into a panda head with ears. Cut cucumber into small strips; arrange to look like a bamboo forest behind panda's head. Toss in bits of orange bell pepper for color.

Using nori, cut out eyes, ears and nose. Punch holes into eyes for pupils. Use cucumber skin to make bamboo shoot the panda is eating.

AARGH BENTO

1 cup plain fried rice; steamed broccoli; cherry tomato; sausage roll slices; store-bought vegetable gyoza, omelette; carrot flowers; french fries. 2-tier bento box.

Fill 1/4 of the top tier with half the fried rice, packing tightly.

Place a line of steamed broccoli down the edge of rice.

Layer 4-6 slices of sausage roll in the remaining space.

Place cherry tomato half on top of the rice.

When remaining fried rice is still warm, gather a large handful and press it into a ball. Put into the bento.

Cut a circle from a slice of mozzarella cheese and use a paper hole punch to cut a smaller circle from a slice of nori.

Place it onto the cheese circle.

Paste the eye into place using a bit of mayo or honey on the back.

Cut an eye patch, bandanna, eyebrows and mouth from the sheet of nori and smooth onto the onigiri.

Fill remaining space with two gyoza, broccoli, a spiralled slice of omelette, french fries and carrot flowers.

Decorate with toy pirate ships.

LUMBERJACK BENTO

Sliced mozzarella; portion deli turkey; 3 strawberries; shredded coconut; 1/2 cup cooked brown rice; leftover Dijon salmon; spinach; mini carrots; cucumber slices; mini red bell pepper; black sesame seeds. 2-tier bento box.

Roll mozzarella and turkey together to form tube shape. Cut into sushi-sized pieces. Arrange to one side of top container.

In other side, line a pile of coconut with fresh strawberries. Cut one strawberry into shape of a heart and place atop coconut. Place salmon to one side of second container. Fill other side with brown rice.

Garnish with spinach leaves and carrot rounds. Cut out a red bell pepper heart.

On rice, use cucumber slices to form lumberjack head, torso and arm. Cut a mouth into the head. Nose is formed by bruising cucumber. Eyes are black sesame seeds.

Use cap of mini bell pepper for hat and thin strips for suspenders. Cut an axe shape out of mini carrot.

28

29

GEISHA BENTO

1 cup long-grain brown rice, cooked; 1 piece reddish-colored lunch meat (e.g. salami); peel of small zucchini; 1 small Indian eggplant; 1 medium-thick slice of white-colored cheese; 1 piece lemon rind; 5 kumquats; cup leftover entree (e.g. vegetable curry); cup shelled edamame; packet green tea Pocky; 1 wood toothpick in a bright color, cut in half; 4 fancy cocktail picks. 2-tier bento box.

Pack rice into the bottom tier of the bento box. Assemble geisha on cutting board. Carve neck and shoulders from cheese; make sure to include shape of make up pattern under hairline.

Use zucchini skin to fashion hairdo and topknot. Use thin slice of kumquat for depth, and an end piece to serve as ornament. Make hair ribbon from thin strip salami and add strip of cheese for collar. Reassemble geisha on rice. Fold and tuck the slice of salami to serve as kimono. Add lemon peel for

color as an accent, wrapped around like collar trim. Quarter eggplant and position in the center of kimono to mimic an obi knot.

Add tiny bits of zucchini flesh and kumquat peel to make a design (smallest gum-paste blossom cutters would make a fancier pattern). Tuck toothpick halves into hair and geisha is complete. Remember to remove toothpicks before eating!

In other tier of box, place paper cupcake cup and fill with leftover entree. Push into far upper corner. Garnish with a blossom cut from remaining cheese and a kumquat-top. Spear edamame on picks and set aside.

Slice tops off remaining kumquats and arrange in empty space of entree tier. Prop edamame-picks on one side and fill in any empty spaces with leftover edamame.

Serve with Pocky as dessert.

ZUCCHINI BENTO

4 strips grilled chicken breast; cup cooked rice; 8 pieces of stir-fried zucchini; 6 slices stir-fried red onion; 6 cherry tomatoes; 2 leftover puff-pastry wraps; 1 small celery stick. 2-tier bento box.

Place two strips of chicken breast on either side of deeper bento tier. Stack zucchini on center-side of each. Fill in middle with rice. Peel off skins of two cherry tomatoes. Gather into rose shape and tuck end into the rice. Place two puff pastries in other tier, long diagonal sides in. Fill gap with cherry tomatoes and slices of celery.

ZUCCHINI VARIATION

Stir-fried zucchini, red onion, eggplant, carrot; cup cooked rice; 2 carrots; 2 leftover puff-pastry wraps; 1 small celery stick. 2-tier bento box.

As above but replace chicken with stir-fried vegetables; cut carrot into flower.

31

AUTUMN BENTO

Leftover cooked chicken breast, diced; 4 mini carrots, 1 cut into rounds; swiss cheese; 2 red bell peppers; ginger cookies; mini fish bottle with soy sauce; 1 cup cooked rice, tinted blue (one drop of blue food coloring); scallion greens; black sesame seeds. 2-tier bento box.

Fill half top container with chicken and garnish with carrot rounds.

Next to chicken, stack small squares of Swiss cheese and bell pepper.

Complete top box with a couple of ginger cookies

Place cookies in a small muffin cup if you want to protect from chicken juices.

Fill entire bottom of the lower container with rice.

Using a paring knife, cut out lobster shape from red bell pepper.

Cut mini carrots into small fish shapes. Arrange on top of rice.

Cut tubular section of scallion green open so it lies flat.

Cut thin slices into sheet to give appearance of seaweed; arrange in box to create a seabed scene.

Sprinkle black sesame seeds along the bottom edge of container.

Place a fish-shaped soy sauce bottle on top of the chicken.

AQUARIUM BENTO

1 cup long-grain white rice, cooked; 1 zucchini, split lengthwise; 2 gummi clown fish; 1 handful rainbow Goldfish crackers, crumbled; cup leftover meat entree (e.g. leftover Thai peanut chicken); 1 piece wrapped melon candy. 2-tier adult bento box.

Press rice into shallow tier of bento box.

Cut long slices of peel from zucchini and carve seaweed shapes. Carve two small circles for fishes' eyes.
Place seaweed shapes carefully on rice (assemble them on cutting board and reassemble on rice).

Arrange two fishes on rice.

Carefully add zucchini-skin eyes.

Make sure rice is cool before you add these.

In deeper tier, place eclair cup and fill with meat entree.

Fill in remaining space with orange pieces in cupcake cup.

Place melon candy elsewhere.

Spread cilantro out along diagonal center of the bento box. Carefully arrange tomato pieces: first claws and arm-strips, then head, then thorax, then slices of abdomen, and finally, tail. Very gently press sharp ends of cloves into lobster head to make eyes. Squeeze out one drop of black gel on each one; these make great beady eyes. Arrange two long cayenne pepper strips on either side of head as antennae. Dab on black gel as accent, along lines of abdomen, to make band marks on the claws, and so forth. Using paring knife, peel the skin of each cherry tomato off in as long and thin a continuous piece as you can. Pinch and wrap pieces, fanning them out at top, until you have a rosette shape. Tuck this in on one side of lobster. Mash mayonnaise, egg yolks and mustard together in a small bowl until very fine. Swirl into condiment cup to make 'butter sauce'. Press into rice on other side of lobster. Push in sprigs of cilantro to fill in any gaps.

LOBSTER BENTO

1 cup white long-grain rice, cooked; 5 'yellow pear' cherry tomatoes; several sprigs of fresh cilantro; 4 large Roma tomatoes; 2 whole cloves; 1 tube black gel icing; 2 hard-boiled egg yolks; 2 tsp mayonnaise; 1 tsp yellow mustard; 1 cayenne pepper, seeded, and cut into long strips; 1 small plastic condiment cup. 1-tier bento box, rounded-square shape.

Using rice paddle, press white rice into bottom of bento tier. Cut one Roma tomato in half lengthwise and cut small wedge-pieces out, with the

point situated a little over halfway in. These will be claws. Cut second Roma tomato widthwise 1/3 off the end. Take remaining 2/3 and, using paring knife, shape a mouth at tip. Pinch it slightly to give it shape. This larger piece is lobster head; smaller piece is thorax, which will go right behind it. Cut a third Roma tomato widthwise into slices, mashing them down slightly with your hand as you do so. This forms segments of abdomen. Take last Roma tomato, cut off tip of end so it's square, cut it in half lengthwise, and place on cutting board cut-side down. Making slits that go 2/3 of piece's length, spread out into a fan-tail. Conserve remaining tomato half for strips to join the claws to the thorax.

TORII GATE BENTO

2 cups of mashed potatoes, divided into two; neon blue food color, regular blue food color, black food color; 1 baked Okinawan sweet potato, scooped out mashed; 1 tbsp mashed sweet potato; scraps of potato peel; 1 red bell pepper, cut into long strips; steamed mixed vegetables e.g. Chinese leftover takeaway vegetables; pinch sesame seeds; 1 serving of leftover baked chicken; handful whole almonds; cup of strawberry mousse dessert. 2-tier bento box, rounded-square shape.

In one bowl of mashed potatoes, drip in one drop of neon blue food color and swirl lightly. Don't stir it all the way; it'll

be your cloudy sky. In other bowl, use 3 drops of blue food color with 1 small drop of black. Mix thoroughly. Fill lower half of larger box tier with darker blue mashed potatoes. Fill in top half with lighter blue swirled mashed potatoes; leave small space between the two layers.

Fill in gap with purple Okinawan sweet potato, pulling upward with a spoon to make mountain peaks.

Arrange strips of red pepper to construct a torii gate. Where gate touches the 'water', add dabs of orange sweet potato to make water-reflections.

Add more sweet potato to 'water' here and there to make patches of sunlight.

Cut elongated V shapes from potato skin to make birds, and arrange them above gate. Take one rounded carrot piece from steamed vegetables and cut so that it fits into top as a sun.

In other tier, arrange remaining items. Clockwise: steamed broccoli with a scattering of sesame seeds, assorted mixed vegetables, the mousse dessert, and chicken in the silicone cup atop the almonds.

GOLDEN GATE BENTO

2 cups of mashed potatoes, divided into two; neon blue food color; regular blue food color; black food color; 1 baked Okinawan sweet potato, scooped out mashed; 2 tbsp mashed sweet potato; scraps of potato peel; 1 carrot; minced beef. 1-tier bento box.

Cook minced beef, layer in bento box. Prepare potatoes and arrange as in Torii Gate Bento (see left). Cut carrot into strips arrange across box in shape of Golden Gate Bridge. Dab sweet potato in 'water' as reflections.

35

BALLOON BENTO

1 cup cooked jasmine rice; steamed broccoli; steamed baby corn; mangosteen; green seedless grapes; cherry tomatoes; black olive and baby corn skewers; lemon slices; raw carrot flowers, cucumber peel, tomato peel, lemon peel. For noodles: soba noodles, 1 cucumber, 1 carrot, 1 onion, black sesame seeds. For soba sauce: 1 tbsp sesame oil; 4 tbsp black sesame seeds; 1 tbsp tamari; 1 tbsp soy sauce; 1 tbsp balsamic vinegar, 1 1/2 tsp sugar. 1/2 tsp cayenne powder, 1/2 tsp salt, 1/4 tsp white pepper, 1 tbsp vegetable oil, 3 tbsp vegetable stock. For parmesan Chik'n Strips: 1 packet Morningstar Farms Meal starters Chik'n strips; 1 stick butter; 4 oz grated parmesan cheese; 1 tbsp garlic powder; 1/2 tsp salt; 1/2 tsp pepper; 1/2 tsp dried basil; 1 tsp ground paprika; lemon slices. 3-tier bento box.

For the noodle tier, cook noodles, drain, rinse with cold water. Combine all the sauce ingredients together and whisk until well mixed. Arrange cold soba noodles with chopped onion, carrots

and cucumber around the edge. Flower cut a cherry tomato, place in the center, sprinkle the black sesame seeds in lines from the tomato to the corners. Pack the sauce in a side container and pour it over the noodles just before eating. Prepare parmesan Chik'n Strips: sauté the Chik'n Strips in a dry skillet until they are just thawed. Mix together the parmesan with the spices and seasoning in a large bowl. Melt the butter in the microwave. Dip the Chik'n Strips in the melted butter and then in the cheese and spice mixture, making sure to cover as much as possible. Place onto a baking pan and cook in a hot oven for 5-7 mins, or until cooked through.

Fill the rice tier box with jasmine rice, packed tightly. Cut bunny shape from a slice of cheese. Using a face punch, cut the facial details from origami paper put on with tweezers. Once rice cools, place bunny onto the rice. Arrange three soba noodles for the balloon strings. Make a bow shape from cucumber peel and put it into place where the strings are gathered. Cut balloon shapes from lemon peel, tomato peel and cucumber peel. Place on top of the soba noodle strings.

Pack vegetable and chicken tier with steamed broccoli, grapes still on the vine, baby corn and a silicon cup with canned mangosteen (drain the syrup before removing the fruit from the can). In the empty corner lie a large piece of lettuce. Fan out the Chik'n Strips and lemon slices on the lettuce leaf, making two layers. A large cherry tomato goes in the corner for color, place another next to grapes. Recline bamboo skewers of baby corn slices and black olives over the top of the tomato. Cut several carrot flowers and place them over the grapes.

BOUQUET VARIATION

See ingredients list from Balloon Bento. 3-tier bento box.

Prepare and pack the noodle tier and vegetable and chicken tier as in Balloon Bento recipe. Fill the rice tier box with jasmine rice, packed tightly. Arrange 8 soba noodles for the flower stalks. Cut leaf shapes from cucumber peel and arrange along stalks. Cut daisy shapes from lemon peel, and tulip shapes from tomato peel. Add carrot flowers from vegetable tier; group at the top of soba noodle stalks.

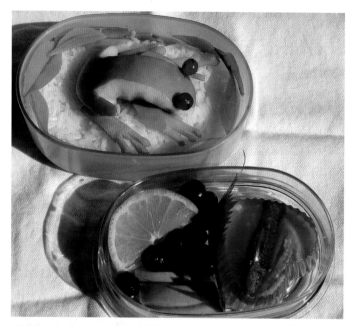

GIRAFFE BENTO

1 cup polenta or corn meal mush, cooked very thick and cooled; 1 cup long-grain white rice, tinted sky-blue (1 drop neon blue food color in rice cooker water, stirred before cooking; 1 slice roast beef lunch meat, darker rind still in place; 2 cloves; 1 scrap nori; 2 small sprigs fresh cilantro; 1 serving steamed mixed vegetables; 1 serving leftover meat entree (e.g. Thai peanut chicken); 1 piece pumpkin dessert; black decorating gel. 2-tier bento box.

Spray hands with nonstick cooking spray and pick up polenta (it should work just like modeling clay).

Make the neck, head and ears of a giraffe and lay in bottom tier of bento box.

Using a rice paddle, fill in empty space with the cooled rice.

Use fingers to add pinches of rice to hard-to-reach areas.

Tear off pinches of roast beef slice to use as giraffe's spots. Place on neck.

Use longer pieces along ridge of nose and to accent shape of ears.

Push in cloves to serve as eyes.

Use shreds of darker rind of roast beef as eyelashes, bases of ears and top tufts of hair.

If rinds are too thick, you can cut small pieces of nori to serve as lashes. Use additional bits of nori for nostrils.

TREE FROG BENTO

1 cup rice; 1 Granny Smith apple; lemon juice; 2-3 drops neon blue food color in lidded condiment cup; 10-12 snow pea pods, washed, split open, peas removed; 1 carrot; 2 fresh red currants; scrap of nori; 2 half-rounds sliced navel orange; handful blueberries; 1 prepared gelatin wagashi. 2-tier bento box, oval shape.

Press rice into bottom tier of bento box. Create a flat surface. Using 1/2 apple carve rounded arrow shape of tree frog, show flashes of white on frog's sides. Brush surfaces with lemon juice so they don't brown. Blot dry. Brush food color to draw blue stripes on frog's sides. Blot dry and arrange in center. Cut four flat slices of carrot and carve out wedges to fashion into toes. Tuck carrot-feet under frog, adding short green arm pieces from the other half of the apple; brush with lemon juice. Snip off each end of toothpick, push pieces into front of apple. Push currants onto toothpick. Cut two elongated diamond shapes from nori to form pupils. Spread out pea pods and, using the center fold as the stem cut out small leaves. Arrange in garland around frog. Place the wagashi and other ingredients in other tier.

Push one small sprig of cilantro into either side of mouth.

Use flexible toothpick, dipped in black decorating gel, to add accents to mouth and throat.

In the divided tier of bento, position remaining ingredients.

Clockwise: pumpkin dessert, leftover meat entree, and steamed vegetables.

Pumpkin Dessert: mix up your favourite pumpkin pie recipe, but bake in a glass dish instead of a pie crust.

Just like a pumpkin pie, a knife will come out clean when it's done.

Chill in fridge until very firm, then scoop out individual servings with a melon-baller.

The leaf accent is made by cutting pieces of ready-made pie crust with a leaf-shaped cutter and baking until golden-brown.

Press one onto the top of each scoop.

TREASURE ISLAND VARIATION

See ingredients list from Giraffe Bento (left), add 5 small broccoli spears; 1 chocolate coin.

Mold polenta into island shape as if seen from above. Place in box; fill empty space with cooked rice. Arrange broccoli spears to create wooded areas. Cut roast beef slices; lay as paths. Cut nori into X shape to mark treasure spot; bury coin below it.

CHERRY BLOSSOM BENTO

1 cup sushi rice; 1 piece fried tofu; 1 hard-boiled egg; red food coloring; black sesame seeds. 1-tier bento box.

Press rice into box. Cut fried tofu; place to represent tree branch. Slice hard-boiled egg; cut into flower shapes. Dip flowers in small dish containing 1/4 cup water and four drops red food coloring. Leave some for ten seconds, others for 15 seconds, to get color variation. Arrange on tofu branch and falling from it. Sprinkle sesame seeds onto flowers for detail.

ORCHID BENTO

1 cup prepackaged deli noodle salad; 1 medium cucumber; 1 edible orchid; 3 slices kiwi fruit; 1 orange or tangerine wedge; 8 pieces pea-flavored crunchy snacks; 1 serving vanilla pudding; pink and purple decorating icing. 2-tier bento box, oval shape.

Use a mandoline slicer to cut cucumber lengthwise into long, thin ribbons. Pinch and bend ribbons and place around border of bottom tier. Add noodle salad as a mound in middle, using tongs.

Place edible orchid on top as decoration. Ensure noodles aren't piled too high so that orchid is not crushed when lidded. Scoop vanilla pudding into the triangular cup. Squeeze dabs decorating icing over surface. Use toothpicks to swirl patterns into icing (the purple and pink should echo shades of the orchid). Place the cup in upper tier of bento box.

Arrange kiwi fruit, orange wedge and pea snacks around pudding cup.

TIGER LILY VARIATION

See ingredients list from Orchid Bento (left), replace edible orchid and pink and purple decorating icing with 1 small bright-orange carrot, black sesame seeds, 1/8 sheet of yellow mamenori; orange decorating icing.

Create tiger lily by following instructions in Hive Bento (see right). Place on noodles. Color vanilla pudding with orange icing to match.

HIVE BENTO

1 cup hummus; small slice of zucchini-peel; 1 stick chocolate dessert-garnish; 1/8 sheet of white mamenori (soy paper); 1/8 sheet of yellow mamenori; 1 piece whole-wheat pita bread, cut into quarters; Green Goddess dressing; 1 small daikon radish, washed and peeled; 1 small bright-orange carrot, washed and peeled; pinch of black sesame seeds; colorful fruit chunks; 1 small pastry as dessert (a ladoo is pictured). 1-tier bento box, with side cups for side dishes and dessert.

Turn down 'collar' of zip-top sandwich bag for easy loading and fill with the hummus. Gently press out excess air, close top of bag and snip one bottom

corner off to make into a piping bag. In middle of the bento box, pipe a rounded beehive shape (think extra-curvy Christmas tree with no trunk).

Cut half-round shape from the zucchini skin and press it into the hive shape as the opening.

Cut small slices from garnish-stick; chunks from rounded ends work best. Use scissors to cut elongated heart-shapes from white mamenori. Arrange slices of garnish-stick on top of hive and press points of heart-shapes in on either side to serve as bees' wings.

Arrange quarters of pita on either side of hive. If you're afraid they might press hive out of shape, package them separately.

Using a mandoline slicer or wide-blade vegetable peeler, cut long, thin, flexible ribbons of daikon. Arrange like noodles in bottom of one of side-dish containers.

Cut six long, thin strips of carrot. If you cut a lengthwise cross-section, you'll get pretty striping on the petals. Arrange strips on daikon-ribbons, curving them as you tuck them in. This is the base of your tiger lily.

Sprinkle black sesame seeds over petals and cut a few thin strips from the yellow mamenori. Tuck into center of flower to make stamens. Pack bottle of dressing alongside, to serve with vegetables.

Fill a second small cup with fruit. Keep pastry alongside as dessert.

PAINTER'S BENTO

1 whole-wheat pita; 3 hard-boiled eggs, shelled; 1 wedge steamed butternut squash with coconut/raisin garnish; 2 servings deli-prepared salads, e.g.: bean salad; 2 steamed asparagus spears, upper halves; 1 wrapped Japanese sweet-cake; 5 silicone cupcake cups, filled halfway with water, tinted with food color: red, yellow, green, purple and blue. 2-tier bento box.

Flatten pita piece and cut a palette shape (don't forget hole for the thumb). Slice 6 rounded pieces of egg white off hard-boiled eggs. Keep one aside for white paint; distribute the remaining pieces among cups of food color. Keep curved side up to avoid uneven coloring. Soak for at least 5 mins. Assemble other tier of the bento. Clockwise: deli salads, wrapped sweet-cake, steamed squash and asparagus. When egg white pieces are as dark as you'd like, pinch silicone cups and pour off the colored water and blot dry. Transfer gently onto pita and arrange to look like artists' paint.

DRAGON BENTO

Zaru soba noodles (see p 37 for recipe); 1 carrot; 1/2 cucumber; 1 onion; 1/2 cup jasmine rice; checker board apple; 1 large head of broccoli, already steamed; 1/2 cup vegetable broth; vegetable oil; 7 oz tofu. For sweet love sauce: 1/2 cup water; 1 cup sugar; 1/2 cup rice vinegar; 1 tbsp garlic powder; 1 tsp salt; 1 tbsp chili oil; 1 tsp cayenne powder. 2-tier bento box.

First make the sweet love sauce; bring the first 5 ingredients to a boil, lower heat and simmer 20 minutes, stirring frequently. Add chili oil and cayenne to mixture, cook for 3 minutes and pour into a container to keep.

Heat oil in skillet. Add broccoli and cook for a few minutes until it begins to wilt. Add vegetable broth and simmer for several mins on high.
Pour sweet love sauce over the broccoli and continue to cook on high for five more mins, stirring frequently. Drain if necessary and eat either hot or cold.

Cut the tofu block into three slices. Place onto paper towels or other absorbent surface. Place paper towels on top and press the tofu firmly with your hands to remove extra liquid. Section slices into triangles by cutting across from corner to corner. Heat oil in a shallow frying pan. Place tofu triangles into hot oil and fry, turning them over every now and then until they are lightly browned on both sides. Remove and drain. In another pan, heat the sweet love sauce gently and simmer the tofu triangles in the heated sauce. Let the sauce reduce to a thick syrup, then remove the tofu. Pack one side

of the top tier with the cooked rice. Make sure to leave enough room for the tofu triangles to be placed on top and have the lid close properly. Arrange the broccoli in half of the other portion of the tier. Take an apple and slice off a side. Trim it into a rough square shape. With a sharp paring knife carefully cut straight lines in first one direction and then the other, just barely through the peel and no further. Using only the tip of the knife slowly slice the peel from some of the squares in a checker board pattern. Soak apple in a mixture of water and lemon juice, dry and place partially on top of the broccoli. Place tofu triangles on rice.

Fill the second tier 2/3 high with the cold soba noodles. Cut a long slice off the cucumber. Shape one end into a curve. Make shallow curving cuts horizontally along its length and two deeper cuts for the eyes. Push one mustard seed into each eye cut. Place dragon's body on top of the soba noodles. For the wings cut two diagonal slices from the remainder of the cucumber. Cut out two curving triangles from each slice, wedge underneath the body with the curved side towards the head. Make several thin peelings from a carrot. On some peelings trim one edge into a taper and on others cut a forked end.
Wedge two tapered carrot pieces between the dragon's body and wings. Arrange the others at the dragon's mouth to make fire.

Cut the onion in half and slice very thinly. Use the smaller, inner ring slices to make clouds on top of the noodles. A double layer of onion slices helps to camouflage where the dragon's body meets the bento box side.

SWEET LOVE BENTO

Zaru soba noodles (see p 37 for recipe); carrot slices; cucumber slices; 1/2 cup steamed jasmine rice; apple flower; sweet love sauce; sweet love broccoli; sweet love tofu (see Dragon Bento for recipes). 1-tier bento box.

Pack the steamed rice tightly into a rough rectangle in the upper right hand of the box. Arrange two to three florets of sweet love broccoli in the lower right corner. Next place one tofu triangle so that it is centered in the green of the broccoli.

Fill the remaining space with soba noodles. Make thin rectangular slices of carrot and cucumber. Layer in a fan shape on top of the noodles. Slice off one side of an apple. Shape into a flower, with a paring knife; place on top of the rice. Cut carrot circle and inset into the center of the apple.
Cut two long slices of cucumber and shape them into leaves,. The broad ends will need to be a little thinner than the tips so that they do not push the flower up when put into place. Make canals along the centers of the leaves, tapering toward the top and remove the peel from them. Gently wedge them under the apple flower, slightly off set from one another.

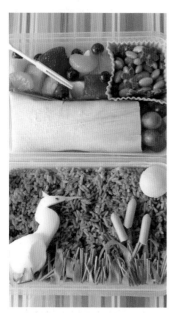

triangular pieces. Arrange among broken soba noodles to make a scene of reeds and marsh grasses. Make three stalks from longer soba pieces and add tips of Pocky as cat tails. Cut one egg in half, taking care not to crumble yolk.

Slice yolk in half and place in top right corner as the moon. Make angled cuts on one half of egg white to resemble body of a bird. Using other half of egg white, cut an elongated S shape for heron's neck. Use a tiny sliver of egg white for crest on head and tiny sliver of the carrot for beak. Take a toothpick and dab tiny dot of yellow mustard as eye. Transfer black sesame seed to center of mustard to make pupil.

In top tier, arrange cooked tamale and grapes. Use a blossom cutter to make flowers of sweet potato slices. Fill silicone cupcake cup with edamame and flowers as contrast. Place sushi grass alongside tamale to section off a waterproof area. Fill in with fruit salad. When you pack up your bento, include bamboo cocktail pick to spear chunks of fruit.

HERON BENTO

1 cup cooked long-grain rice, dyed dark blue (3 drops neon-blue food color and 3 drops neon-purple). 2 hard-boiled eggs, shelled; 1 sheet green mamenori (soy paper); 10-12 uncooked soba noodles, broken into irregular pieces; 3 sticks of green tea or chocolate mousse; yellow mustard; 1 black sesame seed; 1 sliver of carrot; 1 raw Okinawan sweet potato, sliced; 1 cup shelled edamame; 1 frozen tamale; 1 cup of fresh fruit salad; 1 Pocky. 2 small rectangular food-storage boxes.

Using rice paddle pack one of boxes with rice. Take mamenori and cut long

HERON VARIATION

See ingredients list from Heron Bento (left). Replace frozen tamale with 2 slices brown bread; butter; portion of cooked prawns; 1 1/2 tbsp mayonnaise; 2 lettuce leaves. 2 small rectangular food-storage boxes.

Create Heron Bento as above. Cut crusts from bread; butter. Mix prawns with mayo; make sandwich, adding lettuce. Cut into quarters, add to box.

LADYBUG BENTO

1 cup fresh spinach salad; 1 Roma tomato; 1 sheet nori (seaweed wrap); 1 small piece fresh mozzarella cheese, the very white kind; 2 tbsp peanut butter; 1 roasted peanut; 1 small piece mamenori (soy paper); 10-12 wheat crackers; 2-tier bento box, oval shape.

Spread spinach salad in the bottom tier of the bento box. Cut Roma tomato in half lengthwise and choose nicer-looking half. Dampen with a wet paper towel.

Use nail scissors to cut out long strip of nori to go down the center of the ladybug's shell. Carefully place it on tomato – the moisture should cause nori to stick and become very form-fitting.

Cut a second piece of nori to cover end of the tomato half and form ladybug's head. Cut out spots (a hole puncher dedicated to bento use also works well) and stick them to the shell one by one. Place ladybug carefully atop salad.

Cut six elongated triangles of nori and tuck ends of them underneath ladybug to serve as her legs. Cut two circles from small chunk of mozzarella and place carefully as eyespots.

Place rice crackers in one cupcake cup and scoop peanut butter into other. Place in remaining bento tier.

Cut two heart-shaped moth wings from mamenori (when shopping pick color you prefer) and tuck into center of peanut butter. Place peanut in the middle as moth's body.

LADYBUG VARIATION

See ingredients list from Ladybug Bento (left). Replace peanut butter and peanut with 2 tomatoes; 1 avocado; 1 red onion; 2 tbsp lime juice; 1 tsp chili powder; 3 sprigs cilantro.

Create Ladybug Bento as left. Chop avocado, onion, tomatoes, mix with lime juice, chili powder and chopped cilantro. Scoop into cupcake cup, decorate with sprig of cilantro.

GARDEN BENTO

1 cup sky-blue tinted rice, cooked; 1 cup cooked couscous; 10-15 snow pea pods; 4 hard-boiled eggs, shelled; 2 tsp mayo and 1 tsp sugar, mixed, chilled; 6 baby carrots; 1 piece red bell pepper; 1 piece yellow squash; 1 cup spinach salad; 1 cup raspberries; 2 fruit-center cookies; paprika; silicone cupcake-cups, with cool water and tinted with food coloring (pink, purple, yellow, blue). 2-tier bento box.

Fill top of large tier with blue rice and couscous. Remove peas from pod. Cut 20 long, spear-shaped leaves. Press into couscous to leave garden path. Cut thin strips of egg white into flower shapes using gum-paste cutters. Dip some in coloring. Mash egg yolks into mayo. Carve tulip shapes from pepper and carrots. Press gum-paste cutter into squash to make daffodil shapes. Rinse egg whites. Blot dry and arrange. Use a piping bag to add yellow centers to flowers. Cut teardrop shapes from squash for butterfly, use stringy-curls from pea pods for antennae. Arrange remaining tier as shown.

SAKURA GIRL BENTO

1 cup blue-tinted long-grain rice, cooked; 1 cup frozen shelled edamame, thawed; cup frozen cranberries, thawed; 3 fake kamaboko apple slices (see recipe below); hard-boiled egg, zig zag-cut and sprinkled with paprika; slice of white mozzarella cheese; slice of light-colored, medium-sliced turkey lunch meat; several drops of neon-pink food color in a lidded condiment cup; several drops of black food color in a lidded condiment cup; 1 sheet pink mamenori (soy paper); 1 blossom-shaped paper-punch. 1-tier bento box (preferably pink).

Using a rice paddle sprayed with nonstick cooking spray, press rice into half of bento box. Try to make edge into a straight line down middle. Arrange heart-shaped silicone cupcake cup in lower left corner of box; fill with a mix of cranberries and edamame. Tuck egg to upper right, and three slices of fake kamaboko to upper left. Fill in remaining empty space with edamame.

Using paper punch, cut about twelve blossom shapes out of mamenori and set aside. Place turkey and mozzarella on a cutting board. From turkey, cut out an upper torso, neck and head (don't forget room for hair). Use a sure hand on knife and press down firmly so that the turkey doesn't split and become fibrous. Estimate how much mozzarella you will need to make a kimono shape over body and use form to guide the shape you cut. Conserve four tiny pieces of mozzarella to go under the loose blossoms, so they won't be transparent; mamenori goes transparent very easily. Using black food color and

a flexible toothpick, carefully paint on hair, eyes, nose and lip outline. Be very conservative with color as the turkey will absorb it and convert your lines to soft blot-shapes. Once black color has been absorbed, go back with another toothpick dipped in pink and fill in lips.

Carefully arrange on rice, use two additional tiny pinches of turkey for ears. Layer mozzarella kimono over it. Dip toothpick in pink food color and draw accents on center of each blossom shape. Layer eight of blossom pieces over kimono to make a print. If mozzarella is the least bit moist, they should stick. Finish any trim on kimono design with more pink food color.

Place one of tiny bits of mozzarella where you would like girl's hair ornament to be, and place apple-peel leaf on either side of it.

Stick one of remaining blossoms to the bit of mozzarella. Repeat process on blank rice to arrange loose blossoms.

FAKE KAMABOKO RECIPE

One apple, halved; lemon juice and a pastry brush; small bowl water, tinted with neon-pink food color.

Press a flower-shaped vegetable-cutter right into apple chunk, pushing down hard to get it all the way through. Immerse in the food color, soak for 5 mins, rinse well and blot dry with paper towels.

Cut into slices and brush with lemon juice so that the apple doesn't yellow. Arrange in bento any way you like.

FRAPPUCCINO BENTO

1 medium Okinawan (purple) sweet potato, baked, contents scooped out and mashed; 1 cup long-grain rice, tinted green, cooked, and cooled (or brown long-grain rice for a coffee tone); 1 roll of green fruit snack; 5 cauliflower florets; cooked chicken breast pieces; condiment cup of prepared chicken salad; toasted almond slices; chopped seedless grapes; 3 slices cucumber; 3 1/4 slices tangerine; 7 wheat crackers; 2 tbsp mayo; black decorating gel; tube of white royal icing; packet green tea Pocky; plastic drink cup, cut in half lengthwise; plastic straw. 1-tier bento box.

Spray interior of plastic cup-half with nonstick cooking spray; use as mold for rice. Pack cooled rice in firmly with a rice paddle. Place food storage container over inverted mold and flip it; remove mold.

Spoon mashed sweet potato around rice on all sides.

Unroll fruit snack; cut two narrow strips and one small circle (use a biscuit cutter for circle). Drape strips over cup.

Using royal icing and a flexible toothpick, paint a coffee-shop logo on round fruit-snack piece. Once it's dry, use another toothpick dipped in black decorating gel to paint in contrast. Drape over cup.

Arrange upper components of the bento: the chicken salad (add mayo, sesame seeds, almond and grapes) with wheat crackers underneath (you could use a plastic divider to keep crackers from getting soggy), orange slices in oval-shaped paper cup, and cucumber slices.

Poke clipped straw into rice at a slant.

Pack cauliflower in to imitate a mound of whipped cream atop drink.

Be careful that it's not stacked too high, or lid will not close.

Serve with green tea Pocky as dessert.

MANTIS BENTO

1 cup cooked sky-blue tinted long-grain rice; 7 large sugar snap-pea pods; 1 small piece celery; 1 cup shelled edamame; 2 thin strands of citrus peel; pinch of coffee grounds; 3 blueberries; single serving of raita (yoghurt and cucumber); serving of leftover meat (e.g. barbecue chicken). 2-tier bento box.

Press rice into bottom tier of bento box. Using a photo for reference, fashion pea pods and celery into a mantis shape.

Color irregularities and dry spots on pods will make for a realistic appearance.

Work with form of pods and use the stringy sides for legs, etc. Carve out notches for eyes on head, and use blunt side of a knife to press in face-pattern.

Assemble the mantis on a cutting board and move bit by bit to box. Choose two beans of edamame with similar size and color for eyes. Fit

into notches on head-piece; use a dampened toothpick to coffee ground onto each one as a pupil.

Prop the citrus peels near head as antennae. Arrange sliced meat in upper tier and place cup of raita on one side. On surface of raita, add two pea pod-leaves and three blueberries as decoration.

Fill in empty space on either side with edamame.

MANTIS VARIATION

See ingredients list from Mantis Bento (left). Replace serving of leftover meat with: portion tofu; 1/2 tsp cayenne pepper; 1 clove garlic; 1/2 cup lemon juice.

Create Mantis Bento as left. Chop tofu into pieces. Mince garlic, add lemon juice and cayenne pepper. Marinade tofu in mixture for 1 hour, then grill until golden. Arrange in upper tier.

SNOW GLOBE BENTO

1 cup mashed potato; 1 cup mashed Okinawan sweet potato; 8 steamed asparagus tips; 1 cherry fruit leather; 1 slice roast beef lunch meat; yellow mustard; small piece of yellow cheese; pinch of flour; 2 stuffed wine leaves; 1 serving leftover meat entree (e.g. baked chicken); whole-berry cranberry sauce; toothpicks; crescent moon-shaped aspic cutter. 2-tier bento box.

Fill the upper half of bento with mashed Okinawan sweet potato and lower half with regular mashed potatoes. From roast beef, cut rectangle for building and a trapezoid shape for roof. A rectangle of fruit leather forms the chimney; smaller trapezoids make front steps. Assemble on top of mashed potatoes. Place asparagus tips around cabin as trees. Dip toothpick in white potatoes and paint snow onto cabin roof and trees. Drag swirls of white potato outward from chimney as smoke. Dip toothpick in mustard; paint on windows and door and add reflections on snow.

Cut moon from cheese. Sprinkle tiny amount of flour over scene as snow. In other tier, arrange cranberry sauce, stuffed wine leaves and meat entree.

SNOW GLOBE VARIATION

See ingredients list from Snow Globe Bento (left). Replace serving of leftover meat entree with leftover lentil curry; replace roast beef lunch meat with 2 cheese slices; purple food color; black food color.

Create bento (see left). From cheese slices, cut shapes for building and roof. Dip toothpick in purple food color; draw horizontal lines to create log cabin. Dip in black food color; draw tiles on roof. Assemble bento, substitute lentil curry for meat entree.

DESSERT SUSHI BENTO

2 kumquats; 1 large blackberry; 1 mini-size egg roll; 1 serving leftover meat entree (e.g. General Tso chicken); 1 serving leftover vegetable and rice entree; 6-8 medium fresh broccoli florets; 4 cherry tomatoes; 2 canned mandarin orange segments; 2 large marshmallows; 1 piece roll-up fruit snack. 2-tier bento box.

Fill one cupcake cup with meat entree and another with rice and veg. Place in one tier with broccoli and tomatoes between them. Cook egg roll and place in one cupcake cup, kumquats and blackberry in the other. Arrange in half of remaining tier. Unroll fruit snack and cut two long strips, a finger-and-a-half in width. Fold in ends for neatness. Line up marshmallows side by side; place mandarin orange segment on each. Wrap with fruit roll strips; press strip together on underside to seal. Place in cupcake-cup and fit into last half of bento box.

DESSERT SUSHI VARIATION

2 kumquats; 6 large blackberries; plain yoghurt; chopped banana; 2 canned mandarin orange segments; 2 large marshmallows; 2 mini powdered donuts; 1 piece roll-up fruit snack. 2-tier bento box.

For a entirely dessert-based bento, fill top tier of bento with yoghurt, topped with chopped bananas and blackberries. Replace egg roll with donuts and assemble 'sushi' pieces and rest of bento as in Dessert Sushi recipe above.

GREEN EGGS AND HAM BENTO

1 cup cooked rice, tinted orange (2 drops red and 2 drops yellow food color); 1 small medium-thick piece of turkey lunch meat (actual ham will not work, doesn't take the color well); 1 hard-boiled egg, shelled; green food color; neon green food color; black food color; 1/4 cup of frozen shelled edamame, thawed; 2 small baby carrots, chopped into discs; 3 frozen edamame shu mai dumplings; 2 medium kumquats; 4-6 raspberries. 2-tier bento box.

Using a rice paddle or a spoon coated with nonstick cooking spray, fill the box with the orange rice. Try to press it down and create a flat surface.
On the cutting board, trim the piece of turkey into a ham shape that's similar to the famous illustration. Keep a steady hand on the knife and press down firmly - this will keep the turkey from splitting and becoming fibrous.

Wash the blade and cut four small pieces from the boiled-egg white. Cut along the curves of the egg to retain a rounded shape: two oblong pieces for whites, and two smaller rounded pieces to be used as yolks.

You can experiment with the shapes on the cutting board to make sure the 'yolk' sits right. These pieces will be brittle and split easily; sometimes it's easiest to lift them with the edge of a knife. Conserve one tiny oval piece for the 'bone' in the ham.
Carefully dip the turkey piece and the two 'egg yolk' pieces into the green colored water. Make sure they do not touch; if they touched, they would come out with lighter spots that might ruin the effect. After making sure all pieces are submerged, put the bowl in the refrigerator and let it soak for at least five minutes.

While you're waiting, prepare the top tier. Cook dumplings and line up down the middle as a divider. Fill in one side with the carrots and edamame; arrange the kumquats and berries in the other.

When the five minutes are up, check on the progress of the pieces. If they are as green as you like, rinse gently in cool water and turn out onto paper towels. Make sure the rinse water runs clear so that the color won't bleed onto the other items. Blot well to remove all excess moisture. The egg pieces, especially, will be very delicate, so handle those with extra care.

Place the two 'egg whites' on the right side of the rice tier and carefully arrange the green 'yolks' on top of them.

After making sure the turkey piece has been patted thoroughly dry, return it to the cutting board. Pour a few drops of black color into a condiment cup. Using a flexible toothpick as a brush, dip it in the black coloring and carefully color in the edge of the meat. Once you've colored all the way around, draw in the design on top.

If you're not used to working with black food coloring, it can blot and spread. When you're first starting out, it's best to experiment on a piece of paper towel to see how the food color behaves and what sort of pressure/amount you need to apply to get the result you want. Then experiment on different food scraps you weren't planning to use.

Black food color can also stain teeth and tongues, and it tends to give food a bitter taste, so it's best used in very small doses!

After use, the condiment cup can be easily sealed and put away for next time. If the drops inside dry, you can rehydrate them with a bit of warm water.

Once finished, rinse the toothpick well and use it to deposit the tiny piece of egg as the 'bone' on the 'green ham'.

GREEN EGGS VARIATION

See ingredients list from Green Eggs and Ham Bento (left). Replace dumplings with 3 slices ham; 3 tbsp cream cheese.

Create bento (see left). Spread 1 tbsp cheese on each ham slice. Roll slice to create swirl, cut in half. Position in upper tier in place of dumplings.

GREEN EGGS VARIATION

See ingredients list from Green Eggs Bento (left). Replace dumplings; baby carrots; edamame with 2 eggs; spinach; ham.

Create bento (see left). Whisk eggs and pour into heated pan. Allow to cook slowly for 2 mins then add spinach and chopped ham. Flip omelette over, allow both sides to brown. Cut into 4 quarters and stack in upper tier of bento box.

JAWS BENTO

2 pieces whole wheat bread; 1 slice cheese; 6 slices corned beef; 6 broccoli florets; 2 corner-pieces of dark-colored fruit leather; handful rainbow-colored Goldfish crackers; green grapes; strawberry; 3 gummy-shark candies; packet shark-shaped fruit snacks. 1 divided rectangular box.

Line box with blue cupcake cups. This forms a blue background for the shark. Stack 2 pieces of bread; cut a torpedo-like shark shape. Press bent chrysanthemum-shaped cutter to create shark mouth. Assemble sandwich; keep meat as top layer so the red shows through. Press two nuggets of fruit leather into either side of shark's head to serve as eyes. Arrange two tiny pieces of the meat as nostrils. Camouflage bottom edge of the shark's head with broccoli florets. Fill in top section of box with Goldfish crackers, grapes, strawberry slices and gummy sharks.

TOUR EIFFEL BENTO

1 cup cooked and cooled blue 'tie-dye' rice; 2 slices white cheese (e.g. white American processed slices); 1 kumquat, sliced in half; 1 slice mottled cheese (e.g. Colby Jack); 7 small broccoli florets; 1 tbsp Grape Nuts cereal; tinted rice or coconut for color, or pink mamenori (soy paper); sliced fruit; 1 cookie cutter, Eiffel Tower-shape. 1-tier bento box.

Using a rice paddle or spoon sprayed with cooking spray, spread rice in bottom of box. Pack it down to create a flat surface. Cut slice of the white cheese in half. Trim curves in lower corners so that it will fit into box. Fit as closely to lower side of bento box as possible. Use cookie-cutter to cut an Eiffel Tower-shape out of mottled cheese slice. Place it with base overlapping white cheese. The top should be well-clear of upper end of box.

Cover sides of white cheese slice with broccoli florets. Pull apart if necessary, in order to fill in blank spaces and to make them fit. Try to create effect of a

tree-lined avenue leading up to Tower.

Add the Grape Nuts cereal to make the rest of the visible white cheese into a path shape.

Sprinkle grains of tinted rice (or coconut, or mamenori blossoms) over trees to mimic blooms.

Cut free form clouds out of remaining white cheese. Add half a kumquat, cut side down, where sun should go. Slice it down to 1/3 if lid won't fit.

See ingredients list from Tour Eiffel Bento (left). 1-tier bento box.

Create bento as left. Instead of Eiffel Tower shape, cut city skyline from mottled cheese slice. Turn bento box 90 degrees and arrange skyline 1/3 way up rice. Add Grape Nuts, broccoli florets, tinted rice to create trees and roads. Add cheese clouds and kumquat sun as described left.

CUTE BENTO

PACMAN BENTO

1 cup cooked rice; 1 tablespoon seaweed furikake (can be found in Asian supermarkets); black sesame seed; 1 small piece each of a red, a green and an orange bell pepper; yellow cherry tomatoes; sliced cucumber; sliced red bell pepper; 1/2 passion fruit; cherry and banana candy; cress leaves. 2-tier bento box.

Separate a little rice from the rest and hold it to one side. Mix remainder of rice with furikake. Put furikake-mixed rice into the lower tier. Leave a spot open for the 'pacman' by placing a yellow tomato in the rice. Cover the furikake-mixed rice with a layer of white rice. Take tomato out. Make a pacman labyrinth by placing small sticks of uncooked spaghetti on the rice in the shape of the labyrinth walls. Sprinkle on lots of sesame seed, until every part of the rice is covered. Remove the sticks to leave white labyrinth walls. Cut a pacman out of a yellow tomato by cutting a triangular wedge out of the tomato below where the stalk was attached; the mark the stalk has left can be used as the eye. Place pacman on top of the sesame seed-covered rice. Use leaves of garden cress to create dots that will be eaten by the pacman, spacing them at regular intervals in front of the pacman mouth. Cut ghost shapes out of the red, green and orange bell peppers. Arrange them on the rice and stick two sesame seeds on each of the ghosts as eyes. Fill other tier with a muffin liner containing cucumber and bell pepper slices. Next to it, place a layer of yellow cherry tomatoes and layer 1/2 a passion fruit next to cherry candy and banana candy pieces.

PEEPING MICE BENTO

1 cup cooked rice; frozen peas; frozen corn and carrots; 1 tbsp butter; parsley; ready-to-cook glazed pork loin or any sliced meat e.g. ham/sliced pot roast; half an orange; fresh or canned pineapple; pink and white kamaboko. 1-tier bento box.

Cook the rice and frozen peas. Defrost frozen corn and carrots; sauté lightly in butter and add a pinch of parsley. Lightly fry ready-to-cook glazed pork loin. Slice half an orange into wedges and a fresh pineapple into bite-sized pieces or use canned pineapple pieces. Steam or blanch store-bought fancy fish balls. If using kamaboko, cut into a mouse-like shape then dot with nori eyes. Fill the bento box 3/4 deep with rice. Layer meat slices and mice. Make the mice look like they are peeping out of the bento by covering half of them with the meat, so that their faces remain visible.

Fill space with corn and carrots, and then peas, arranged in colorful stripes across the bento box. Place oranges and pineapples in separate section of the bento box; either use a compartmentalized box, muffin liners or bento cups.

59

SLEEPING BEAR BENTO

1/2 baked potato; Havarti or other white cheese; yellow bell pepper; carrot, cut into circles and strips; leftover sirloin steak; cherry tomatoes; salad greens; nori. 1-tier bento box.

Use a plastic divider to separate the container. In smaller half, place sliced sirloin and garnish with tomato wedges and salad greens. Cut small portion from the end of the baked potato, keeping the skin intact (to use for bear face, ears and paw). Mash remaining potato, fill second half of container. Cut saved portion of potato into a circle for the head, half-circles for ears and paws. Trim a slice of Havarti to form the quilt; decorate with carrot. Place bear head, ears and paw above the cheese. Place small circle of Havarti on the bear face for 'snout'. Cut small circle of yellow bell pepper to make the chicken. Use piece of carrot as beak. Finish off faces with small nori pieces.

UNDER THE SEA BENTO

1/2 cup koshihikari rice; salt; 3 ready-to-cook chicken fingers; 4 cocktail hot dogs; iceberg lettuce; salad dressing; dipping sauce. 1-tier bento box.

To make the onigiri: cook koshihikari rice. While warm, use wet fingers to mold into a triangular shape. Make diagonal cuts in the base of each cocktail hot dog, taking them 1/3 of the way up the hot dog. Pull these back to create 8 tentacles. Use a drinking straw to poke circles out of sliced cheese, for eyes. Using a sharp pair of kitchen shears, cut eye and mouth shapes from

nori. Top cheese eyes with nori details. Decorate onigiri with nori eyes and the cooked chicken fingers with cheese and nori eyes. Shred iceberg lettuce leaves for the salad.

Decant dressing into a sauce bottle, to be carried separately. Pour some chicken finger dipping sauce into a covered sauce container. Prop onigiri in one corner of the box. Place chicken fingers beside the onigiri and octodogs and sauce cup opposite them, propping octodogs and chicken fingers against the wall of the box. Fill the empty spaces with salad.

OCEAN VARIATION

1/2 cup koshihikari rice; salt; fry or bake ready-to-cook chicken fingers; 4 cocktail hot dogs; iceberg lettuce; salad dressing; dipping sauce. 1-tier bento box.

Cook rice, pack into bento box. Cook chicken fingers and place at bottom edge for sand. Make octodogs as in Under The Sea Bento (left) and lie flat on rice, angled as if swimming. Arrange shredded lettuce leaves on rice in seaweed shapes, with bases touching sand. Place sauce as sunken treasure.

CUCUMBER TAIL BENTO

Kumquats; blueberries; raspberries; sugar snap peas; small cucumber; adzuki beans (canned); sushi rice (koshihikari); umeboshi; furikake; honey. 2-tier bento box.

Cook rice. Peel small cucumber; remove a thin ribbon of the flesh so you can see the seeds inside. Slice into medallions, keeping together and placing into box. Add two kumquats at front to form a head.

Select three pea pods; use a toothpick to hold them together in a fan shape. Place at the end of the cucumber to form a tail. Slice one kumquat in half and take one of those halves and cut it into half again. This is the base of the tail. Place raspberries and blueberries around cucumber.

Mash a few adzuki beans into a paste and sweeten with honey to taste. Use the paste as a filling when making the onigiri. Sprinkle furikake on the onigiri in thin lines. Place halved kumquat and two pea pods on top of the onigiri.

FISHTANK BENTO

Kumquats; blueberries; raspberries; green seedless grapes; cucumber; baby zucchini; ginger root; sushi rice (koshihikari); umeboshi; sesame seeds. 1-tier bento box.

Cook rice. Start with an onigiri stuffed with umeboshi. Slice a single kumquat in half, end to end. One half will form the goldfish body, the other the tail. Slice the tail piece into three, place on onigiri. Add sesame seed for an eye and light sesame seeds for bubbles coming from the mouth. Skin half a cucumber and using a paring knife, cut slivers length-wise to look like flowers.

Place rounds at the base of the onigiri. Save slivers for sea grasses. Cut zucchini into matchstick sized slivers; add to cucumber slivers. Nestle around the onigiri. Add a layer of grapes to cover the bottom of the bento. Add blueberries and raspberries. Slice a bit of fresh ginger, notching the edge to create the illusion of a fish body and tail. Use notched pieces as fins and add sesame seed eyes.

CIRCLES BENTO

Kumquats; green seedless grapes; blackberries; baby tomatoes; sushi rice (koshihikari); umeboshi; furikake. Bamboo steamer.

Small steamers meant for dim sum can be transformed into a bento box using parchment paper and kitchen twine. Using the underside of the steamer as a template, cut a circle of parchment paper to fit the bottom and lid of each steamer.

Make onigiri; put down one layer of rice, add a bit of stuffing for the middle, add one more layer of rice and press them together so they seal into a rice ball. A popular onigiri has a pitted umeboshi center and is sprinkled with furikake on the top for decoration. Use pieces of parchment paper as masking tape to create sharp designs when sprinkling furikake on the top of your onigiri.

Using round items in a repeating pattern in the circular steamers adds visual punch.

SAVORIES BENTO

Champ (mashed potato with onion and peas); spinach and pomodoro radiatore pasta with dill Havarti cubes; 3 strawberries; 1 black olive; HP sauce in a small cup. For Forfar Bridies: 2 1/2 cups all purpose flour, 1 tsp salt, 1 tbsp ground pepper, 1 ½ sticks regular butter, 4-5 tbsp cold water, 3 tbsp butter, 1 package Morningstar Farms crumbles; 1 onion; 1 cup mushroom broth; 1/2 tbsp ground mustard; 1 tbsp garlic powder; 2 tbsp dried parsley; salt and pepper to taste. For savory dill and olive cheese ball: 8 oz. cream cheese; 4 oz. Dill Havarti; 1/2 cup shredded sharp cheddar; 2 dashes HP sauce; 1 tbsp garlic powder; 1 tsp onion powder; 10 black olives, very finely chopped; white and black sesame seeds. 1-tier bento box.

Bridies are Scottish meat pies that are delicious when warm or cold. These are vegetarian. Sautée crumbles and onion in butter. Add mushroom broth, mustard, garlic and parsley. Simmer until the broth is gone, then stir over medium heat for 3 more minutes. Let cool completely. In a large mixing bowl combine flour, salt and pepper for the crust. Add butter, a few pats at a time, rubbing it into the flour by hand until the mixture resembles coarse bread crumbs. Add water to the flour and butter mixture, one tbsp at a time. Make the dough into a large ball, adding more flour if necessary. Wrap in wax paper and refrigerate for 1 hour.

Separate the ball of dough into three roughly equal portions. Roll each portion, one by one, out to ¼ inch thickness. Cut 6 inch rounds from each,

kneading and re-rolling as necessary. Put 3 large teaspoonfuls of crumble mixture in the center of the pastry rounds. Wet edges with a little bit of water; fold over. Crimp edges together with a fork. Cut three slits into top of each bridie, or for extra cuteness cut happy faces! If cooking immediately, cook in a hot oven for 10-12 minutes. If freezing, place in freezable container separating layers with wax paper. Place directly from the freezer into the oven and cook on a high heat for 18-20 minutes.

For cheese balls: stir cream cheese until softened. Tear small bits of Havarti off by hand and stir into the cream cheese.

Add shredded cheddar mix well. Add HP sauce, garlic and onion powders to cheeses, mix by hand. Make tablespoon of cheese into a small ball and roll it in a plate of white and black sesame seeds until fully covered.

Pack champ tightly into the bottom right corner so that it forms a solid triangle. Place strawberries in the opposite corner to prop up the bridies. Place pasta in bottom left corner, and two bridies, one on top of the other in the center. Wedge in blue cup of HP sauce and scatter dill havarti cheese cubes over the pasta, place mini cheese ball in corner and add olive.

and the blooms in the pink. Keep an eye on them; when they are as dark as you'd like, drain and rinse well (until water runs clear). Blot well with paper towels until each piece is very dry. Reassemble the blossoms. Place one blossom atop each of the wraps. Slice 5-6 discs of cucumber and fan out alongside the wraps. In a small bowl, stir the yogurt and salt together. Grate the remaining cucumber into the mixture and stir. Transfer to the silicone cupcake cup and use a little conserved cucumber for garnish.

GARLIC PRAWN BENTO

3 raw, shelled prawns; 1/2 clove garlic; small piece of butter; small portion pickled Chinese cabbage; rolled omelette; tomato; lettuce; cooked Japanese rice; black sesame seeds. 1-tier bento box.

Make garlic prawns. Mix minced garlic with softened butter. In a hot pan, sear prawns on one side for one minute, then turn and add the butter. Allow to bubble for another minute. Remove, cool, and thread onto a food pick.

Line the top of the bento with lettuce, then place the garlic prawns on a skewer at one end. To make the rolled omelette into a heart shape, cut it on a sharp diagonal about half an inch from the top. Then turn one half around and place the two pieces cut side together. At the other end, place the pickled Chinese cabbage in a bento cup, then fill the remaining space with omelette heart and cherry tomato. Fill the bottom of bento with cooked rice, decorate with a line of black sesame seeds.

DAIKON SAKURA BENTO

Green peppers stir-fried with peanut butter sauce; 1 piece of sesame mamenori, cut into quarters; 1 fresh daikon radish; 1/3 cup cooked white long-grain rice, still warm; neon pink food color; yellow food color; 1 sakura-shaped vegetable cutter; 1 star-shaped aspic cutter; 1 small tangerine, peeled and divided in half; 1/2 small cucumber, 1/4 cup plain yogurt; pinch of salt; handful of dried cranberries; 1 packet green tea Pocky. 2 rectangular food storage boxes.

Spread out the pieces of mamenori. While rice is still warm, spoon 2 or 3 teaspoons into the center of each piece, along the diagonal. Top rice with green pepper mixture (tongs work well for this); quickly bring the top and bottom edges together. The heat and steam of the food should seal the wraps shut. Set aside until cool; when cool, add to box (usually 3 will fit). Slice 3-4 discs of the daikon radish and use the sakura-shaped cutter to cut a blossom shape from each. Use the star-shaped cutter to cut a star-shaped hole in the center of each one. Place the stars in the dish of yellow food coloring

ELEPHANT BENTO

2 cups cooked white long-grain rice, cooled; nonstick cooking spray; 1 small piece pink mamenori (soy paper), neon blue food color; 1 serving prepared Thai peanut chicken, cooled; 1/3 small zucchini; 9 or 10 green seedless grapes; 1 mushroom-shaped chocolate snack; strawberry flavor (available in Asian grocery stores). 2-tier bento box.

First, prepare elephant-shaped cookie cutter for mold. Spray well with nonstick cooking spray. Densely pack with rice, leaving a small hollow. Insert a teaspoon or so of Thai peanut chicken.

Fill the rest of the mold with more densely packed rice, ensuring that contents are not leaking. When the mold is full, press it once more, firmly, with the palm of your hand.

Slip a hand underneath and carefully transfer the entire mold to the bottom tier of the bento box. Press gently with your fingers to extract.

The cooking spray should ensure that it slides right out. If you get hung up on a small part like the trunk, nudge at it gently with a chopstick.

Dip a toothpick in the neon blue food color and make a single dot for the elephant's eye.

Use a blossom punch to cut three pink blossoms from the mamenori and place atop the rice. If the mamenori curls or will not stick, you can "glue" it with dots of light corn syrup.

Fill in the area around the elephant with the green seedless grapes. Using your favourite method, prepare four sushi rolls using remaining rice, half of remaining Thai peanut chicken, and diced zucchini.

Since rolls do not have a wrapper, be careful not to crush them as you cut.

Arrange four rolls in the second tier; use the small mushroom-shaped chocolate to fill the blank space in between (a spare grape also works).

Fill in the remaining space with the rest of the peanut chicken and garnish with julienned zucchini peel.

HAMBURGER AND PEPPER EGG BENTO

Blanched broccoli and cauliflower; tomatoes; cheese; lettuce; fried egg pepper; edamame bean skewer; cooked rice mixed with black sesame seeds. For teriyaki burgers: 1 onion; butter; 7 oz minced pork; 10 oz minced beef; 1 oz bread crumbs; 1 1/3 pt milk; 1 egg; salt and pepper; 4 tbsp mirin; 4 tbsp soy sauce; 4 tsp sugar 1-tier bento box.

Cook teriyaki burgers: sauté onion in butter.

Add to pork and beef, mix with milk and bread crumbs, add egg and seasonings.

Form mixture into bento sized hamburgers.

Chill in fridge for an hour, remove; fry gently in oil.

Heat mirin in a pan, add soy sauce and sugar. Simmer until thickened, pour over the burgers.

Line box with sushi grass and lettuce.

Put rice into divider cup, top with edamame bean skewer and fried egg pepper.

Place three teriyaki burgers.

Cut out a heart shaped piece from a thin slice of cheese, and use a food pick to secure it.

Fill the spaces with the tomatoes and the blanched broccoli and cauliflower.

Jasmine Rice; veggie hot dog flowers; steamed broccoli; baby corn; baby tomatoes; mochi; lemon cream puff biscuit. For Japanese curry: 2 cubes Golden Curry Brand curry mix; 3 Idaho potatoes; 3 large carrots; 1 onion; 8 oz. extra firm tofu; butter; 2 tbsp vegetable oil. 2-tier bento box.

Cut the tofu into 5 slabs, placing them upon several paper towels and covering them with more paper towels. Squeeze the extra water out. Cut into cubes. Heat the oil in a large skillet on medium high. When the oil is hot, put in tofu cubes; brown on each side. While the tofu is browning, chop the onion in large pieces. Add them to the pan with the tofu and stir until the onions are clear.

Peel and cube potatoes. Set aside. Peel and chop carrots into thick rounds. Set aside. Remove the tofu and onions from the pan. Replace with potatoes and carrots, sauté with butter for 3 minutes. Put in enough water to cover the vegetables allow to simmer until the potatoes are cooked through.

Break apart and add the cubes of curry mix to the potatoes and carrots, adding enough water to just cover the vegetables again. Stir curry mix while it melts into the water. Add tofu and onions back into the mixture, stirring thoroughly. Again, add more water if the sauce seems too thick. Or if you like a thick sauce, just let it simmer for a few more minutes so that the flavor can absorb into the tofu. Serve over rice.

Fill 1/2 of the bento with jasmine rice and layer a thin covering of rice on the

EGG CHICK BENTO

2 burger balls; 1 cup rice; salmon furikake; blanched asparagus; carrot, cherry tomatoes; sliced cheese cut into shapes; a boiled egg; black sesame seeds; apple; parsley; soy sauce bottle. 2-tier bento box.

Boil an egg for ten minutes. Remove from the heat and cool under a tap. Using a sharp knife, cut in a zig zag pattern around the middle of the egg, taking care not to push the knife in too far and cut the yolk. Pull the two halves apart to expose the yolk. Add triangular piece of carrot for a beak and black sesame seeds for eye. Cut a red apple into eight equal segments. Score a V-shape halfway up the rabbit. Peel the skin away from the flesh with the knife until you get to the tip of the V. Remove the middle part, leaving two flaps either side, which will become ears. Soak in water and a little lemon juice, to prevent browning. Fill one tier with cooked rice, add a line of furikake down the middle. Add burger balls to one side, topped with a slice of cheese secured with a food pick. Add apple rabbit and a cherry tomato, and soy sauce bottle. Finally, add egg chick and asparagus spears. Fill gaps with parsley, sprinkle with carrot shaped into stars.

bottom of the other half. Spoon the curry into the other half. Cut steamed sugar snap peas into flower stems and leaves with a paring knife, laying them onto the rice. Take a tiny fondant cutter and cut flowers out of veggie hot dog rounds. Place them over the snap pea stems then put brightly colored sugar dots into the centers.

For the other set of flowers cut rounds from steamed baby corn and place several together over the snap pea stems.

Cut a veggie hot dog into thirds. Take two of the thirds and slice 3/4 down the length in sixths. Put the long, thin ends of baby corn in the center to make the 'petals' separate a bit. Place hot dog flowers into the bento at one end. Shore up hot dog flowers by packing steamed broccoli tightly around them, following up with steamed baby corn.

Place a paper cupcake cup into the other end and fill with one mochi and one cookie. Fill remaining space with baby tomatoes.

HEARTS BENTO

Jasmine rice; carrots; teriyaki tofu; steamed peas; cherry tomato half. For teriyaki tofu; 4 oz. extra firm tofu; 2 tbsp soy sauce; 2 tbsp teriyaki sauce; 1 tbsp olive oil. 1-tier bento box.

Cut tofu into thick slices. Marinate in a bowl with soy sauce and teriyaki sauce for at least 10 minutes. Heat olive oil in a small frying pan. Sauté tofu in oil until just browned on all sides. Pour in marinade; continue to sauté until sauce is gone.

Fill half of box with rice, packing tightly. Place moisture proof cupcake cup next to the rice. Cut circles of carrot; stand on edges in cupcake cup and pour in steamed peas. Using a fondant or vegetable cutter, cut one large carrot heart and one small. Lay onto rice. Wedge three teriyaki tofu sticks into the space. Place a pick into one tofu stick to aid in picking them up. Cut a cherry tomato in half and place one half on top of the tofu sticks.

SMILEY FACE BENTO

Open-face cheese sandwich; corn; steamed pea skewer; tomato; cucumber slices; rice; turquoise food color gel; Morningstar Farms Broccoli and Cheddar bite; 2 Sanko cheese and almond rice crackers. 1-tier bento box.

Make a round onigiri; place into bento.

Across from it put an aluminum cupcake cup and filled halfway with cooked corn.

Lay one sliced and one uncut broccoli bite into the box.

Layer slices of cucumber and two rice crackers in front of broccoli bite halves.

Using graduated cookie cutters, cut a large circle of bread and a smaller circle of cheese.

Spread a filling onto the bread, covering with cheese circle.

Cut a smiley face from a sheet of nori

DUCKY BENTO

1/2 cup Japanese rice; 1 tablespoon red shiso furikake; nori seaweed, cut in duck shape; red daikon pickles; cucumber, sliced; 1/2 pack firm tofu; 3 tablespoons soy sauce; 2 tablespoons mirin; shichimi to taste. 2-tier bento box.

Cook rice. Drain tofu for 10 minutes by placing a heavy object on top, so that the water is pressed out slowly.

Chop into bite sized slices. Mix soy sauce with the mirin. Marinate tofu in this mixture for at least 10 minutes. Put a little bit of oil in a skillet and bake the tofu on both sides on medium heat until golden brown.

Mix rice with furikake. Put rice in the lower lid of the bento box. Make a flat surface with a rice spoon. Arrange nori ducks on top.

In other part of bento, arrange tofu, cucumber and pickles as shown.

with a face punch and place the eyes and mouth onto the cheese.

Gently lay the sandwich into place.

With a paring knife, cut a large cherry tomato into a flower by making small diagonal cuts up and down all the way around and pulling upper and lower halves apart.

Skewer three sweet peas on a plastic toothpick; arrange across the corn cup.

CRAYFISH BENTO

1/2 cup Japanese rice; 1 tablespoon seaweed furikake; nori seaweed, cut in fish shapes; 3 1/2 oz crayfish; 1 clove of garlic; 1 tablespoon soy sauce; mixed lettuce; small container with sesame dressing. 2-tier bento box.

Cook rice. Heat oil in a skillet. Chop garlic and stir-fry until lightly browned. Add crayfish and stir-fry for two more minutes.

Add soy sauce, stir, and remove from heat.

Mix rice with furikake. Put into the lower part of bento box.

Arrange nori fish on top. Place crayfish next to rice, with a plastic divider in between.

Fill upper part of bento with lettuce and what is left of the crayfish. Include the container with dressing.

FUN HEARTS BENTO

2 Heart shaped onigiri; 2 chicken nuggets; 3 gyoza; carrot circles; apple slice; steamed broccoli; baby tomato skewers. 1-tier bento box.

Make minature onigiri.

Take freshly steamed rice and place in onigiri mold.

Place into the bento, followed by the chicken nuggets which go into a corner.

Add raw carrot circles and gyoza, stacking one on top of the other two.

Slice off an entire side of an apple.

Take a fondant flower cutter and cut just through the apple peel.

Rock it from side to side in order to cut through the lower part where the apple curves.

Use a sharp paring knife to cut away the peel in the flower shaped cut.

Soak in a mixture of lemon juice and water for a minute, and place in bento.

Fill space next to the apple with steamed broccoli florets.

Make baby tomato skewers. Angle them to lean beside the onigiri.

Take a sheet of origami paper and use a face punch to cut eyes and mouths.

Place them onto the hearts using a pair of tweezers. Remove before eating.

LION BENTO

1 tofu bite; 1 Yves meatless hot dog; kichdi; 2 Mrs. T's Potato and Cheddar Mini pierogies; steamed broccoli; lemon wedge; mozzarella stars; cherry tomato; 1 nori sheet. 1-tier bento box.

See Holiday Fun Bento for recipes.

Tightly pack kichdi to fill up half of the bento.

Make sure to leave enough room so that the lion face will fit within the confines of the box.

Place the tomato in the upper left corner, followed by two broccoli florets.

Lean two pierogies against the broccoli and tomato with the curved ends up.

Gently nestle a small wedge of lemon next to the tomato.

Place tofu bite in the bottom center of the kichdi area.

Cut a lion face from a sheet of nori using a face punch or scissors.

Transfer nori details onto the tofu bite with tweezers.

Cook hot dog according to package directions.

Slice most of the way through down the entire length.

Remove both ends with diagonal cuts.

Curve the hot dog around the tofu bite.

Place the two end pieces in the kichdi touching the curved mane, diagonal slices upright.

Make several tiny mozzarella stars.

Place stars around the broccoli and pierogies to garnish.

LION VARIATION

1 chicken nugget; 1 hot dog; kichdi; 2 gyoza; steamed broccoli; lemon wedge; mozzarella stars; cherry tomato; 1 nori sheet. 1-tier bento box.

Cook chicken nugget according to instructions, stir-fry cooked gyoza in a little soy sauce. Prepare remaining ingredients as in Lion Bento (left) and arrange as above to create a bento box for meat-lovers.

CATERPILLAR BENTO

Near East roasted garlic and olive oil couscous; cucumber and carrot caterpillar; fruit cup with blueberries, pineapple chunks and kiwi; pasta salad leftovers; Morningstar Farms broccoli and cheddar bites; 2 French fries; lentil pate heart; black olive. 2-tier bento box.

Fill top tier with couscous, packing it down tightly. Slice rounds of cucumber and carrots, then layer them onto the couscous. Alternate between them, trying to keep the smaller carrot rounds in the center of the cucumbers.

Take two small cuts of red bell pepper and wedge them underneath the last cucumber round to make antennae.

With a face punch, make eyes and a mouth from a sheet of nori and use tweezers to put in place on the last cucumber slice.

Put the silicon cup in the bottom tier and fill with the blueberries and pineapple chunks. Slice a kiwi and cut out the butterfly shape with a small cookie cutter. Place on top of the fruit cup.

Place two broccoli bites on the opposite side of the tier. The two French fries go beside them, propped up upon the broccoli bites.

Fill remaining space with pasta salad. On top of the pasta place a lentil pate heart cut with a cookie cutter and a second, smaller carrot heart. A black olive sits in the tiny space left beside the fruit cup.

BEEF STEW BENTO

Leftover beef stew; sprig parsley; 1/2 cup brown rice; 1/2 cup white rice; cucumber kim chee; 1 sheet nori. 2-tier bento box.

Stew carrot, thinly slice and cut into flowers, using vegetable cutters. Fill top tier of bento box with stew; gently place the carrot flowers in top left corner on top of parsley sprigs. Cook rice and mix brown and white rice together. Fill half of the lower tier of bento box with the brown/white rice mix. Place paper food cup in remaining half, fill with stewed carrots and cucumber kim chee. Make star-shaped paper template and cut two stars from nori to top the rice.

KOALA BENTO

1/2 cup Jasmine rice; Korean rice snacks; steamed broccoli; carrot heart; Babybel cheese. For vegetables and somen noodle stirfry: 1 pack somen noodles; 1/4 onion; 1/2 green pepper; 1/2 red pepper; 1/2 yellow pepper; 1 tbsp sesame oil; 1 tbsp soy sauce. Child's bear-shaped bento box.

Chop and stirfry the onion and peppers in sesame oil until the onion has turned clear. Cook the somen noodles then add to the pan with vegetables, add soy sauce and stir for 3 minutes.

Take two to three Babybel cheese rounds and let them warm up a bit to soften them. Press them into a bear-shaped egg mold, trying to get them to conform as completely as possible. Putting cheese in just one side works well, or in both sides can make a double mold. Close the mold.

Steam it in a steamer basket over a small amount of water for a very short time, about 3-4 minutes. Let cool on the counter for a few minutes and then place into the fridge for at least a half hour. Open the mold and tap out the cheese.

Fill half of the bear face with the rice, packing it down tightly. Gently spoon the somen noodle stirfry into the remaining space.

Cut the stems from steamed broccoli florets; fill in nose and add carrot heart on top. Place crunchy rice snacks into the ears. The cheese bear goes in the corner of the bento box as a last touch.

KOALA VARIATION

3 strawberries; 1 serving rice pudding; handful blueberries; handful raspberries; pinch sugar; handful raisins; handful dried apricots. Child's bear-shaped bento box.

Fill half of bear face with rice pudding. Mix blueberries and raspberries together, sprinkle with sugar. Add next to rice.

Use strawberries to fill in nose, place apricots in ear sections. Make eyes, nose and ear accents from raisins.

PEANUT BUTTER BENTO

Peanut butter sandwich, cut into half moons; Okinawan sweet potato, baked and cubed; mango, cubed; 1 wedge Laughing Cow light Swiss cheese; 4 low fat Triscuit biscuits. 1-tier bento box with divider.

Bake sweet potato; slice into cubes. Make peanut butter sandwich and using a circle cookie cutter, cut out three half moons. Place in bento box. Add sweet potato to fill empty space. Add cheese wedge to the other side and place the Triscuit crackers next to it. Chop mango into cubes and place.

ALMOND SAKURA BENTO

1 cup long-grain white rice, cooked and cooled; 1/2 cup prepared Thai peanut sauce; 13 pieces of sliced almond, well-shaped, with good, dark borders; 5 fresh broccoli florets; 1 large fresh strawberry; 1 pink red-bean rice cake; 2-pack Sakura Kit Kat; 1 2-tier adult size bento box, sakura-shaped.

Press the rice into one tier of the bento box. Spray sakura vegetable cutter thoroughly inside and out with nonstick cooking spray. Press into the rice firmly, but don't grate it against the bottom. Carefully pull the cutter upward and out, pressing on the rice around it if you need to. Repeat elsewhere on the rice in whatever design you choose, spraying the cutter again with cooking spray if the rice sticks. Two perfect cherry-blossom shapes should be cut into the rice.

Carefully spoon the peanut sauce into the holes; nudge it around so that the bright orange sauce fills all the space. Fill both holes all the way to the top. Add three tiny dabs of sauce in the blank rice-space to anchor the loose petals. Carefully arrange the almond slices in cherry-blossom patterns on the two deposits of peanut sauce and press the loose petals onto the dabs of sauce. If you press down gently, it should squeeze out an orange border around each petal to set it off.

Arrange remaining ingredients in the other tier. Clockwise: fresh strawberry in mini cupcake paper, broccoli, sakura kit-kat, red-bean rice cake in mini cupcake paper.

FOX IN THE HENHOUSE BENTO

1 cup colored shortgrain rice; powdered Japanese color mix; 1 sheet nori; carrot, lettuce; 3 chocolate mushrooms; parsley; 2 cherry tomatoes; tangerine; 2 quails' eggs. 2-tier bento box.

Press rice into cube-shaped rice mold to create 3 chicks and into star-shaped rice mold to create fox. Use white rice on fox cheeks to create differentiation. Arrange the fox in the right side of the bottom tier on a leaf of lettuce.

Place a piece of plastic grass beside the lettuce. Line the left half of the box with a paper cup, and arrange tangerine sections and cherry tomatoes speared with picks. Add parsley accents.

In the upper tier, place a thin layer of shredded cabbage, then arrange the chicks on top. Leaf lettuce accent behind the chicks.

Boil quails' eggs and cut tops off leaving jagged edges to make egg chicks. Cut carrot beaks into beak and feet shapes, place on chicks. Add nori eyes to chicks and nori eyes and whiskers to fox. Dot 3 chocolate mushrooms into gaps.

THREE PIGGIES BENTO

5 sausages; 2 tablespoon soy sauce carrot; baked beans; 1 oz broccoli; 1 teaspoon grated garlic; plum flavorings for cooked rice; potato starch; 7 oz cooked rice; 1 tbsp sake; 1/2 cup plum vinegar; ketchup; 2 oz chicken leg; 3 quails' eggs (2 boiled); lettuce; 1 lemon; 1 small tomato; 1 nori seaweed sheet; fish sausage; flower shape pasta. 1-tier bento box.

Cut chicken into bite-size pieces. Marinade with soy sauce, grated garlic, sake and one beaten quail's egg for 30 mins. Boil two quails' eggs, then marinade with plum vinegar until they turn pink. Put lettuce into bento box.

Divide broccoli into small fringes. Boil broccoli and flower shaped pasta.

Make 3 cuts into tops of sausages, boil about 20-30 seconds with boiling water. Keep 2 sausages for mushroom stalks. Peel carrots and cut into thin round slices. Boil until tender.

Make three onigiri with plum flavorings. Place in bento box. Use fish cake to make snouts and ears, pin on using spaghetti. Cut nori seaweed sheet into eyes, nose and mouth shapes. Add to piggies.

Heat pan, drain chicken and cover with potato starch. Deep-fry chicken for five mins until browned. Make quails' egg mushrooms. Cut holes using thin straw. Cut eggs in half. Fix to sausages with food picks.

Add sausage, carrot, lemon, broccoli, fried chicken in bento box.

CHICKEN AND EGG BENTO

1 frozen hamburger steak; 1 quail's egg; 1 carrot; kabocha squash; mayonnaise; 1/2 oz broccoli; plum flavoring for cooked rice; 1 egg; salt; 2 sausage; 2 snow peas; lettuce; 1 nori sheet; 6 oz cooked rice; 1/4 tomato; sliced cheese. 1-tier bento box.

Cook hamburger, put into bento box with lettuce. Boil broccoli and snow peas. Peel skin of carrot and cut into slices. Boil. Simmer squash and snow peas. Cut sausage into flowers and boil about 20-30 seconds. Boil quail's egg. Cut egg with zig zag. Stir together plum flavorings and cooked rice. Make two onigiri and add nori seaweed stripes. Put into bento box. Make Japanese style omelette; cut into chicken and flower shape with cookie cutter. Put chicken onto hamburger stalk, flowers onto onigiri. Make chicken's crest, feather and beaks with carrot and eyes from nori. Cut carrot into circle, place on flowers. Fill gaps with broccoli and tomato.

PANDA BENTO

1/2 egg; 3 sausages; 1 medium potato; 1 teaspoon cut green onions; 4 green soy beans; 1/2 cup rice; 1 small tomato; 1 nori seaweed sheet; lettuce; salt; butter; pepper; soy sauce. 1-tier bento box.

Put some lettuce into bento box. Cut sausage and boil for about 20 or 30 seconds. Cut tomato. Beat egg in the bowl with a little salt and pepper. Heat the skillet or wok (med-high), add oil; stir-fry the tomato first. Pour in the egg mixture until it becomes slightly firm. Season with salt, pepper and soy sauce. Top with boiled green soy beans. Cut a potato into quarters; stir-fry potato with some butter. Top with cut green onions. Cook rice. Make two oval shaped onigiri. Put onigiri into bento box. Cut nori seaweed sheet into eyes, nose and mouth, belt and ears for pandas. Cut sausage with thick straw and put it on onigiri as cheeks. Add sausage and stir-fried potatoes to bento box. Include picks to make easy to eat.

CHECKED FLAG BENTO

1 frozen bear shaped onigiri; 2 frozen gyoza; 1 quail's egg, boiled; 2 small cheese stars; 1 stalk of asparagus, cut into thirds; 2 broccoli florets; 2 snow peas, halved; 1 carrot triangle; 2 squares cut from apple, 1/2 tangerine, divided into wedges; 1 strawberry, sliced; 2 blackberries; 5 blueberries; 1 small circle and 1 small oval cut from thinly sliced ham; 1 nori sheet; 2 black sesame seeds; lemon juice; 1 tbsp canola oil; 1 small bottle of gyoza dipping sauce (half soy sauce, half rice vinegar). 1-tier bento box.

Microwave onigiri until warm (about 45 seconds). Place in bento, cut nori nose and mouth, place on ham circle, cut ham oval and cut in half. Position on face. Fry gyoza; place, with bottle of sauce, in corner of box. Steam asparagus, broccoli, snow peas. Place in box with quail's egg chick, apple checker boards, (rubbed with lemon juice to keep from browning), strawberry slices, blackberries and blueberries. Add cheese stars for decoration.

PEEK-A-BOO BENTO

Kumquats; blueberries; blackberries; green seedless grapes; sugar snap peas; grape tomatoes; 1/2 cup sushi rice (koshihikari); umeboshi. 1-tier bento box.

Mold your rice either using your hands or an onigiri mold, stuffing the center with a pitted umeboshi. Place this in center of bento. Surround with alternating tomatoes and blackberries,

use green grapes at sides. Remove tips of pea pods; use to fill empty nooks. Slice top and bottom of kumquats to expose flower-like pattern; place them on at edges of bento. Take two similarly sized baby tomatoes and cut them in half to create flower petals to sit on top of the onigiri. Cut single pea pod in half, lengthwise following the seam. Place halved pod on the onigiri between the tomatoes. Cut base from one of the kumquats and add a pea half in the center of the tomato and pea pod flower.

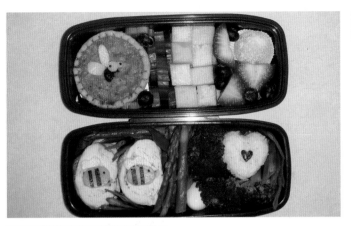

1 Portobello mushroom; 1 cup spinach; pinch polenta; 1 cup rice; 1/4 cup shredded umeboshi; 1 tbsp red edible glitter; 4 broccoli florets, 1/2 orange pepper; 1 Hawaiian purple sweet potato; 4 pretzels; 1 slice cooked beef; 3 beans. 2-tier bento box.

Cook spinach, broccoli and sweet potato. Mash potato and add to box. Cook rice, make onigiri stuffed with umeboshi and potato.

Decorate onigiri with pepper slice and food glitter. Cut boot from mushroom. Make moth and lamp from pretzels, meat, pepper, beans.

Arrange remaining ingredients.

BEE BENTO

1 small frozen heart shaped onigiri; 1 mini sweet potato pie; 1 leftover chicken portion; 3 stalks asparagus, cut in half; 3 to 4 broccoli florets; 6 to 8 snow peas, cut in half; 1 quail's egg, boiled; 2 slices carrot; 1/2 slice cucumber; 8 small cubes of pineapple; 8 small cubes of melon; 2 strawberries, cut in half; 8 to 10 blueberries; 1 small daifuku; slice mozzarella; slice cheddar; 1 sheet nori; 5 black sesame seeds. 2-tier bento box.

Microwave onigiri until warm. Place nori heart in center.

Steam asparagus, broccoli and snow peas.

Make bees: punch two ovals from cheddar with a cheese cutter and two hearts from mozzarella, remove bottom points of hearts to make wings.

Place nori strips and sesame eyes on cheddar ovals. Add two stacks of chicken slices, asparagus, quail's egg, onigiri to lower tier.

Place one bee on each stack of chicken slices. Put sweet potato pie in left side of the top tier.

Slice cucumber and arrange in three rows. Put pineapple and melon in columns, alternating colors.

Place daifuku in the top right corner in a foil cup. Fill remaining space with berries.

Cut carrot flowers, place with blueberries to fill gaps around the pie.

To make the fly, cut wings and eyes out of cheese.

Use a nori oval as the body and press two sesame seeds into the cheese for eyes; use remaining sesame seed for the fly's nose.

PIG AND STAR BENTO

Green and purple string beans; 1 cup rice; broccoli; green pepper; carrot; yellow plum; red plum; shrimp; cucumber; black sesame seeds. 2-tier bento box.

Cook rice.

Pack molds with rice to create pig-shaped and star-shaped onigiri.

Stuff onigiri with a mixture of shrimp, cucumber, and vinegar.

Decorate with black sesame seeds.

Place in top tier, fill the empty space with broccoli florets.

Layer green pepper strips across the bottom tier.

Add carrot coins and strips to decorate the left side of box.

Cut plums in half and use sakura-shaped cookie cutter to take a flower out of each.

Swap red flower into the hole left by the yellow flower.

Lie in box on pepper bed.

Use remaining half of the yellow plum to cut radial, pie-shaped pieces to serve as the sun-ray shapes.

Lay around the edge of the yellow-and-red half.

Cut remaining red plum to fill the far right side.

ANGRY PEACH BENTO

1 cup rice; 1/4 cup shredded umeboshi; 1 small sweet potato; 1 tsp garlic powder; 1 tsp crushed red pepper flakes; 1 cup edamame beans; 1 peach; 1/2 cucumber; 3 yellow cherry tomatoes; 3 red cherry tomatoes;. 2-tier bento box.

Cook rice. Cook sweet potato, mash.

Mix mash with shredded umeboshi.

Use mold to make one star onigiri and one flower onigiri.

Stuff with umeboshi and potato mixture.

Dust star onigiri with garlic powder.

Top flower onigiri with pepper flakes. Cook edamame beans.

Cut peach in half.

Cut pieces of plum skin into eye and hair pieces.

Place two peach pieces and two cornflake crumbs as eyes.

Peel cucumber, cut into flower shapes using cookie cutters.

Arrange ingredients as shown in image.

the other half of the container, arrange the remaining items: cookies in a paper cupcake cup, the cup of dressing, and the remaining carrots and edamame.

Place green goddess dressing in a paper cup. The fruit leather fits perfectly on its side. Cut a long, wide strip from the last carrot and cut your letter from that using a cutter or by hand. Rest it gently on top of the dressing.

TERI BURGER BENTO

1 1/2 cup chopped lettuce; handful edamame beans; 1 carrot; 1 hamburger; 1 tbsp teriyaki sauce; 1 slice white cheese; 1 slice nori. 1-tier bento box.

Put chopped lettuce into box. Grate carrot and sprinkle with edamame onto lettuce.

Cut two circles out of cheese for eyes and a mouth shape.

Cut out nori detail, add to eyes. Place onto cooked hamburger soaked in teriyaki sauce, and put on top of salad.

GROUCHY BOY BENTO

2 slices multi grain sandwich bread; 1 slice luncheon meat; 1/2 cup shredded lettuce; 2 slices Swiss cheese; handful frozen, shelled edamame; 2 small slivers red pepper; 6 small broccoli florets; 6 baby carrots; 2 small biscuits; 1 wrapped fruit leather; 1 tbsp green goddess dressing. I-tier plastic food-storage container, with divider.

Make a sandwich by buttering bread and filling with one slice Swiss cheese, luncheon meat and lettuce. Use a paring knife to cut a jagged mouth. Place in the larger compartment of the food storage container. Cut two ovals from the slice of Swiss cheese. To make them match, cut one freehand, stack on the cheese, then use it as a template for cutting the second piece. Add the ovals to the sandwich for eyes, accenting with thawed edamame. Cut the bell pepper slivers to form angular eyebrows and arrange above the eyes to make a scowl. Tuck broccoli along the sandwich's lower border. Choose the widest carrot and set to one side. In

SCARED SARNIE BENTO

2 pieces whole wheat bread; 2 slices bologna; 1 slice cheddar cheese; 1 tsp yellow mustard; 1/2 slice Swiss cheese; 2 frozen and shelled edamame; 7 baby carrots; 1/2 cup snack mix; 1 mini-muffin; 1 wrapped Japanese sweet-cake; 1 mini-pack of fruit snacks (the ones shown here are shark-shaped); 1 handful roasted, salted peanuts; 1 tbsp caramel apple dip; 1/2 Granny Smith apple. 2 food storage boxes.

Make a sandwich using bread, bologna, cheddar and mustard. Put cheese between bologna so pink shows

through to look like a mouth. Use a paring knife to carve an arc that begins at the lower, squarish corners of the bread. Place in one box; pull down to make a gap for the mouth. Cut two ovals from Swiss cheese and add edamame to make eyes. Cut a baby carrot in half lengthwise; taper with paring knife to make eyebrows. Arrange on the sandwich. Fill space with snack mix.

Arrange remaining ingredients in the four-compartment bento. Clockwise: mini muffin; wrapped sweet-cake, and fruit snacks; apple wedges; peanuts and dipping sauce; baby carrots.

MONSTER BENTO

2 pieces whole grain bread; 3 slices pastrami; 2 slices Swiss cheese; 2 edamame beans; 8 baby carrots; 1/2 cucumber; 3 tsp cream cheese; handful red seedless grapes, 2 frosted mini-cupcakes; 1 packet bite-size chips. 2 medium rectangular food storage boxes.

Make a sandwich using two slices pastrami, one slice Swiss cheese. Slice in half along the diagonal. Place in lower left corner of one box. Fold and tuck the extra piece of lunch meat in center of diagonal cut so it protrudes like a tongue. Cut four sharp, angular teeth from a piece of the cucumber; prop across cut.

Cut two ovals from cheese, position as eyes. Accent with edamame, top with eyebrows made from baby carrot slices. Slice remaining cucumber into discs; make three sandwiches from cucumber slices and cream cheese. In the other tier, arrange the remaining items: grapes and carrots; mini cupcakes; chips.

pepper. Pack into one side of bento box.

Boil quails' eggs, then simmer with curry powder and bouillon cube until colored yellow. Put yellow quails' eggs on to rice with food picks.

Beaks are made with carrot pieces, glued on using mayo. Cut nori seaweed sheet for eyes.

Place broccoli, fried chicken and remaining ingredients into bento box as shown in image.

HAPPY TOMATO BENTO

8 honeydew melon balls; 1 small bunch red currants, 1/4 cup romaine lettuce; 1 'yellow pear' cherry tomato; 1 scrap nori; leftover meat entree (e.g. barbecue chicken); 1 small sweet potato; 1 pinch toasted almond slices. 2-tier bento box.

Subdivide the top bento tier with two eclair cups. In one cup, arrange the melon balls in a pile.

Drape currants across the top. In the other cup, arrange the lettuce.

Dampen cherry tomato with a bit of water. With bento-dedicated nail scissors, cut two V shapes and a triangle shape from the nori. Arrange on tomato to form eyes and a mouth. Prop tomato atop the lettuce.

Bake and mash sweet potato. In lower tier, arrange the meat entree on one side and the mashed sweet potato on the other. Scatter almond slices over the sweet potato.

THREE CHICKS BENTO

3 quails' eggs; 1 chicken breast; 1 lemon; 2 grapes; 1 cheese stick; 1 sheet nori; 1/4 cup bread crumbs; 1 sweet potato; 1 tsp black sesame seeds; 1 carrot; pinch salt; 1 baby tomato; 1 tsp curry powder; 1 tbsp flour; pinch pepper; 1/2 oz broccoli; 1/2 cup rice; 1 tbsp ketchup; 2 lettuce leaves; 1 bouillon cube; 1 egg; 1 tsp mayonnaise. 1-tier bento box.

Line bento box with lettuce. Divide broccoli into small fringes. Boil in salted water for two mins. Peel carrot; cut into thin round slices. Boil carrot slices until tender. Cut with fish shaped cookie cutter. Keep small pieces to one side for chick beaks.

Flatten chicken breast with rolling pin. Roll cheese stick and nori seaweed sheet together with chicken breast. Sprinkle salt and pepper on chicken. Dust chicken with flour and dip in beaten egg. Roll chicken in bread crumbs mixed with black sesame seeds. Fry chicken in hot oil until cooked and golden brown. Cut in half.

Peel sweet potato into chequered pattern and boil for six mins. Cook rice, then stir-fry with ketchup, salt and

CHICKEN FINGERS BENTO

2 ready-to-cook chicken fingers; 1/4 cup frozen peas; 3 quails' eggs; 2 umeboshi; 1 tbsp dipping sauce; 1 sheet nori; 1/2 carrot. For chicken couscous: 1/4 cup couscous; 1/2 cup chicken broth; 1 tsp lemon juice; 1 tbsp butter; pinch sea salt. 1-tier bento box.

Make chicken couscous. Bring chicken broth to boil. Add lemon juice and sea salt. Turn off heat. Add couscous then cover. After 5-10 minutes, fluff up couscous with a knife. Add butter and toss until evenly coated. Boil quails' eggs, allow to cool then peel. Bake chicken fingers until cooked. Boil peas. Fill half of bento box with couscous. Line 1/4 of the box with a foil cup, then add chicken fingers. Place peas in a reusable bento cup. Fill gaps with one quail's egg and umeboshi.

On the couscous bed, position dipping sauce in cup, two quails' eggs, a piece of sushi grass and a toothpick to look like the eggs are carrying the sauce cup. Add details like eyes, beaks and tails with nori and carrots.

HAMBEARGER BENTO

1/2 cup rice; 1 radish; 1 tomato; 1 orange; 1 tsp mayonnaise; 2 chives. For hamburgers: 8 oz ground beef; 1/2 cup fresh bread crumbs; 1 egg; pinch salt; pinch pepper; 1/2 onion; a little oil. 1-tier bento box with section dividers.

Make hamburgers. Chop onion then sauté in a little oil. Cool. Beat egg. Mix together beef, onion, bread crumbs, half the beaten egg, salt and pepper. Fry lightly until cooked. Place in one section of box. Cook rice. Shred radish. Rub with rock salt, then rinse thoroughly. Slice tomato. Create a pattern on orange by running a lemon zester along the skin. Sprinkle zest on burgers. Slice orange into wedges, place in another section.

Place rice in empty compartment of box. In the last compartment, sit tomato slices and radish in a bento cup. Place bear shaped burger on top of rice. Add facial details using mayonnaise. Create tulip using tomato for bud and chives for stalk.

CUTE BENTO

1-2 tbsp crumbled feta cheese; 1 small plum tomato; 1 slice Swiss cheese; 1 sheet nori; pinch denbu flakes. For beef couscous: 1/4 cup couscous; 1/2 cup beef broth; 1 tbsp lemon juice; pinch salt; pinch pepper. For mock bifteki: 4 oz ground beef; 1 tbsp sour cream; 1 tsp dried thyme; pinch salt; pinch pepper; 8 feta cheese cubes. 1-tier bento box.

Make mock bifteki. Mix together beef, sour cream, thyme, salt and pepper.

Place small amount of beef mix in palm, add a piece of feta.

Wrap beef around the feta, rolling gently into a ball.

Repeat until mix is used up.

Grill for 10-15 minutes in a broiler on high. Stack in bento.

Make couscous. Boil beef broth. Remove from heat.

Add lemon juice, salt and pepper to taste.

Add couscous then cover. Leave for 5-10 minutes.

Fluff with a fork, place in bento.

Mix together crumbled feta and diced tomato, place in gap in box.

Cut cheese and nori to make eyes for meatballs and bear design.

Color bear mouth with denbu oboro.

SKELETON BENTO

3 ready-to-cook chicken fingers; 4 quails' eggs; 1 dragon fruit; 1 sheet nori. For chili pepper fusilli: 2 tbsp olive oil; 3 cloves garlic; 1/2 tsp chili pepper flakes; 3/4 cup diced fresh tomatoes; 3 tuyo fillets; 1 tsp shredded fresh basil; 3/4 cup fusilli; tsp salt. 1-tier food storage box.

Fry or bake chicken fingers. Peel and slice fresh dragon fruit. Hard boil and peel quails' eggs. Make fusilli. Cook pasta until al dente. Lightly sauté garlic in olive oil. Add chili flakes, sauté a little before adding tomatoes. Add shredded tuyo, cook until tomatoes soften. Add basil. Add pasta to pan, sauté until well coated. Fill half of bento with pasta. In one compartment, pack chicken fingers and place dragon fruit in another. Thread together two quails' eggs using toothpick to form skeleton. Use kitchen shears to cut face eye and mouth details from nori. Wet quail's egg with a little water to make nori stick. Repeat and place in box.

NEST BENTO

1/2 cup rice; 1 tomato; 2 quails' eggs; 1 small piece carrot; 4 sesame seeds. For tapa: 2 pieces sirloin steak; pinch salt; oil for frying. For kani and pea scrambled eggs: 1 egg; pinch salt; 1 stick kani; 1 tbsp peas; oil for frying. 1-tier bento box.

Make tapa: thinly slice sirloin steak. Lightly salt both sides of meat.

Place in an airtight container then let cure in refrigerator for a couple of hours or overnight.

Lightly panfry, until nicely browned.

Cook rice. Make scrambled eggs: lightly stir-fry the sliced then flaked kani and peas.

Add beaten egg, mixed with salt.

Work a wooden spoon into the egg mix, to make rough, crumbly pieces. Cook until just set.

Hard boil quails' eggs then peel. Fill 3/4 of the box with rice, topped with tapa.

In a separate compartment, add diced tomato.

Line half of the separate compartment with a foil cup. Fill with scrambled eggs.

Add carrot beaks and sesame seed eyes to the quails' eggs.

Position upright on tapa, anchoring bases between meat slices.

SALAD MONSTER BENTO

1 small potato; 1 tbsp butter; 1 tbsp milk; 2 romaine lettuce leaves; 1 tomato wedge; 5 circular croutons; 1 slice cheese; 1 sheet nori. For mini burgers: 4 oz ground beef; pinch salt; pinch pepper; 1 tsp butter. 1-tier bento box.

Make mini burgers.

Season beef with salt and pepper.

Handling as little as possible, shape into two patties. Pangrill in butter.

Boil and then mash potato with butter and milk. Lay the mashed potato diagonally in corner of bento box.

Place burgers next to the mashed potato, with edges resting on potato mound.

Fill in space with torn lettuce leaves.

Cut eyeball circles from cheese and

pupils from nori, then place one on each burger patty. Cut the tomato wedge nose.

Arrange croutons along the upper right corner of the box, making them look like a hand pulling the salad blanket down.

Slice cheese into semicircles and add as nails.

Place tomato wedge as nose.

1 egg; 2 lettuce leaves; 2 black sesame seeds; 2 sprigs parsley; 1 heart shaped onigiri; 1 triangle shaped onigiri; 4 tomberries; 1 strip cucumber peel; sprinkling furikake; 1 sheet nori; 1 slice ham; 1 slice cheese. For teriyaki salmon: 1 piece salmon; 2 tsp sugar; 2 tsp soy sauce; 2 tsp mirin; 2 tsp sake; oil for cooking. 1-tier bento box.

Sauté the salmon on both sides in a frying pan. When browned, add the rest of the ingredients and simmer until glazed. Hard boil egg. Peel, make slits for bunny eyes with a knife, insert black sesame seeds. Cut thin slices of cucumber into wedge shapes for ears, and balance on his back. For skewers: layer nori, ham and cheese, slice into rounds. Secure with a toothpick. Line bento with lettuce, place salmon and skewers at one edge and the egg bunny and onigiri (sprinkled with furikake) at the other. Fill any gaps with curly parsley and tomberries.

BREAKFAST BUNNY BENTO

2 tbsp maple syrup; 1 tbsp white cake icing; 2 small sausages; 1 potato; 1 tsp mixed herbs; 1 tsp minced garlic; pinch salt; pinch pepper; 1 egg; 1 orange. For pancakes: 1 cup flour; 1 tsp baking powder; 1 tbsp sugar; pinch salt; 1 egg; 1 cup milk; 1 tbsp vegetable oil; oil for cooking. 1-tier bento box.

Make pancakes. Mix flour, baking powder, sugar and salt in a bowl. Lightly stir in egg, milk, and vegetable oil. Heat cooking oil in a non-stick frying pan over medium heat, cook stack of small pancakes. Stack pancakes in the top right corner of bento box. Decorate pancakes with white cake icing. Put maple syrup into a small sauce container and place it next to pancakes. Cook sausages in frying pan over medium high heat.
Chop potatoes into bite-size pieces and season with herbs, garlic, salt, and pepper. Line baking tray with oiled tin foil. Bake potatoes in oven until they turn golden. Place potatoes into a small divider cup in the bottom left corner of bento box. Make scrambled eggs in frying pan and season with salt and pepper. Slice orange. Fill gaps in bento box with scrambled eggs, sausages, and oranges.

TOFU VARIATION

1 egg; 2 lettuce leaves; 2 black sesame seeds; 2 sprigs parsley; 1 heart shaped onigiri; 1 triangle shaped onigiri; 4 tomberries; 1 strip cucumber peel; sprinkling furikake; 1 sheet nori; 1 slice cheese. For teriyaki tofu: 1/2 block tofu; 2 tsp sugar; 2 tsp soy sauce; 2 tsp mirin; 2 tsp sake; oil for cooking. 1-tier bento box.

Slice tofu and marinade in remaining ingredients for 30 mins. Stir-fry and place in bento box with remaining ingredients prepared as above.

SUNNY MONDAY BENTO

2 eggs; 1/2 cup rice; 3 mini carrots; handful spinach; 1 chunk cheddar cheese; 1 sheet nori. 1-tier bento box.

Cook rice. Fill half of the box with rice, patting down to create a flat surface.

Scramble two eggs in a small, flat-bottomed bowl.

Microwave eggs until cooked; this shapes them into a patty. Place in bottom center of box.

Grate cheese. Arrange the spinach and cheese around the egg patty.

Cut carrots into slivers using vegetable peeler.

Use the carrot to create sun rays, arrange around the egg patty and rest on rice.

Cut a smiley face out of nori using a punch and place on the egg.

95

OMELETTE BENTO

1 mini hot dog; 1 cube cheddar cheese; 2 cherry tomatoes; 2 lettuce leaves; sprinkling furikake; 6 black sesame seeds; 1/2 cup rice. For Indian omelette: 3 large potatoes; 1 onion; 4 oz pepperoni; 2 tsp garam masala; handful cherry tomatoes; 2 tbsp cilantro leaves; 8 eggs; oil for cooking. 1-tier bento box.

Cube and boil potatoes. Fry the onions until softened in the oil (around five minutes), add the sliced pepperoni and garam masala. Cook for around a minute, then add the potatoes and cherry tomatoes. Beat eggs, whisk and season well before adding to the pan. Once the omelette is set on the bottom, move to a hot oven to finish off, before sprinkling with cilantro. When cooled, cut a slice to fit in bento.

Line bento with lettuce, pack the omelette in to leave a diagonal space. Cook rice and separate into three portions. Mold one small onigiri and place on bottom of bento. Make another onigiri by mixing the furikake with the rice, and another by dipping the onigiri directly into furikake.

Make tomato faces, cutting two small slits in a cherry tomato with a sharp knife, then positioning black sesame seeds to make eyes. Shred the end of hot dog into six equal parts to make an octopus. Push hot dog down onto the segments, then boil until cooked. Turn upside down and allow to cool, letting gravity pull the legs apart. Add eyes as with tomato faces. Place hot dog and cheese on top of onigiri platform, then place extra two onigiri on either side.

ZEBRA BENTO

2 iceberg lettuce leaves; 2 romaine lettuce leaves; turkey cold cuts; 1 avocado; 2 slices whole wheat bread; 1 serving kim chee crab; 5 grape tomatoes; 6 carrot sticks; 1/2 red bell pepper; 1/2 orange bell pepper; 1 Swiss cheese slice; 1 sheet nori; pinch toasted sesame seeds. 1-tier bento box.

Line half of bento box with dark green romaine lettuce leaves. Finely chop iceberg lettuce leaves and add to other half of box. Top iceberg lettuce with avocado cubes, kim chee crab, and

grape tomatoes. Using whole wheat bread, turkey cold cuts, and thinly sliced avocado, make a turkey avocado sandwich. Add to bento box.

Cut the zebra's head out of the Swiss cheese. Cut stripes, mouth, ears, and hair out of nori. Place on cheese. For eyes, press two toasted sesame seeds vertically into the cheese. For the nose, press two toasted sesame seeds flat into the cheese.

Using various colors of bell pepper slices, cut out a sweater and message in letters. Add to sandwich. Add carrot sticks to empty space.

MOUSTACHE BENTO

1/2 cup long grain rice; 1/2 cup peas; 1 onion; 1 tsp ketchup; pinch salt; pinch pepper; 1 egg; oil for cooking; 3 frozen mini burgers; 1 tbsp tonkatsu sauce; 1 cherry tomato; 1 broccoli floret. 1-tier bento box with divider.

Cook rice. Finely chop onion. Heat oil in a frying pan over medium high heat. Stir-fry rice, green peas, and onion.

Season fried rice with ketchup, salt, and pepper. Fill one section of bento box with fried rice. Beat egg in a bowl. Heat oil in a non-stick frying pan over medium heat. Spread egg out in pan and make a thin crepe. Remove egg crepe from heat carefully. Make a cartoon face on egg crepe by cutting out eyes and mouth with a knife.

Cover fried rice with egg crepe, tucking in the sides. Draw eyebrows and moustache with ketchup.

Heat frozen mini burgers in a pan over medium high heat. Brush the burgers with tonkatsu sauce. Remove burgers from heat when completely heated through. Blanche broccoli in salted water. Fill remaining space in bento box with burgers, cherry tomato, and broccoli.

TIGER VARIATION

1/2 cup long grain rice; 1/2 cup peas; 1 onion; 1 tsp ketchup; pinch salt; pinch pepper; 1 egg; oil for cooking; 3 frozen mini burgers; 1 tbsp tonkatsu sauce; 1 cherry tomato; 1 broccoli floret. 1-tier bento box with divider.

Prepare ingredients and add to bento as in Moustache Bento recipe (left). When crepe is made, cut tiger eyes, nose, mouth and ears from crepe using a knife. Cover fried rice with egg crepe, tucking in the sides. Draw whiskers onto tiger face with ketchup.

FLATPIE WEDGE BENTO

3 broccoli florets; 1 Morningstar Farms parmesan chik pattie; 2 Morningstar Farms broccoli and cheddar bites; 4 baby tomatoes; 1 tbsp ketchup; 5 blueberries; 1 carrot; 1 baby bok choy leaf; 1 slice of Scottish flat pie (see below right); 1 slice mozzarella. 2-tier bento box.

Cook chik pattie and broccoli and cheddar bites, allow to cool. In the center of the top tier place a large cookie cutter. Lay the chik patty on top of the cookie cutter so that it will be raised and not hidden by the rest of the food. Put three steamed broccoli florets at points around the patty, cutting the stems to shorten them if necessary. Take one broccoli bite and cut it diagonally. Stand halves beside the Chik patty, in between two of the florets ,with the cut sides up. Fill a container with ketchup and place next to another piece of broccoli.Place baby tomatoes in any spaces left around the perimeter of the bento.Cut a shooting star from a slice of mozzarella with a mini cookie cutter and gently lay on top of the patty.

The wedge of flat pie goes in first, followed by a cupcake cup on one side and a diagonally halved broccoli bite on the other. Place one leaf of baby bok choy in the cup. With a tiny flower fondant cutter, make raw carrot flowers to go on top of the bok choy leaf. Take a plastic toothpick and sandwich it between two stickers to make a decorative pick. Slide on several fresh blueberries. Rest against broccoili bites. Place baby tomato beside the blueberries.

FLAT PIE RECIPE

For filling: 2 tbsp olive oil; 1 onion; 4 potatoes; pinch salt; pinch pepper; 1 1/2 tbsp garlic powder; 1 tbsp dried basil; 1 tbsp dried tarragon. For crust: 2 cups flour; 1 1/2 tsp baking powder; 1 tsp black pepper; 1/2 tsp salt; 2 1/2 tbsp butter; 1/3 cup vegetable broth. For topping: 2 cups shredded cheese (mixture of mild cheddar, sharp cheddar, Colby and Monterey Jack).

Heat oil in a skillet. Slice onion into strips and add to oil with peeled and thinly sliced potatoes, salt, pepper, garlic, tarragon and basil. Cook until potatoes are golden brown. Heat oven to medium high. Mix flour, baking powder, pepper and salt. Add butter and rub into the flour mixture with fingers until it resembles coarse crumbs. Add broth and stir until dough pulls away from sides of bowl. Turn out dough onto waxed and floured paper, roll into flat circle, transfer onto a cookie sheet. Ladle cooled filling into center and spread out leaving about 1 and a half inches around the edge. Fold edges over the filling in a rough fashion. Cook for 20 mins. Cover potato and onion area with shredded cheese, bake for 8 minutes.

2 pieces whole grain bread; 2 tsp smooth peanut butter; 1 tsp jam; 1 small piece nori; 2 tbsp frozen shelled edamame; 1 tsp yoghurt; 1 tsp apple sauce; 6 frozen grapes; 1 mini cherry pie; 1 handful rainbow-colored, star-shaped children's cereal. 1-tier bento box.

Use a round biscuit-cutter to cut the crusts from the bread. Be careful not to tear. In the exact center of each piece, deposit a tiny amount of peanut butter (about 1 tsp) and a tiny bit of jam (about 1/2 tsp). Carefully arrange the circle of bread in the gyoza press so that the filling lines up with the pocket-hollow. Fold the bread over when closing the press to ensure that the piece doesn't slip. Once press is closed, push down hard on handles to ensure a good seal. Repeat with the other piece of bread and set the sandwich-dumplings aside.

Divide thawed edamame between the two heart-shaped cups. Divide frozen grapes between two diamond-shaped cups and set aside. Carefully spoon yoghurt into one oval-shaped cup and apple sauce into the other (these are easy to eat – pinch the cup closed and the contents will fall right into your mouth).

Place cherry pie in the bottom center of the box and the grape-cups on either side. Carefully prop gyoza near the top and spread out remaining cups near the middle. Fill in blank spaces with rainbow-colored cereal. Use a smile face punch to punch two faces out of the nori and carefully transfer them to the gyoza.

SMALL PACKAGES BENTO

1 gyoza-pressed peanut butter sandwich (see Gyoza Girls Bento, right, for technique); 4 cherry tomatoes; 1 oval-shaped paper baking cup filled with frozen grapes; 1 oval-shaped paper baking cup filled with frozen edamame; 1 mini caramel apple; 1/2 serving shop-bought butternut squash soup; 1/2 tsp sour cream; 1 bag green tea. 1 sandwich-size chip and dip container.

Arrange contents clockwise around the central well: cherry tomato, frozen grapes, cherry tomato, mini caramel apple, cherry tomato, edamame, cherry tomato, gyoza sandwich.

Fill the central well with the butternut squash soup, garnish with sour cream, and seal with inner lid.

The container can be heated and the soup eaten after you're finished with the other contents.

Place the outer lid over container. Serve with green tea bag.

This is a very space-efficient lunch; the whole thing fills the space of a regular-sized sandwich.

HEDGEHOG BENTO

Handful spinach; 1/4 cup shredded cheddar cheese; soy sauce; Japanese melon bread; 1 sheet nori. For pearl balls: 1 lb ground pork; 1 tbsp soy sauce; 1 clove garlic; 1 tbsp rice wine; 1 onion; 1 tbsp sesame oil; 1 tsp Chinese Five Spice Powder; 2 tbsp corn starch; 1 cup sushi rice. For vegetable stir-fry: 1 carrot; 1 green bell pepper; 1 onion; 1/2 cup chopped Chinese cabbage; 1 clove garlic; oil for cooking; pinch pepper. 1-tier food storage box with side-dish cup.

Make pearl balls. Mix ground pork with soy sauce, minced garlic, rice wine, diced onion, sesame oil, Chinese Five Spice Powder and corn starch. Wash rice. Soak rice in fresh water for 15 minutes. Drain and pat dry (rice should have absorbed some water, but have a mostly dry exterior).

Make little meatballs and roll them in rice. Line a bamboo steamer with parchment paper and steam for about 45 minutes.

Stir-fry slivered carrots, sliced green bell pepper, diced onion and Chinese cabbage in a little oil and minced garlic. Season with ground black pepper.

Place the side-dish cup into main box. Fill the bottom of the main container with vegetable stir-fry. Arrange three pearl balls on top. Cut out small nori circles to form the faces of the hedgehogs. In the side container, place the spinach to form a bowl shape; fill with shredded cheddar. Fill a small plastic bottle with soy sauce. Pack melon bread on the side.

PENGUIN BENTO

1 egg; 1 slice cheddar cheese; 1 slice white cheese; 1 carrot; pinch pepper; 1 tsp sake; 1 hot dog; 1 quail's egg; 1 lettuce leaf; 1/2 cup potato starch; 1 garlic clove; 1 oz broccoli; 1 snow pea; 1 sheet nori; 1/2 tbsp green seaweed flakes; 1 oz chicken leg; soy sauce; 1/4 cup lotus roots; 1 cup rice; 1/4 cup hijiki seaweed; pinch sugar; pinch salt. 1-tier bento box.

Grate garlic. Marinade chicken with soy sauce and sake. Line bento box with lettuce. Boil broccoli and snow peas.

Peel carrot and slice. Boil until tender. Cut with fish shaped cookie cutter. Boil hot dog for 30 seconds with boiling water. Cut chicken into bite-size pieces and roll in potato starch. Deep-fry in hot oil until cooked and golden brown. Cook rice, stir-fry with ketchup, salt and pepper. Pack into half of bento box. Beat egg with salt and seaweed flakes. Make tamagoyaki. Cut in half. Sauté hijiki and lotus roots. Season with soy sauce, sugar and sake. Cut penguin from nori and cheese slices, with carrot cheek. Cut snowflakes from nori using paper punch. Add to cheese circles. Place on rice. Pack remaining ingredients. Toss chopped snow peas with stewed hijiki.

OCTODOG VARIATION

1/2 cup rice; sprinkling furikake; 1 sheet nori; 3 hot dogs; 1/4 cup soy sauce; 1/4 cup sugar; 1 lettuce leaf. 1-tier bento box.

Prepare ingredients and pack bento as in Crab Hot dog Bento (above). Cut hot dogs in half and make four slices into the cut end of each hot dog piece. Boil for one minute so tentacles open up. Make cuts for eyes. Place in bento box.

MINI CARAMEL APPLES

1 large Granny Smith apple; 1/2 cup lemon juice; prepackaged caramel apple dip; 1/4 cup crushed peanuts.

Peel apple. Use the melon-baller to extract balls of apple. One large apple should yield about six.

Brush each apple-ball with lemon juice and blot dry with paper towels.

It's important that apple pieces are dry, or caramel won't stick.

Spear each apple ball on a wooden skewer-half and dip in the caramel by twirling gently.

Dip in crushed peanuts, then transfer each caramel apple to a mini paper cupcake cup.

Chill in refrigerator until caramel is set.

These make great bento-sized sweet snacks, and appear in Small Packages Bento.

CRAB HOT DOG BENTO

1/2 cup rice; sprinkling furikake; 1 sheet nori; 3 hot dogs; 1/4 cup soy sauce; 1/4 cup sugar; 1 lettuce leaf. 1-tier bento box.

Cook rice, mix with furikake.

Mold to make two onigiri.

Wrap with nori strips.

Line box with lettuce leaf.

Place onigiri in box, propping it up against the box's back edge.

Use crab and tulip hot dog cutters to cut hot dogs.

Simmer in sugar and soy sauce mix until hot dogs begin to curl.

Arrange crab and tulip hot dogs at front of bento box.

SANDWICH KIT BENTO

1/2 cup finely chopped lettuce; 5 black olives; serving kim chee flavored imitation crab salad; 1/2 avocado; 5 cherry tomatoes; 2 slices whole wheat bread. 1-tier bento box.

Cut bread with Christmas tree-shaped cookie cutter.

Place chopped lettuce in the left half of the bento box.

Spoon a serving of kim chee crab salad into the back of the box on the right half.

Slice avocado lengthways. Place slices on and in front of the crab salad, keeping them together to add a band of color.

Prop a few cherry tomatoes between the avocado and the front of the bento.

Tuck olives next to crab salad. Place the two bread slices on top and add more cherry tomatoes into spaces.

MINI SANDWICH BENTO

3 slices whole wheat bread; 2 tbsp peanut butter; 2 tbsp jelly; handful fresh blackberries; 1 apple; 1 lettuce leaf. 1-tier bento box.

Cut bread with holiday-themed mini cookie cutters, making twelve pieces for mini sandwiches.

Spread a layer of peanut butter on six of the bread pieces and a layer of jelly on the other six. Assemble.

Place divider into box, placing slightly off-center.

Line larger section with lettuce leaf.

Carefully place the mini peanut butter sandwiches into the bento, on top of the lettuce, arranging them so that each is visible.

Tuck as many blackberries as you can fit into the remaining area.

Cut apple into thin slices; use mini cookie cutters in other festive designs.

Place apple slices in empty section, making every few slices face skin out.

CROQUETTE BENTO

1 lb ground turkey; 1 onion; 1 carrot; 2 eggs; 1 packet instant mashed potatoes; 1/2 cup flour; 1/2 cup panko; oil for cooking; 2 broccoli florets; 1 frozen onigiri; sprinkling furikake; 2 slices tomato; handful salad greens. For seasoning: 2 tbsp sugar; 2 tsp garlic salt; 1 tsp ground ginger; 2 tsp oyster sauce; 2 tsp tonkatsu sauce; 1 tbsp mirin. 1-tier bento box.

Combine seasoning ingredients, mix well.

Mince onions, heat oil and fry until soft.

Add ground turkey and cook until done. Add seasoning mixture. Simmer for five minutes.

Add grated carrot and one chopped boiled egg. Simmer for five minutes.

Prepare mashed potatoes, using 3/4 cup less water than directions specify.

Add to turkey mixture and mix well.

Refrigerate. When ready to cook, form patties.

Prepare dipping bowls: a bowl with one egg beaten with two tbsp water, a bowl with flour, and a bowl with panko.

Dip patties in flour, egg and coat with panko.

Fry until golden brown on both sides. Pack bento.

PINK FLOWERS BENTO

1/2 cup leftover fried brown rice; 1/2 cup peas; 1 tbsp soy sauce; 1 piece ham steak; 1 slice cheddar cheese; 3 eggs; 1 tamagoyaki; 1 portion pipi kaula (smoked beef); 1 grape tomato; 3 cucumber slices; 3 carrot sticks. 1-tier bento box.

Fry peas together with fried rice, adding soy sauce for flavoring.

Add a small amount to bento box.

Push to the side until rice level is just below the top of the bento box.

Use plastic food dividers if desired.

Boil egg. Slice in half and place in small food cup. Add to bento box.

Make tamagoyaki, cut two wedges and add to bento box.

Add cucumber slices and chopped carrot sticks to a cupcake cup.

Place in bento box. Add finely chopped pipi kaula pieces and a grape tomato.

Using a vegetable cutter, cut three ham flowers from a ham steak.

If the flowers are too thick, cut them in half to obtain more flowers.

Add to bento box.

With a straw, cut out three flower centers from cheese and place on ham flowers.

BURGER BEAR BENTO

1 red sausage; 1/2 egg; 1/4 small tomato; pinch salt; 1 lettuce leaf; 1 frozen hamburger; 1/2 cup rice; 1 slice cheddar cheese; 1 fish sausage; 1 small carrot; 1 thin slice ham; 2 caps shimeji mushroom; soy sauce; 1 slice cheese; pinch pepper; 2 grapes; 1 tsp margarine; 1 sheet nori; 1 tsp mayonnaise. 1-tier bento box.

Cook rice. Line half of box with lettuce and place cooked rice in remaining half of bento box.

Divide broccoli into small fringes. Boil broccoli. Peel carrot and cut into thin round slices. Boil until tender. Cut carrot into flower shapes with cookie cutters. Cut end of sausage into 4 pieces to make flower shape, boil for 30 seconds. Roll slices of ham around cooked broccoli pieces, use mayo to hold in place.

Make mesh-usuyakitamago (mesh shaped Japanese style crepe omelette). In a mixing bowl, beat egg well. Strain egg with tea strainer. Drip egg into oiled pan on medium heat, adding little by little and drawing it in a mesh shape. Put the mesh shaped omelette on top of rice. Stir-fry the shimeji mushroom caps with margarine, salt, pepper and soy sauce. Cook the hamburger and place onto mesh omelette.

Cut cheese and nori to make face details and arrange on burger. Put the shimeji mushrooms beside the hamburger as ears. Place broccoli, sausage, grapes and remaining ingredients in bento box as shown in image.

STAR PANCAKE BENTO

1 cup bisquick; 1/2 cup milk; 1 tbsp sugar; 1 egg; 3 tbsp jam; 2 lettuce leaves; 2 breakfast sausages; 1 tangerine; 2 strawberries; 4 mini star hash browns. 2-tier bento box.

Blend bisquick, milk, sugar and egg. Pour onto hot griddle to make six four-inch pancakes. Cook until edges are dry, turn; cook until golden.

Cut pancakes into star shapes with a cookie cutter. Using a smaller cutter, cut stars out of the center of three of the pancakes. Spread jam on the three whole stars; lay a cutout star on top of each.

Cook sausages and hash browns, peel tangerine. In bottom tier, arrange star pancakes in a wax paper cup.

Line other half of tier with a green lettuce leaf. On top of the leaf, arrange two cooked breakfast sausages and some tangerine sections.

In the upper tier, place fruit at one side in a wax paper cup. Line the right side with a lettuce leaf and fill with mini star hash browns.

BUN OF STEEL BENTO

1 cabbage bao; 6 baby tomatoes; 6 black olives; 3 miniature corn croquettes; teriyaki tofu and onions (see recipe below right); 1 Japanese wheat cookie; 1 gyoza wrapper; 2 drops blue food coloring gel; 1 sheet nori; 1 slice cucumber. For vegetable fried rice: 1 cup of pre-cooked cold rice; 1/4 cup steamed peas; 1/2 cup chopped onions; 1/2 cup chopped carrot; 1/4 cup canned corn; serving eggless omelette mix; 3 tbsp vegetable oil; 5 tbsp soy sauce; oil for cooking. 2-tier bento box.

Make vegetable fried rice. Pour vegetable oil over the cold rice. Mix well with a rice paddle, adding more oil as necessary until each grain of rice is coated with oil.

Heat 1/2 tbsp oil in a skillet. Sauté the omelette mix, treating it just like scrambled eggs. Remove from pan.

Sauté the vegetables until the onions are clear. Remove from pan. Add the rice to the hot pan, stirring to release any clumps of rice. Cook for five minutes.

Pour three tbsp soy sauce over the rice and stir several times. Cook for five minutes.

Add vegetables and omelette to the rice with two more tbsp of soy sauce. Cook for five minutes. Remove from heat and serve hot or cold. Fill one bento tier with vegetable fried rice. Cook steamed bun according to package directions.

Place at the top of the tier, then fill up the rest with more fried rice.

Use the back of a spoon to 'paint' blue food coloring gel onto a gyoza wrapper.

Take scissors and cut a rough tunic shape from the wrapper and place it on top of the fried rice, trying to curve it under at the edges a little.

Cut nori eyebrows, nose, moustache and belt. Use small cucumber slices for sleeves and natural colored gyoza wrapper for hands.

Use section of tomato peel for mouth. Fill remaining space on top of the fried rice with baby tomatoes.

Place an aluminium cupcake cup at one side of the second tier. Fill with teriyaki tofu.

Add Japanese wheat cookie, corn croquettes, baby tomatoes and two picks filled with black olives to remaining space in box.

TERIYAKI TOFU RECIPE

2 tbsp soy sauce; 2 tbsp teriyaki sauce; 1 onion; 1/2 pack extra firm tofu.

Chop onion and cube tofu. Marinate the tofu in the soy and teriyaki sauces for 15 minutes. Stir every now and then to make sure that all the pieces get to soak. Heat a skillet on high. Remove tofu from the marinade with a slotted spoon and sauté. When pieces of tofu begin to stick and brown, add onion and marinade to pan. Stir well and cook until the marinade has been absorbed.

BOUQUET BENTO

2 slices white bread; 1 slice soy turkey; 1 slice cheese; 1 tsp mayo; 1/2 tsp mustard; handful pretzels; 3 baby tomatoes; 1 slice mozzarella; 1 tbsp steamed peas; 1 tbsp canned corn; 3 carrot sticks; 1 serving tomato soup; 1/2 cucumber; pinch sugar dots. 1-tier bento box with side bowl.

Cut bread into rectangular shape so sandwich will fit box.

Make sandwich, using cheese slice, mayo, mustard and soy turkey as filling. Place in bento.

Pack a few pretzels at the top and bottom of bento.

Fit baby tomatoes and a few slices of raw carrot along side gaps.

Skewer corn and peas onto two animal picks, alternating for color.

Lay next to tomatoes and carrots at either side of the sandwich.

Cut cheese flower using flower-shaped cookie cutter.

Lay on bread, add sugar dots.

Place pea on bread with corn piece petals around it.

Cut slices of cucumber peel to create flower stems.

Place on the bread, tucking underneath the flower shapes.

Add soup in side bowl.

ZOO BENTO

1 serving yaki soba; 3 hot dogs; 1 tbsp soy sauce; 1 tbsp sugar; 1 1/2 cups rice; 1 tin Spam; furikake; 1 fish cake; 3 sheets nori; 1 tsp shrimp flakes; 2 lettuce leaves. 1-tier picnic size bento box.

Cook rice. Simmer Spam slices in soy sauce and sugar, flavor with furikake.

Use special mold to make Spam musubi. Add musubi halves to right side of box.

Mold remaining rice into two round onigiri. Decorate with nori faces. Brush cheeks with red shrimp flakes.

Add lettuce leaves to remaining space in box. Place onigiri next to musubi.

Cook yaki soba. Layer in remaining space. Cut hot dogs into crab shapes and boil for 30 seconds. Place crab hot dogs on top of yaki soba.

Slice fish cake and carefully arrange at bottom edge of box.

SMILEY HEART BENTO

1 serving Knorr's cheddar broccoli pasta; 1 slice Swiss cheese; 1 tbsp steamed peas; handful blueberries; 1 baby tomato; 1 veggie hot dog; 1 sheet light blue origami paper. 1-tier bento box.

Cook cheddar broccoli pasta. Place in half of bento box. Cook veggie hot dog; cut into 3 sections, removing the ends. Stand the sections upright and cut down 3/4 of their length 3 times to make 6 sections of hot dog that can be pulled apart but are still attached at the bottom. Put hot dog flowers into the bento, insert two steamed peas in the center of each of the sections.

Place a cupcake cup in space beside hot dog flowers, fill with blueberries. Wedge a baby tomato into gap. Using fondant cutters, cut large and small hearts from Swiss cheese; lay on top of the pasta once it has cooled. Skewer several peas on a plastic pick place on pasta. Cut a smiley face from origami paper using a paper punch, make sure to remove before eating.

HEARTS BENTO

2 oz soba noodles; 1 1/2 oz tofu; olive oil for frying; 1 oz mushrooms; handful green beans; 4 small pak choi leaves; small piece ginger; 1 garlic clove; pinch roasted sesame seeds; 1 tbsp sesame oil; 1 tsp maple syrup. 2-tier bento box.

Use cookie cutters to make mushroom stars. Chop tofu into small pieces. Fry in hot olive oil until crispy. Set aside. Fry mushrooms in same pan with ginger and garlic for about four minutes. Boil green beans until cooked but still crunchy. While beans are cooking, drop the pak choi in the boiling water and immediately remove and set aside. Cook soba noodles according to instructions. When all the above are cooked, mix thoroughly together, dress with sesame oil and maple syrup and put into bottom tier. Sprinkle with sesame seeds. Cut cucumber into slices, then cut hearts using cookie cutter. Use cut cucumber slice to garnish noodles. Place cucumber hearts, sliced strawberries, grapes and plum in top tier.

BUTTERFLY BENTO

4 oz easy cook couscous; vegetable stock; 1 oz sultanas; 3 cubes feta cheese; 2 asparagus stalks; 1 red pepper; 1 small onion; 2 carrots; 1 zucchini; olive oil for frying; 1 slice lime; 1/2 cucumber; 2 strawberries; handful grapes; 1 tbsp mung beans; 1 stuffed olive. 2-tier bento box.

Soak couscous. Leave it covered until ready to use. Heat a little oil in a pan and add the chopped pepper and onion, cook on a medium heat for approximately 5 minutes. Slice one carrot, add to pan, cook for three minutes and add sliced zucchini. Add chopped garlic.

Fluff up couscous with a fork and pack into bento. Cut 3 flower shapes out of feta. Place steamed asparagus at bottom of couscous, and feta flowers with pepper accents at left. Peel and chop remaining carrot, cut one slice into butterfly shape, place on couscous. Add the stir-fried vegetables to bento and top with a slice of lime.

In top tier place sliced carrots; cucumber, cut into shape with a cookie cutter; strawberries; sliced grapes; mung beans; olive.

RADISH HEART BENTO

2 lettuce leaves; 1 inch cucumber; 2 small tomatoes; 3 small new potatoes; 1 1/2 oz green beans; 1 egg; 4 black olives; 1 tbsp salad dressing; 1 tsp low fat mayonnaise; pinch salt; pinch pepper; 1 radish; 1/2 carrot; 1 slice kohlrabi; 2 strawberries; handful grapes. 2-tier bento box.

Line bottom tier with lettuce. Chop cucumber and tomatoes. Steam green beans; boil egg and quarter. Arrange on lettuce, ending with boiled egg. Dress salad. Cut carrot, kohlrabi and radish hearts, add with fruit to top tier.

RADISH HEART VARIATION

1 serving yaki soba; 1 scallion; 1/2 red pepper; 3 mushrooms; 1/2 cup shrimp; 1 tsp chili flakes; soy sauce; oil for cooking; 1 radish; 1/2 carrot; 1 slice kohlrabi; 2 strawberries; handful grapes. 2-tier bento box.

Cook yaki soba noodles. Slice pepper, chop mushrooms and scallion. Heat oil, stir-fry shrimp with soy sauce and chili. Add scallion, mushrooms and pepper. Place in bottom tier of bento, garnish with radish. Cut carrot, kohlrabi and radish hearts, add with fruit to top tier.

SCOTTIE DOG BENTO

4 oz pasta shapes; 1 small sweet potato; 1 onion; 1 red pepper; 1 small tomato; 2 oz green beans; 2 scallions; pinch salt; pinch pepper; 1 tbsp grated parmesan; 1 slice parmesan; olive oil for cooking; 1/2 carrot; 1 piece kohlrabi; handful taro chips; 1 kiwi fruit. 2-tier bento box.

Put chopped onion, sliced pepper, cubed sweet potato in a roasting tray with a little olive oil and roast for ten minutes. Add chopped green beans, scallions and tomato and roast for a further 15 minutes or until cooked. Cook pasta. Mix vegetables and pasta together and add parmesan. Season to taste. Place in bottom tier and garnish with slice of parmesan cut into star shape.

Place taro chips and carrot (cut into heart shapes with a cookie cutter) in sections of top tier. Cut kohlrabi into a dog shape, add a carrot collar and sesame seed eye, place in box. Peel kiwi fruit and cut into star and flower shapes, stack in remaining section.

BRATWURST BENTO

2 Mrs. T's potato and onion pierogies; serving leftover spaghetti; 1 tbsp spaghetti sauce; 6 black olives; 1 frozen BOCA soy bratwurst; 2 cups vegetable broth; 2 strawberries; handful grapes; 2 Japanese crackers; 1 Morningstar Farms broccoli and cheddar bite; 1 broccoli floret; 1/2 carrot; 1 slice Swiss cheese. 2-tier bento box.

Cook the vegetarian bratwurst. Heat vegetable broth in a skillet.

When hot, add sausage straight from the freezer.

Simmer, turning sausage over every few minutes to make sure it cooks evenly.

Make the spaghetti cup, twirling pasta into a silicon cup.

Heat spaghetti sauce and place on top of pasta. Garnish with a black olive. Place at left side of top tier.

Place strawberries in the top tier. Pack grapes, crackers and black olives in spaces.

Cook pierogies and place two at an angle at right side of bottom tier.

Chop broccoli into smaller pieces and steam. Cut carrot into slices and boil until tender.

Fill the other half of bottom tier with broccoli and carrots.

Cook broccoli bite according to instructions.

Wedge the broccoli bite at front of box and fill gaps with small pieces of broccoli.

Cut the bratwurst into circles and put them on bamboo skewers. Lay the skewers over the steamed vegetables.

Cut tiny stars from Swiss cheese using cookie cutter. Place one on each sausage round.

If the bratwurst are still a little warm the cheese will melt just enough to keep them from falling off. Fill any remaining spaces with black olives.

RABBIT BENTO

1/2 cup rice; 1 stick string cheese; 1 blue food marker; pinch sakura denbu; 1 kiwi fruit; 1/4 cup tinned mandarin oranges; handful asparagus; 1 serving leftover barbecue pork. 1-tier bento box.

Cook rice, mold into rabbit-shaped onigiri. Make eyes and mouth from string cheese colored with food marker, cheeks from sakura denbu. Arrange in box with flower cut out kiwi, mandarin oranges, steamed asparagus, paper cup containing pork.

PIGGY ONIGIRI BENTO

3 red sausages; 1/8 kiwi; handful grapes; 1 spring roll wrapper; 2 sheets nori; 2 cheese sticks; 1/4 small tomato; 1 tbsp sugar; 1/2 tsp ketchup; 1 fish sausage; 1/2 egg; 1 oz broccoli; 1/2 tbsp sake; 2 lettuce leaves; plum flavoring for cooked rice; 1 cup rice; 1 tbsp soy sauce; 1 kabocha squash. 1-tier bento box.

Line bento box with lettuce. Divide broccoli into small fringes. Boil broccoli for two minutes. Cut sausages into four pieces at ends, boil for 30 seconds.

Cut Kabocha squash into bite-size pieces. Put water, sugar, soy sauce and sake in a sauce pan. After boiling, add Kabocha squash. Simmer on a low heat until tender.

Make cheese and nori spring roll. Wrap nori seaweed sheet around cheese sticks, wrap again in spring roll wrapper. Deep fry until browned. Cut into halves. Cook rice, gently stir together cooked rice and plum flavorings. Mold two onigiri. Tie three nori seaweed sheet belts around onigiri. Put into bento box.

Make crepe-style Japanese omelette. Beat egg in a bowl. Add salt and mix well. Strain egg with tea strainer and stir-fry on low heat. Cut omelette with piggy shaped cookie cutter. Put the piggy onto onigiri. Cut nori seaweed eyes, nose and rose patterns for back using paper punch. Place on piggies, add dab of ketchup to cheeks.

Arrange sausage, broccoli and other ingredients in bento box.

RICE ANIMALS BENTO

1 cup brown rice; handful salad greens; 4 broccoli florets; 1 slice cheddar cheese; 1 slice Swiss cheese; 1 sheet nori. 1-tier bento box.

Cook rice and allow to cool. Making rice balls with brown rice is not easy, use white rice for easier construction.

To make a rice ball by hand, prepare a small bowl of salt water to keep hands moist so rice sticks to itself.

Wet hands. Take a small handful of cooked rice. Pat it into a small mound, then shape into a triangle. Repeat to make three rice balls.

Line the bottom of box with salad greens. Arrange rice balls on top.

Cut broccoli into smaller pieces and steam. Place in front and behind of rice balls.

Cut nori into smiley faces for the rice balls. Cut Swiss cheese into teardrop shapes to form ears. Place on rice balls.

Decorate with small pieces of cheddar cheese.

STARRY BENTO

2 star-shaped frozen onigiri; 2 Aidell's teriyaki pineapple meatballs; 6 slices sanbaizuke; 1/2 red bell pepper; 1/2 orange bell pepper; 1 Okinawan sweet potato; 2 lettuce leaves; 1 sheet nori. 1-tier bento box.

Line rectangular bento box with lettuce leaf.

Carefully place two star onigiri with nori faces on their sides, propping up with halved toothpicks if needed.

Cook meatballs. Skewer two meatballs on a food pick and place into box. Add slices of sanbaizuke to a food cup and add to bento box.

Take thin slices of assorted colors of bell pepper and cut into star shapes, using a paper cutout to trace.

Boil Okinawan sweet potato and cut into thin slices. Cut into star shapes. Arrange the bell pepper and potato stars in the box.

RUSSIAN DOLL BENTO

2 red sausages; 2 snow peas; 1 1/2 tbsp flour; pinch salt; 1 simeji mushroom; 1 oz broccoli; 1 1/2 oz chicken breast; 1/4 cup milk; pinch pepper; 1 tbsp potato starch; 2 eggs; 1/2 cup rice; 1 slice cheddar cheese; 1 tsp dried parsley; 1 tsp mentsuyu; plum flavoring; 1/8 onion; 1 tsp butter; 1 sheet nori; handful wakame seaweed; pumpkin flavoring; 1 slice cheese; 1 kani kama fish cake. 1-tier bento box.

Line bento box with lettuce. Boil broccoli and snow peas. Cut off top of sausage and slice into cross. Boil for 30 sec until opens. Make small gratin. Stir-fry sliced onion and sausage with butter. Add flour and milk, mix well. Season. Put into paper cup. Add cheese on top and grill until browned. Put in bento box. Beat egg with some salt. Add sliced wakame seaweed. Pour into pan and stir-fry over low heat. Roll egg in pan, make tamagoyaki. Cut in half. Cut chicken into bite-size pieces. Sprinkle with salt and pepper and cover with potato starch. Stir-fry with simeji mushroom until tender. Dilute mentsuyu with three times water, pour in and stir-fry until cooked. Cool, put in bento box. Cook rice, divide in half. Stir together half with pumpkin flavorings for doll's face. Stir rest of rice with plum flavorings for dress. Make into doll-shaped onigiri. Make usuyakitamago. In a mixing bowl, beat egg with some salt and mix well. Pour into pan, stir over low heat. Roll around onigiri for hood. Cut kani kama fish cake to make muff, nose and flower, use white parts for lace. Cut nori eyes, mouth and hair. Use asterisk paper punch to cut nori for pattern of dress. Pack box.

CLOCK BENTO

2 hot dogs; 1 slice cheddar cheese; pinch pepper; 1 oz broccoli; 1 thin slice ham; 1 sheet nori; 1 tbsp flour; 1/2 cup rice; umeboshi; 1 slice white cheese; 1 bouillon cube; 1/4 sweet potato; 1 daikon radish; pinch salt; 1 pickled plum; 1 simeji mushroom; soy sauce; 1/4 cup bread crumbs; 1 quail's egg; 1 carrot. 1-tier bento box.

Put cheese slice onto ham and roll up. Rest in refrigerator for one hour. Boil broccoli for two mins. Peel section of sweet potato into chequered pattern and boil for six mins. Cut sausage into 4 pieces at end and stir-fry until sausage begins to open. Cook rice. Make onigiri with umeboshi filling. Wrap strip of nori around onigiri. Put into bento box. Cut circle from white cheese for clock face. Cut numbers from nori, hands from ham and cheddar cheese. Place. Cut daikon radish and carrot into bite-size pieces. Simmer daikon, carrot and simeji mushroom with bouillon cube, soy sauce and pepper for 15 mins or until tender. Drain and put in cup in box. Dust ham and cheese roll in flour, dip in beaten egg then bread crumbs. Fry in oil for a few mins. Cut in half. Place with remaining ingredients in bento.

PINK PIGS BENTO

2 sausages; 1 small yellow tomato; 1 tbsp sake; 1 stick dry spaghetti; 1 oz broccoli; 2 oz chicken leg; 1 sheet nori; pinch salt; 1/2 cup rice; 1 tsp grated garlic; 1 fish sausage; 1/4 cup potato starch; 1 cauliflower floret; 1 quail's egg; 1 slice cheddar cheese; 1 tsp ketchup; 1 small red tomato; 2 tbsp soy sauce; 1 lettuce leaf; plum flavoring. 1-tier bento box.

Cut chicken leg into bite-size pieces. Marinade with soy sauce, sake grated garlic and beaten quail's egg for 30 mins. Divide broccoli and cauliflower into small fringes, boil. Cut end of sausage into four pieces. Boil for 30 secs.

Cook rice, stir together with plum flavoring. Make 2 onigiri. Put into bento box. Make snouts and ears with fish sausage. Stick to onigiri with pieces of spaghetti. Make eyes and mouth with nori seaweed sheet. Drain chicken and dust with potato starch. Fry chicken in hot oil until cooked and browned. Place remaining ingredients into box.

PIGGY BENTO

3 fish sausages; 2 red sausages; 1 carrot; 1 slice sweet potato; 1 oz broccoli; 1/2 cup rice; 1/4 boiled quail's egg; okra; 1 thin slice bacon; 1 tsp ketchup; 1 tsp mayonnaise; pinch salt; pinch pepper; 1 lettuce leaf. 1-tier bento box.

Put lettuce into bento box. Boil broccoli and okra for two mins. Peel carrot and slice, boil. Cut red sausages into four pieces at end, boil for 30 secs. Roll cooked okra with bacon, stir-fry over medium heat, season and cut in half. Cut strips of skin from sweet potato to make stripes. Stir-fry with butter and soy sauce. Cut boiled carrot with flower shaped cookie cutter.

Cook rice. Lightly salt, mold into two onigiri. Put in bento box. Cut fish sausage into ears and snouts for pigs. Glue onto onigiri using mayo to stick. Cut nori seaweed sheet with smiley paper punch for eyes and mouths. Put them onto onigiri. Make cheeks by dotting on ketchup using a chopstick. Add broccoli, okra and other ingredients to bento box.

BUNNY BENTO

2 frozen croquettes; 1/2 cup rice; 1 carrot; 1 nori seaweed sheet; 1 1/2 oz broccoli; 1 lettuce leaf; umeboshi; 1 fish sausage; 1 slice cheese; 1 eggplant; 1 small piece of apple; plum flavoring; 1/2 small tomato; 3 string beans; 1 tsp mentsuyu. 1-tier bento box.

Dilute mentsuyu with water. Line bento with lettuce. Divide broccoli into small fringes, boil. Peel carrot and slice, boil. Cut with flower-shaped cookie cutter. Cut eggplant into round slices. Deep fry eggplant and string beans until tender. Drain the oil and marinade eggplant and string beans into mentsuyu for 20 mins. Cook rice, stir together with plum flavorings. Make two onigiri. Put into bento box.
Make face of bunny, cutting sliced cheese and nori for eyes and mouth. Nose, cheeks and ears are cut from fish sausage. Put them onto bunny onigiri. Cut umeboshi in half and put them onto onigiri. Make branch with string beans. Dice apple and peel the skin with cookie cutter. Place remaining ingredients in bento box.

FUNNY MAN BENTO

1 inarisushi; 2 frozen hijiki seaweed dumplings; 1 sheet nori; 1 grape; 1 slice cheddar cheese; 1 tsp mayonnaise; 1 red sausage; 1 slice white cheese; 1 lettuce leaf; 2 small slices sausage; 2 frozen potato pieces with faces. 1-tier bento box.

Put lettuce into half of bento box. Divide broccoli into small fringes. Boil for 2 mins. Cut end of sausage into six parts and boil for 30 seconds.

Put inarisushi into bento box. Make eyes with nori seaweed sheet and sliced cheese.

Make cheeks with sausage slices. Cut mouth and eyebrows from nori.

Nose is made with cheddar cheese cut with a straw. Put onto inarisushi.

Cut cheddar cheese with flower shaped cookie cutter. Arrange remaining ingredients in bento box.

CHESTNUT BENTO

2 red sausages; 1 oz sweet potato; 1 tbsp dried bonito flakes; 1 oz broccoli; 1 slice cheddar cheese; 1 sheet nori; 1/2 cup rice; 1 slice white cheese; soy sauce; 1 lettuce leaf. 1-tier bento box.

Put lettuce into bento box. Divide broccoli into small fringes and boil. Cut end of sausage into four parts and boil for 30 seconds. Peel sweet potato into chequered pattern and boil for six mins.

Cook rice. Gently stir together 1/3 cooked rice with soy sauce. Stir together 2/3 cooked rice with soy sauce and dried bonito flakes. Put rice together, shaping onigiri into a chestnut shape. Put onigiri into bento box.

Cut nori into eyes, nose and mouth shapes. Put the nori seaweed eyes, nose and mouth onto white or cheddar cheese. Cut cheese around nori outline. Put onto onigiri. Arrange remaining ingredients in bento box.

CATAPIL BENTO

1/2 cup rice; 1 orange bell pepper cap; 1 slice green bell pepper; 1 slice Swiss cheese; 1 sheet nori; handful salad greens; 1 piece red bell pepper; 1/4 cup blue cheese crumbles; 1 tbsp crushed walnuts. For fajita chicken with peppers: 6 chicken strips; 1 clove garlic; oil for cooking; 2 green bell peppers; 1/2 onion; 14oz canned green chilies; 2 tbsp lime juice; 1 tbsp cumin; 1/2 tsp oregano; 1/2 tsp paprika; 1/2 tsp chili powder; 1/2 tsp sugar, 1 tsp salt; 1 tbsp cilantro. 2-tier bento box.

Make fajita chicken. Marinate chicken strips in lime juice, spices, sugar, salt and herbs. Cut bell peppers, onion and chilis into strips. Heat skillet with a little oil and minced garlic. Stir-fry chicken until cooked through. Add vegetables. Cook rice, place in bottom tier with chicken. Cut cap of orange bell pepper into caterpillar shape. Use green pepper to decorate. Cut face from cheese and nori. Fill top tier with salad greens, red bell pepper cut into heart shape, blue cheese and walnuts.

HAPPY WORM BENTO

Portion leftover mashed potatoes; 1 leftover kielbasa sausage; handful spinach; 1 carrot stick; 1 sheet nori; handful green beans; 1/4 cup trail mix with banana chips; 10 cherry tomatoes; 3 cloves garlic. 2-tier bento box.

Stir-fry green beans. Roast garlic in oven. Fill the bottom tier half full with mashed potatoes. Cut sausage in half and cut two slices for faces.

Push the sausages and faces into the mashed potatoes to keep them from rolling about. Cut out smiley faces for worms from nori, use a craft punch. Cut the carrot into pieces to form a sun. Garnish with spinach.

Fill half of the top tier with stir-fried green beans. Decorate with cherry tomatoes. Place roasted garlic along the edge of your green beans. Place trail mix in separate container at top of tier.

124

NOT SO CUTE BENTO

Serving leftover spaghetti; 2 mini yellow bell pepper; 1 slice mozzarella; pinch black sesame seeds; handful salad greens; 1 leftover cooked Italian sausage; 1 mini orange bell pepper; 1 mini red bell pepper. 2-tier bento box.

Fill the bottom of top tier with spaghetti. Cut out shape of a mouth with an overhanging nose from one pepper. Use a small paring knife to pierce skin for eyes, insert black sesame seeds. Cut second bell pepper to make body. Use cookie cutter to make mozzarella ghosts, add sesame seed eyes. Slice peppers, arrange in second tier with salad greens and mozarella slices to form bouquet. Dice sausage.

NOT CUTE VARIATION

See ingredients list from Not So Cute Bento (left). Replace leftover spaghetti; 1 leftover Italian sausage with 1/2 cup rice; 2 frozen mini burgers; 1 scallion. 2-tier bento box.

Cook rice, place in top tier. Cook burgers. Dice scallion and slice burgers. Arrange in second tier next to bouquet.

PEPPER PEOPLE BENTO

Serving leftover yaki soba; 1 clove garlic; 2 tbsp tomato sauce; 2 tbsp Worcestershire sauce; 1 tbsp fish stock; 1 tbsp soy sauce; 1 tbsp honey; oil for cooking; 2 mini red bell peppers; 1 scallion; handful salad greens; 1 mini carrot. For tortilla rolls: 1 red chili tortilla; 1 tbsp cream cheese; 1 slice deli turkey; 1 scallion. 2-tier bento box.

Lay tortilla flat, spread entire surface with cream cheese. Lay a slice of turkey on top. Roll tortilla around scallion stalk. Cut into bite-sized pieces. Arrange into rows in top tier of bento. Fill the remaining side with salad greens and sliced carrot.

Cook yaki soba noodles and drain. Stir-fry with a little oil, minced garlic and sauce made from tomato sauce, Worcestershire sauce, fish stock, soy sauce, honey. Fill the bottom container with yaki soba. With a pairing knife, cut faces into the mini peppers. Garnish with diced scallion.

AIRPLANE BENTO

1/2 cup rice; 2 drops blue food color gel; 1 egg; 1 slice American cheese; 1 slice cucumber; 1 sheet green mamenori; 1 sheet orange mamenori; 1 sheet nori; 5 red grapes; 1 cherry rice bar; 4 sweet cocoa flavor mini fried dough twists; 1 rice cracker; 2 cucumber slices; 1 Morningstar Farms broccoli and cheddar bite; 1 tomato; 1 tbsp corn; 1 slice white bread. 2-tier bento box.

Hard boil egg. Cook rice with food coloring. Fill the bottom tier with blue rice, packing it down well. Cut clouds from hard boiled egg whites and place on top of the rice. Cut airplane shape from American cheese. Place plane onto rice, making certain rice is fully cooled first. Shape cucumber slice into a wing and place onto plane.

Use scissors to cut a line of green mamenori, lay it across the plane. Cut windows from orange mamenori, and detail from nori using paper punch and place using tweezers. Partially squash a grape. Cut away excess with a paring knife to leave bird shape. Place under cloud. Use torn lettuce and bits of broccoli and cheddar bite to make tree tops.

Cook broccoli and cheddar bite, place next to cucumber slices, skewered corn and tomato in top tier. Slice cherry rice bar into pieces, place in cupcake cup in bento. Put dough twists and red grapes in gap, slot rice cracker in front of cucumber slices. Cut a small rectangle of white bread. Use scissors to cut the letters from the mamenori rectangle and place on the bread. Use honey to stick if necessary.

KOREAN BBQ CHICKEN BENTO

1 serving chicken pieces; 1/2 cup rice; 2 tbsp Korean barbecue marinade; 1 scallion; 1 tsp sesame seeds; sesame oil; 5 frozen takoyaki; 1/2 cup bean sprouts; 1 tsp oyster sauce; 1 tsp oil; 1 tbsp mayonnaise. 2-tier bento box.

Lightly sauté chicken in Korean barbecue marinade and a little oil.

Just before it has cooked, add sesame seeds, diced scallion and a few drops sesame oil.

Cook rice. Reheat frozen takoyaki in microwave. Pack mayonnaise in sauce cup.

Heat oil in pan, quickly sauté bean sprouts. Add oyster sauce before bean sprouts wilt.

Fill half of top tier with rice. Fill remainder of rice tier with Korean barbecue chicken. Add more diced scallion to garnish.

Place takoyaki and sauce container in the other tier. Add a bento divider.

Put sautéed bean sprouts in remaining space beside takoyaki.

WHALE BENTO

1/2 cup rice; 1 small tomato; 1 slice lemon; 1 sheet nori; 2 frozen fried chicken pieces; 1 fish sausage; 1/2 cucumber; 1 slice cheddar cheese; 2 sausages; 1 sliced white cheese; 1 kani kama fish cake; 1 lettuce leaf; 1 oz broccoli; 1 tsp mayonnaise; 1/4 cup baked beans. 1-tier bento box.

Place lettuce in bento box. Cook rice. Make onigiri in semicircle shape. Cut nori seaweed sheet for whale skin, place on onigiri. Put whale onigiri into bento box. Cut strips of nori and add to whale's jaw. Make cheeks with fish sausage. Cut mouth from Kanikama fish cake, and eyes from cheese and nori.

Divide broccoli into small fringes and boil for two mins. Cut end of sausage into six pieces. boil for 30 secs.

Reheat frozen chicken pieces, place at bottom of bento as rocks. Add cucumber cut into seaweed shapes.

Cut cheese into stars with cookie cutter. Put them onto fried chicken rocks. Place remaining ingredients into bento box. Add the splash, cut from white cheese.

WHALE VARIATION

See ingredients list from Whale Bento (left). Replace 2 frozen fried chicken pieces; 2 sausages with 2 fish fingers; 2 croquettes. 1-tier bento box.

Prepare ingredients and arrange in box as in Whale Bento. Cook fish fingers and croquettes according to package instructions.

Add croquettes in place of sausages. Slice fish fingers and place in bento in place of chicken pieces, as rocks. This gives the bento a more fishy taste.

MINI COOPER BENTO

1 quail's egg; 1 slice cheese; 1 tsp mayonnaise; 1 small tomato; 1 carrot; 1 oz broccoli; 1/2 cup rice; 1 tbsp ketchup; 2 thin slices ham; pinch pepper; 1 small sweet potato; 1 frozen hamburger; 1 sheet nori; pinch salt; pinch black sesame seeds; 2 baby corn; 1 lettuce leaf. 1-tier bento box.

Put lettuce in bento box. Divide broccoli into small fringes and boil. Dice sweet potato. Boil for six mins. Drain broccoli and sweet potato and mix with mayo, black sesame, salt and pepper. Peel carrot and slice. Boil and cut with car shaped cookie cutter. Roll ham slices around baby corn. Stir-fry with salt and pepper. Cut in half. Boil quail's egg. Cut out star shape using cookie cutter. Stick Union Jack on toothpick into egg. Cook hamburger, top with 1/4 slice cheese and car-shaped carrot. Microwave to melt cheese. After cooling, add window and tires made from nori and cheese; use mayo to stick. Cook rice, then stir-fry rice with ketchup, salt and pepper. Make onigiri in Mini Cooper shape. Make eyes, nose, front window and mouth with cheese and nori, use mayo to glue. Make Union Jack with ham and cheese, add to Mini Cooper. Place ingredients into bento box as shown below.

FLAT PIGS BENTO

1 frozen croquette; 1 small tomato; 1 slice ham; 1 lettuce leaf; 1 1/2 oz broccoli; 1 slice white cheese; 1 slice cheddar cheese; soy sauce; 2 red sausages; 1 sheet nori; 1 tsp ketchup; 1/2 cup rice; 1 tbsp canned corn; 1 tsp margarine. 1-tier bento box.

Line bento box with lettuce. Divide broccoli into small fringes and boil. Cut end of sausage into six pieces. boil for 30 secs. Cook rice, make noriben by placing rice in bento box and covering with nori sheet dipped in soy sauce.

Cut cheese into two pig shapes using cookie cutter. Place on noriben. Cut stars, eyes and snouts, using sliced ham and nori. Cut cheddar cheese flowers and leaves from broccoli stalk. Add to bento. Make pig cheeks with ketchup.

Cut ham into dice. Stir-fry with corn and margarine, salt and pepper. Arrange sausage, frozen croquette and remaining ingredients in bento box.

2 Morningstar Farms broccoli and cheddar bites; 1 slice Swiss cheese; handful black olives; 1 large potato and onion pierogy; 1 BOCA soy bratwurst; 1 broccoli floret; 1/2 carrot; 2 strawberries; 1 baby bok choy leaf; 1 tsp mayonnaise; 4 pink sugar dots. 1-tier bento box.

Steam broccoli and carrot. Cook pierogy and place at back of the bento, with two pieces of baby bok choy on either side.

Cook broccoli and cheddar bites, lean on the pierogy. Cut the main part of the face out of Swiss cheese, apply a tiny bit of mayo to the back and stick it in place. Do the same with the eyebrows and noses. Slice black olives, cutting some into half circles, some into thin circles, and some in half along the length rather than round.

Take a plastic toothpick and spear broccoli bites at ear height. Place halved olives on toothpick ends. Dot rounds and half circles of olives with mayo and stick to face. Do the same with pink sugar dots for the cheeks. Gently wedge two strawberries in front of the monkeys. Fill remaining space with pieces of steamed broccoli and carrots. Cook bratwurst and slice. Skewer two bratwurst slices on a bamboo skewer and lay on top of the vegetables.

Cut two tiny Swiss cheese stars out with a fondant cutter, place on the still warm bratwurst to melt just enough to stay in place. Remove toothpicks before eating.

LITTLE COWS BENTO

2 sausages; 1 oz sweet potato; 1 tsp ketchup; 1 kabocha pumpkin squash; 1 serving pasta; 1 bouillon cube; 1 lettuce leaf; 1 carrot; pinch salt; 1 slice cheese; 1 slice pork; 1 nori seaweed sheet; 1 fish sausage; pinch pepper; 1/2 cup rice; 1 shimeji mushroom; 1 tsp black sesame seeds; 1 tbsp potato starch; soy sauce; 1 brussels sprout; 1 tsp margarine. 1-tier bento box.

Line bento box with lettuce. Cut sweet potato into rectangles and boil. Drain and roll with thin sliced sausages. Season and stir-fry until cooked and browned. Cut into half. Boil kabocha pumpkin until tender. Drain and mash, add salt and pepper, black sesame seeds and potato starch. Mix, form into rounds and stir-fry with margarine and soy sauce. Cook rice, add salt. Make two onigiri. Wrap nori around bottom halves, add to box. Cut fish sausage into horns and snouts. Cut ears from cheese, eyes, eyebrows, eyelashes and mouth from nori. Put onto onigiri, dot on ketchup for cheeks. Cut sausage in half and into cross. Slice carrot and brussels sprouts. Simmer with simeji mushroom and bouillon cube until vegetables are tender. Drain and put in bento box, add remaining ingredients.

Black Rabbit & A White Rabbit

132

MEATBALLS BENTO

1 egg; 3 Swedish meatballs; 2 baby plum tomatoes; 1 cup rice. For sesame peppers: 1/2 green pepper; 1/2 red pepper; 1/4 tsp salt; 1/2 tbsp sesame seeds; 1/2 tbsp sesame oil. 2-tier bento box.

Deseed and thinly slice peppers. Add salt, and leave to stand for 20 minutes.

Toast sesame seeds and add to the peppers when still hot. Drizzle on sesame oil and leave to stand in the fridge for at least one hour.

Cook rice, mold into onigiri and place in top tier (not shown).

Hard boil egg, then place in heart-shaped mold to shape. Cook meatballs.

Add peppers to diagonal cup, place in bento. Slice egg and place in the middle of box. Alternate meatballs and tomatoes around egg. Garnish with food pick.

WRAP SANDWICH BENTO

1 sundried tomato tortilla wrap; 1 slice turkey; 1 lettuce leaf; 1 thin slice smoked gouda; 1 red leaf lettuce leaf; 1/4 avocado; 1/2 tomato; 2 mini onigiri; 1 sheet nori; 5 strawberries; handful blueberries; 4 tangerine sections. For lime-wasabi mayonnaise: 1/2 cup mayonnaise; 1 tsp lime juice; 1/4 tsp wasabi paste. 2-tier bento box.

Make wrap sandwich, filling wrap with sliced turkey, green lettuce, sliced tomato and avocado, thin sliced smoked gouda, and lime-wasabi mayonnaise. Slice and pack in bottom tier of bento.

Divide upper tier of bento in half. Line the left side with a piece of red leaf lettuce.

Arrange two shaped mini onigiri with nori faces on top of the lettuce. Line the right side with a wax paper cup, and fill with fresh fruit, arranging in a pattern. Place a plastic pick in the fruit for easy eating.

TODDLER BENTO

1 Morningstar Farms Chik'n nugget; 1 lettuce leaf; 3 crinkle cut french fries; 2 Ritz crackers; 2 slices mozzarella cheese; 1 soy bologna; 1 tbsp steamed peas; 1 small portion roasted garlic and olive couscous; 1 cherry tomato; 1 tbsp ketchup. 1-tier bento box.

Prepare couscous according to the directions on the package. Fill half of the bento with couscous, packing it down tightly. Cook Chik'n Nugget. Place a small leaf of lettuce in the upper left corner and stack the nugget against it. Use cookie or vegetable cutters to cut a sun and a heart from slices of mozzarella. Repeat with slices of soy bologna. Stack together Ritz crackers, cheese and bologna and place in bento on their edges. Prop french fries into corner next to couscous, shortening to fit as necessary. Place container of ketchup in front of cracker stack. Steam peas. Place some on top of couscous. Spear peas onto two picks, place next to ketchup container. Cut tomato in half and place on top of couscous.

RED SANDWICH BENTO

2 slices white bread; 1/2 tbsp peanut butter; 1 tbsp jelly; 1/2 tbsp cream cheese; 1 lettuce leaf; 1 blood orange; handful red fruit snacks; 2 koala cookies; 1 mini Babybel cheese; 2 Laughing Cow cheese blocks. 1-tier sandwich style bento box.

Line box with lettuce leaf. Make sandwich. Half with jelly and peanut butter, the other half with jelly and cream cheese. Slice in half diagonally, remove crusts. Place in left half of bento. Slice a blood orange into quarters and put into upper right of the box. Add a paper divider cup filled with red fruit snacks and koala cookies. Add Babybel and Laughing Cow cheeses to gap in center.

RED SANDWICH VARIATION

Replace 1/2 tbsp peanut butter; 1 tbsp jelly with 2 slices salami.

Make salami sandwich; place as above.

134

PRETTY RABBIT BENTO

1/2 Morningstar Farms Chik'n patty; 1 hot dog bun; 1 hamburger bun; 1 small portion broccoli macaroni cheese; 1 piece pickled ginger; 1 green bell pepper; 2 cherry tomatoes; 1 sweet midget pickle. For tonkatsu sauce: 2 tbsp sugar; 2 tbsp ketchup; 2 tbsp soy sauce; 2 tbsp HP sauce. 1-tier bento box.

Combine tonkatsu sauce ingredients and mix well. Refrigerate any leftovers.

Cook Chik'n patty, place in hamburger bun with generous dollop of tonkatsu sauce.

Cut sandwich in half and place one half along bottom wall of the bento.

Fill the remaining space with macaroni cheese, wedge cherry tomato into the corner.

Cut hot dog bun in half. Place the havles on top of macaroni cheese as the rabbit's ears.

Cut Swiss cheese into ear and eye pieces. Put in place gently.

Cut pupils from a sheet of nori and place on cheese with a pair of tweezers.

Fold pickled ginger into triangle and place as nose.

The bow is made made by slicing off the bottom of a green bell pepper and slicing into shape.

A halved cherry tomato makes the center.

Use a toothpick to keep it in place.

Cut two small rectangles of Swiss cheese.

Make slits in the hamburger bun to wedge them in as teeth.

Place the pickle beside the tomato. Remove toothpick before eating

BOY RABBIT BENTO

See ingredients list from Pretty Rabbit Bento, replace 1 cherry tomato with 1 orange bell pepper. 1-tier bento box.

Create bento as in Pretty Rabbit Bento.

Once bunny is assembled in bento box and nori and cheese eyes and teeth and ginger nose have been added, create baseball cap for bunny.

Slice green bell pepper into semicircle and place over left ear.

Cut orange bell pepper to make peak of cap and place.

PRETTY RABBIT VARIATION

See ingredients list from Pretty Rabbit Bento (left). Replace Chik'n patty; tonkatsu sauce with 2 slices smoked salmon; 1 tbsp cream cheese; handful fresh spinach leaves. 1-tier bento box.

Spread hamburger bun with cream cheese, layer smoked salmon and spinach on top. Cut in half and place in bento. Prepare ingredients and pack bento as in Pretty Rabbit Bento.

PANDA SUNDAE BENTO

3/4 cup rice; plum flavoring ; 1 lettuce leaf; 1 tsp ketchup; small piece ham; 1 sheet nori; 1 tsp mayonnaise; pinch salt. 1 plastic cup, 1 paper Chinese box.

Cook rice. Stir together 1/3 rice with plum flavoring. Put into cup. Stir together remaining rice and salt. Put 1/2 rice into cup. Top with lettuce. Make onigiri with rest of rice. Put onto the lettuce. Make eyes, ears and mouth with nori. Make nose with ham. Put onto onigiri with mayo as glue. Dab ketchup on as cheeks. Carry in paper Chinese box.

THREE PIGGIES BENTO

2 sausages; 2 tbsp soy sauce; 1 carrot; 1 tbsp baked beans; 2 oz broccoli; 1 tsp grated garlic; plum flavoring; 1/2 cup potato starch; 1/2 cup rice; 1 tbsp sake; 1/2 cup plum vinegar; 2 oz chicken leg; 2 quails' eggs; 1 lettuce leaf; 1 slice lemon; 1 baby tomato; 1 sheet nori; 1 fish sausage; 4 pieces flower shaped pasta. 1-tier bento box.

Cut chicken into bite-size pieces. Marinade for 30 mins with soy sauce, grated garlic, sake and 1 beaten quail's egg.

Boil 1 quail's egg, marinade with plum vinegar until pink. Put lettuce into bento box.

Divide broccoli into small fringes. Boil broccoli and flower shaped pasta until tender.

Cut end of sausages into four parts and

boil for 30 seconds. 1 sausage is kept for mushroom stalk. Peel carrot and slice into rounds. Boil until tender.

Cook rice, mix with plum flavoring. Mold into three onigiri with plum flavorings. Put into bento box.

Cut piggy faces and piggy tail from fish cake. Cut nori seaweed sheet into eyes and mouth. Cut cheese into tail shape and carrot into cheeks for faces. Add to piggies.

Make Japanese style fried chicken. Heat the pan. Drain chicken and cover with potato starch. Deep fry chicken for five mins until cooked and browned.

Make quail's egg mushroom. Cut holes in egg white with thin straw. Cut egg in half. Add sausage as mushroom stalk. Put a food pick into the mushroom.

Add sausage, carrot, lemon, broccoli, and fried chicken to bento box, and arrange as shown.

THREE PIGGIES VARIATION

See ingredients list from Three Piggies Bento. Replace 1/2 cup rice; plum flavoring with 2 frozen mini burgers; 1 slice cheddar cheese

Prepare ingredients and arrange bento as in Three Piggies Bento (left). Cook frozen burgers. Top with circular slices of cheese, grill until melted. Add to bento in place of onigiri, placing piggy faces cut from fish cake on top.

LADYBUG BENTO

4 sausages; 1 oz broccoli; 1 sheet nori; 1/2 cup plum vinegar; 1 quail's egg; 1/2 cup rice; pinch black sesame seeds; pinch salt; 2 ozsliced salmon; 1 oz sweet potato; 1 lettuce leaf; 1 hampen fish cake; 1 egg; 1 cheese slice; 1 tbsp ketchup; pinch pepper. 1-tier bento box.

Boil quail's egg, peel. Soak with plum vinegar until turns pink. Line bento box with lettuce. Boil broccoli.

Cut top of sausage off, keep for cloud's cheeks. Cut end of sausage into four parts and boil for 30 seconds. Roast lightly-salted salmon until well done.

Cut sweet potato into sections, peel one section into chequered pattern and boil.

Cook rice, stir-fry with ketchup and some salt and pepper.

Make onigiri in ladybug shape. Add strip of nori for face, put nori dots on back. Make eyes and mouth from cheese slice and nori. Beat egg in a bowl. Add some salt, sesame seeds and rest of sliced cheese, mix well. Make tamagoyaki.

Cut fish cake into cloud shape with cookie cutter. Sauté with soy sauce. Make the cloud's face using sausage for cheeks, eyes and mouth from nori. Put onto cloud fish cake.

Make quail's egg mushroom. Cut holes in egg white with thin straw. Cut egg in half. Add sausage as mushroom stalk. Arrange ingredients in bento as shown left.

LADYBUG VARIATION

See ingredients list from Ladybug Bento. Add 1 slice smoked salmon; 1/2 lime; 1 red chili; 1 tsp soy sauce. 1-tier bento box.

Chop sliced salmon into small strips. Deseed and dice 1/4 chili. Squeeze lime, mix with soy sauce, salmon and chili. When making onigiri, add mix as filling in center. Prepare remaining ingredients and pack.

INDIAN CHICKEN BENTO

1/2 cup rice; 6 pieces precooked deli Indian chicken; 1 egg; 2 lettuce leaves; 2 baby tomatoes. For tuna and wasabi onigiri filling: 1 small can tuna; 2 tbsp Japanese mayonnaise; 1 dab wasabi paste. 1-tier bento box.

Boil egg, cool in cold water, peel.

Place inside flower-shaped egg mold, close mold and leave in cool water 30 mins.

Cook rice. Make tuna and wasabi onigiri filling.

Drain tuna, mix mayo and wasabi.

Taste to see if mix is hot enough; adjust to taste. Add tuna and mix well.

This will make more mixture than needed. Remainder can be used as a sandwich or baked potato filling.

Half-fill heart-shaped onigiri mold with rice.

Make a small dent in the middle and fill with tuna-wasabi mix.

Do not overfill.

Cover with the rest of the rice and mold into onigiri.

Open egg mold and cut flower-shaped egg in half.

Thread Indian chicken onto food picks, placing two pieces on each.

Line bento box with lettuce and assemble ingredients as shown.

cutter. Put faces onto sandwiches using mayo as glue. Cut sliced cheese, and nori into facial features, place with carrot and sausage pieces to make faces.

Make squid dumplings. Mince squid and add potato starch, sake, salt and pepper lightly. Knead well and make small round dumplings. Stir-fry in margarine and soy sauce. Grill boiled corn and coat with soy sauce.

Place remaining ingredients into bento box, arranging as shown left.

SEAMONSTER BENTO

1/2 cup rice; 2 cocktail hot dogs; 1 slice cheese; 1 tomato; 1 sheet nori; 1 scallion. For creamy shrimp and veggie stir-fry: 4 oz shrimp, 1 tsp chopped scallions; 2 tbsp corn and carrots; 1 tbsp cream; 1 tsp butter; pinch salt; pinch pepper. 1-tier bento box with 2 sections.

Make shrimp and veggie stir-fry: peel and de-vein shrimp. Melt butter in pan. Stir-fry the shrimp. Add vegetables. Pour in cream. Season with salt and pepper. Cook rice. Fry cocktail hot dogs. Put shrimp stir-fry in smaller section. Place rice in bigger section, even out the surface.

Cut circles from sliced cheese, add nori pupils. Place three of these on cooled rice. Slice and seed a tomato to make a ring. Place this below the eyes, adding cheese fangs.

Poke the hot dogs into the rice to make them stand upright, making hot dog hands. Thread scallion into ends of hot dogs to make claws.

TWO LIONS BENTO

2 red sausages; 2 cheddar cheese slices; 1 carrot; 1/4 corn on the cob; 3 white cheese slices; 1/2 tbsp grated ginger; 1 tomato; 1/2 egg; 1 sheet nori; pinch pepper; 1 oz broccoli; 2 lettuce leaves; 2 tbsp sake; soy sauce; 4 slices white bread; 1 tbsp margarine; 1 tsp mayonnaise; 1/2 cup potato starch. 1-tier bento box.

Put lettuce into bento box. Divide broccoli into small fringes, boil. Peel carrot and slice into rounds. Boil

until tender. Cut carrot pieces for lion noses. Cut top of sausage for tongues. Cut end of sausage into four parts and boil for 30 seconds.

Spread margarine onto bread slices. Cut tomato into slices. Layer tomato, some salt, sliced cheese and mayo onto bread. Top with remaining bread. Cut sandwiches with flower shaped cookie cutter. Put into bento box.

Make usuyakitamago (Japanese style crepe omelette) for lion faces. Beat egg well. Strain with tea strainer. Stir-fry on a very low heat. Cut usuyakitamago into lion faces with bear-shaped cookie

SEAMONSTER VARIATION

See ingredients list from Seamonster Bento. Replace 1 slice cheese; 1 sheet nori with 4 slices cucumber; 1/2 avocado; 1 black olive. 1-tier bento box with 2 sections.

Prepare and pack bento as in Seamonster Bento. Place three cucumber slices as eyes, slice avocado to create mouth, add cucumber teeth. chop black olives to make pupils.

MEATBALL BENTO

1/2 cup rice; 1 sheet nori; 1 lettuce leaf; 1 tomato; 1 slice ham; 3 Aidell's teriyaki pineapple meatballs; sprig parsley. 1-tier bento box.

Cook rice. Line box with lettuce leaf. Mold rice into two round onigiri. Add nori faces, cut with a paper punch.

Cook meatballs and add to bento box next to onigiri. Slice tomato into four pieces. Stack next to onigiri. Roll ham slice up and cut into three pieces. Add to bento box. Garnish with parsley.

onigiri. Add eyes and mouth cut from nori. Make monkey onigiri. Gently stir together black sesame and soy sauce with rest of rice. Make monkey's face with sliced cheese, eyes and mouth with nori. Cut nose from carrot. Add to face. Put both onigiri into bento box.

Stir-fry lotus root with sesame oil. Season with sugar and soy sauce. Add steamed soy beans and black sesame seeds, place in bento box. Add remaining ingredients to bento box as shown in image.

PIG AND MONKEY BENTO

3 sausages; 1 egg; pinch salt; 1 sheet nori; 1 lotus root; 1 oz broccoli; 2 oz thick sliced pork; pinch pepper; 1 fish sausage; 1 bouillon cube; 1 cheese slice; 1 tbsp flour; 2 lettuce leaves; 1 slice lemon; 1 tsp mayonnaise; 1/2 cup rice; 1 carrot; handful frozen soy beans; pinch sugar; 1/4 cup bread crumbs; plum flavoring; pinch black sesame seeds; soy sauce; 1 tbsp sake; sesame oil. 1-tier bento box.

Put lettuce into bento box. Divide broccoli into small fringes, boil. Peel carrot and slice into rounds. Boil until tender. Cut carrot with flower shaped cookie cutter. Cut ends of sausages into four parts and boil for 30 seconds.

Cut thick sliced pork into bite-size pieces. Sprinkle with salt and pepper, dust with flour. Dip in beaten egg. Roll in bread crumbs and pat down. Fry pork in oil for a few mins. Cut fried pork in half. Cook rice. Make piggy onigiri. Gently stir together plum flavorings and 1/2 cooked rice. Make snout and ear with fish sausage. Put them onto piggy

LITTLE BENTO

1/2 cup rice; furikake; 1 sheet nori; 1 small portion teriyaki beef; 2 small carrots; 1 Okinawan sweet potato; 4 small strawberries. 1-tier bento box.

Cook rice, mix rice with furikake. Using a sushi mold, roll rice in nori and slice into four pieces. Add julienned carrots and teriyaki beef to a cupcake cup and tuck in box. Bake and cube sweet potato. Add cubes to box. Stack small strawberries in the rest of the space.

SMILEY CLOUD BENTO

2 red sausages; 2 oz salmon; 1 cheddar cheese slice; 1/4 tbsp sugar; 1 tsp ketchup; 1 quail's egg; 1 oz broccoli; 1/2 tsp mirin; 1/4 tbsp sake; 1 sheet nori; 1 small tomato; 1 tsp soy sauce; 1 egg; 1 tbsp sake; plum flavoring; 1/2 cup rice; 1 piece cucumber; 1 lettuce leaf. 1-tier bento box.

Line bento box with lettuce. Boil broccoli. Cut ends of sausages into four parts and boil for 30 seconds. Boil quail's egg from cold water for 10 mins. Cool egg and cut zig zag with knife. Cut nori eyes and put on yolk. Make beak from sausage. Cook rice. Stir together with plum flavoring. Make two onigiri and add three thin cut nori seaweed sheet belts to each. Put into bento box. Beat egg, make usuyakitamgo. Cut with small cloud-shaped cookie cutter. Make eyes with nori seaweed sheet. Make cheeks up with ketchup. Stir-fry salmon until cooked. Add simeji mushroom and season with soy sauce, mirin, sake and sugar until stock thickens. Add remaining ingredients to bento box.

KITTY BENTO

1 quail's egg; 1/2 cup rice; pinch salt; pinch pepper; 2 red sausages; 1 oz broccoli; 1 sheet nori; 1 tsp mentsuyu; 1 egg; 1 tbsp potato starch; 1 slice white cheese; 2 lettuce leaves; 3 oz chicken breast; 1 fish sausage. 1-tier bento box.

Dilute mentsuyu with water. Put lettuce in bento box. Divide broccoli into small fringes. Boil in salted water for 2 min. Cut end of sausages into four parts and boil for 30 seconds.

Boil quail's egg. Cut into quarters and sprinkle lightly with salt. Cook rice. Lightly salt cooked rice, make two onigiri. Wrap one onigiri with nori, for black cat. Put both onigiri into bento box.

Make usuyakitamago (Japanese style crepe omelette). In a mixing bowl, beat egg well. Strain egg with tea strainer. Cook strained egg over a very low heat. Cut usuyakitamago into flower shapes with small cookie cutter, and an oval for black cat's nose. Cut cats' eyes, mouth and whiskers from nori and cheese slice. Cut fish sausage into cheeks and nose for white cat. Put them onto onigiri and add flower shapes.

Flatten a chicken breast. Sprinkle lightly with salt and pepper.
Roll the chicken breast up and dust with potato starch. Stir-fry the rolled chicken until cooked and browned. Pour in diluted mentsuyu and cover pan with lid. Sauté for four mins or so. Cut the chicken into bite-size pieces. Add broccoli, sausages and remaining ingredients into bento box as shown in image above.

FRIED NOODLE BENTO

1 packet Chinese noodles; 1 eggplant; 1 sheet nori; 1 green pepper; 3 sausages; 1 lettuce leaf; 1 asparagus spear; 1 fish sausage; 1 egg; 1 piece thin sliced pork mentsuyu; 1 sheet boiled konbu seaweed; 1 oz broccoli; 1 shimeji mushroom; pinch back sesame seeds; 1/2 cucumber; 1/2 small tomato; 1 kani kama fish cake; pinch salt; 1 kamaboko fish cake; 1 slice cheddar cheese. 1-tier bento box.

Dilute mentsuyu. Put lettuce into bento box.

Divide broccoli into small fringes, boil with small pieces of carrot until tender.

Cut end of sausages into four parts and boil for 30 seconds.

Make fried noodles (yaki soba). Cut sliced pork into bite-size pieces. In a pan, stir-fry pork.

Add shimeji mushroom next and then Chinese noodles. Pour sauce for noodles into pan and mix well. Put into bento box after cooling.

Boil egg, cut into zig zag with small knife. Sprinkle with salt and black sesame. Put into bento box.

Deep fry asparagus, eggplant and green pepper. Drain and marinate with mentsuyu in refrigerator for 30 mins

Make two bunnies. Black bunny is made from boiled konbu seaweed sheet with cookie cutter.

Add eyes cut from kani kama, carrot nose, kamaboko fish cake mouth.

Pink bunny is made from fish cake. Add eyes cut from kamaboko fish cake and nori, carrot nose, nori mouth and cheddar cheese ears. Place on noodles.

Place sausage, broccoli and remaining ingredients in bento box as shown below.

145

GREEN TEA BENTO

4 oz green tea soba noodles; 1 scallion; 1 sheet nori; 1 tsp wasabi; 1 tsp grated daikon; 1 tsp dashi no moto (Japanese soup stock); 2 tbsp soy sauce; 1 tbsp mirin; 6 cherry tomatoes; 2 carrots; 1 red apple. 2-tier bento box.

Cook noodles according to directions. Drain and flush with cold water. Drain again.

Make a dressing for noodles: put a dashi powder in a large glass and add 2 fl oz boiling water.

Stir well, then add soy sauce, mirin and daikon. Store in a separate container (not shown).

Put noodles in lower lid of bento box. On top, make flowers of scallion rings keeping one ring aside.

Add wasabi with nori, sliced into strips, arranged around it.

Slice apple and put in upper lid of box, together with enough tomatoes and sliced carrots to fill the space.

Take two apple seeds from core and set aside.

Give your apple pieces a face with the two seeds and half of a scallion ring.

Before eating, take off wasabi and scallions and add to dressing. Then you can either dip your noodles in the dressing (the Japanese way), or pour the dressing over the noodles, mix and eat.

TWO BEAR BENTO

1 lettuce leaf; 5 chicken nuggets; 1 tbsp barbecue sauce; 2 quails' eggs; 2 frozen bear-shaped onigiri; sakura denbu; 1 sheet nori; 3 small cookies; 2 strawberries; 2 cubes Laughing Cow cheese. 2-tier bento box.

Cook chicken nuggets and onigiri according to directions. Line the left half of bottom tier with lettuce. Fill with chicken nuggets. Place a container of barbecue sauce in the middle of box, with two squares of cheese underneath.

Place a paper cup in the far right side of the box, and fill with hard boiled quails' eggs.

In the upper tier, line left side with a wax paper cup, then place two small bear onigiri with nori faces and sakura denbu cheeks.

Line remaining space with another paper cup. Fill with strawberries and koala bear cookies.

SUGARBUNNIES BENTO

2 lettuce leaves; 2 slices sandwich bread; 1 slice ham; 1 slice cheese; 1 sheet nori; 1/2 banana; 1 tbsp peanut butter; chocolate pens to decorate; 2 broccoli florets; 2 strawberries. 1-tier bento box.

Line bento with two small lettuce leaves.

Use one slice of bread to make a ham and cheese sandwich, keeping aside a small piece of ham and a small piece of cheese. Cut into bunny shape with a cookie cutter. Make face with white cheese, nori and ham.

Make a banana and peanut butter sandwich, cut into bunny shape. Draw on face details with chocolate pens.

Arrange the bunnies in the center of the box and fill space around them with two steamed broccoli florets.

Place two strawberries in the lower left corner of the box.

EGG DAISY BENTO

2 slices white sandwich bread; 2 eggs; 2 lettuce leaves; pinch paprika; 1 tbsp mayo; 2 strawberries; 3 snow peas; pinch salt; pinch pepper. 1-tier bento box.

Boil eggs, cool and peel. Slice one egg into pieces, mix with mayo and season. Add to bread with a lettuce leaf to make an egg salad sandwich. Cut crusts off then cut sandwich into 8 sections to make petals. Line bento with lettuce. Arrange sandwich petals around the second hard boiled egg half. Cut in zig zag shape and sprinkle with paprika. Skewer strawberries on a pick and place. The flower's leaves are made from steamed snow peas.

DAISY VARIATION

Replace 2 eggs; pinch paprika; 1 tbsp mayo with 1 tbsp jelly; 3 blueberries.

Make jelly sandwich; cut and arrange as above, placing blueberries in center.

COLORFUL BENTO

BANANA BENTO

1 banana, peeled; 1 jar peanut butter; l low-carb tortilla wrap; 1 bunch redcurrants; small handful frozen red grapes; 1/3 cup yoghurt (e.g. peach flavor); 5 mini fruit-filled biscuits. 2-tier adult size bento box.

Spread out tortilla on a cutting board. Cover entire top surface with a thin layer of peanut butter, right to edges.

Lay frozen, peeled banana down somewhere between center and right edge of tortilla.

Wrap shorter end over banana first, then roll entire rest of tortilla tightly around banana.

Wrap with plastic wrap and let set in freezer for a few minutes; (you can make several at a time and leave frozen until ready to work with them).

When roll is firm to touch, remove from freezer and return to cutting surface.

Use a sharp knife to cut roll into thick slices. Pick three prettiest slices for your bento and re-freeze or snack on rest.

Arrange three slices in shallow tier of the bento boxes. Surround on top and sides with currants.

In deeper tier, place the silicone cupcake cups and fill with remaining ingredients.

From left to right: frozen grapes, yoghurt, biscuits.

GYOZA PUMPKIN BENTO

1/2 cup Japanese rice; 1 tbsp seaweed furikake; 1 sheet nori; 3 1/2 oz pumpkin; 24 gyoza skins; 7 oz minced meat; 1 tsp sesame oil; soy sauce; 1 egg; 2 leaves cabbage; 2 cloves garlic; 1/2 tablespoon white miso; juice of 1/2 lemon; 1 tbsp honey; 2 tbsp mirin; 1 tsp sugar; dashi no moto (Japanese soup stock). 2-tier bento box.

Let gyoza skins defrost; mix minced meat, egg, cabbage, garlic, one tsp soy sauce and sesame oil to make filling. Wet edges, add filling, fold and press firmly; gather edges to make folds.

Fry on high heat for one minute. Add a glass of water, cover pan and steam until water is absorbed. Uncover and fry until brown.

Mix one tsp dashi with 50 ml boiling water. Add mirin, sugar and one tbsp soy sauce; mix until sugar is dissolved. Add pumpkin, bring to a boil then simmer until pumpkin is tender. Cook rice and mix with furikake. Add to box; top with leaf-cut nori shapes. Add pumpkin, four gyozas and bite-sized cucumber pieces. Make a cucumber dip by mixing miso with two tsp water, honey and lemon juice. Leftover gyozas can be eaten within one day.

STRIPES BENTO

1 mini pear; blueberries; raspberries; green seedless grapes; roasted red bell pepper; pickled plum (umeboshi); snow pea pod; ramen noodles; mini toast; double cream brie; 2 oz cooked chicken (in strips); olive oil. 2-tier bento box.

Cook noodles, drain, place in bento, toss with splash olive oil, allow to cool. Slice piece of brie, place in cupcake cup; surround with mini toast.

Put pear in opposite corner. Arrange remaining fruit by size in semi-circular fashion until bento is filled.

Cut roasted bell pepper into strips about same length and width as pre-cooked chicken.

Alternate chicken and pepper strips over noodles. Place umeboshi on top of noodles.

Halve pea pod; shape each into leaves. Add to umeboshi.

TEQUILA BENTO

Fat-free, plain yoghurt; watercress; tortilla; lime; baby tomatoes; 4 oz chicken breast; tequila; garlic; chili pepper flakes; olive oil; chocolate-based dessert item. 2 1-tier bento boxes.

Heat olive oil in pan. Add garlic. Add chicken breast and tequila, cook through, cut into chunks and return to pan.

Allow chicken to get golden on one side; add pepper flakes. Remove from heat and allow to cool.

Place one tbsp yoghurt in cupcake holder. Add mini tomatoes along length of the beanto. Add bed of watercress. Wedge lime slices to hold tomatoes in place.

Place chicken in gaps and layer tortilla on top of chicken. Using a paper punch, punch out designs from extra watercress leaves and decorate yoghurt. Add chocolate dessert in second smaller bento box.

SANTA FE BENTO

Frozen tamale; watercress; grape tomatoes; tequila chicken (as for Tequila Bento); garlic; olive oil; dried red chili pepper flakes; green seedless grapes; raspberries; blueberries; star anise; tea (e.g. black soy bean tea). 1-tier bento.

Cook chicken as for Tequila Bento (left). Thaw single tamale in refrigerator. Slice into quarters right through corn husk wrapper. Place slices in middle of bento. Push cupcake cup into empty space on one side. Start with layer of green grapes, and top with alternating line of raspberries and blueberries.

On opposite side, create bed of watercress leaves with stems removed. Place a few pieces of cooled chicken along with some grape tomatoes on lettuce bed. Allow for a few leaves to peek out around chicken and tomatoes.

Garnish with piece of watercress, single tiny tomato and a star anise.

TRAIL MIX BENTO

Baby carrots; cabbage; grape tomatoes; 4 oz grilled chicken; garlic; olive oil; dried red chili pepper flakes; whole wheat pita bread; fresh mint; pickled plum (umeboshi); dried cranberries; cashews; almond. 1-tier bento box.

Grill chicken after coating with olive oil, garlic, chili flakes.

You will need at least seven mins each side. Allow to cool and cut into bite-size chunks.
Place cupcake cup in corner of bento and fill with dried cranberries and nuts.

Cut cabbage leaf so it fits bento, and place grilled chicken chunks on it.

Line up grape tomatoes between cupcake cup and cabbage leaf (so they are supported).

Add carrots cut into sticks.

Cut pita using cookie cutter, and place along one side of bento.

Add umeboshi as shown and finish with sprig of mint.

PASTORAL BENTO

1 pear; blueberries; green seedless grapes; havarti; whole wheat mini bagels; peanut butter; dried cranberries; fresh mint. 1-tier bento box.

Cut bagels in half. Add layer of peanut butter in center. Slice 1" x 3" block of havarti into thick slices. Place in bento alongside bagels. Rest pear on top bagel and add sprig of mint at top to look like pear leaves. Press cupcake cup into empty area and fill with grapes, blueberries and cranberries.

154

ATOMIC BENTO

1 orange; blueberries; green seedless grapes; baby spinach; baby carrots; cucumber; havarti; mini whole wheat bagel; sushi rice (koshihikari); Japanese pickled plum (umeboshi); crushed red chili flakes; 2 cups sushi rice; 2 1/2 cups cold water. 1-tier bento box.

Cook rice in salted water with chili flakes. Allow to sit for 10 mins. Hand-mold into a ball (onigiri). Line bottom of bento with baby spinach (stems removed).

Halve orange; gently remove inside of one half to create cup. Dice removed flesh; arrange in cup with grapes and blueberries. Place on bed of spinach and add more leaves around cup to stabilize.

Halve mini bagel. Place slice of havarti, spinach leaf and slice of cucumber inside. Use pick to hold sandwich together. Stack two carrot sticks in corner. Place umeboshi at top. Crown bento with onigiri.

MORCON BENTO

1 kg beef round, cut in flat sheets; juice of 10-12 pieces calamansi, approx 1/4 cup, (lemon juice if calamansi unavailable); 1/2 cup soy sauce; sweet pickles, quartered lengthwise; 1/4 cup reserved juice from pickles; hot dogs, halved lengthwise; hard boiled eggs, quartered lengthwise; pimientos, sliced; frozen mixed vegetables; 3 asparagus spears; fresh plum tomato; sunflower oil; beef stock, 1 cup fried rice. 1-tier bento box.

To make Filipino-style Morcon, marinade beef in soy sauce, calamansi juice and pickle liquid for four hrs. Lay beef flat on board, add strips of hot dog, pickles, egg, and pimientos. Roll beef, keeping filling in center. Tie roll with string to hold together. Pan-fry morcon over high heat. When browned, drain off fat. Transfer to pan, fill with beef stock and leftover marinade. Simmer for two hrs. Drain, fry to crisp outside and slice into 1/2 in-thick slices. Make fried rice, with day-old cooked long grain rice and frozen mixed vegetables, in hot wok. Drizzle with soy. Steam asparagus. Cut tomato into wedges. Spread rice in main bento box. Top with morcon. Add tomatoes and asparagus spears.

MORCON VARIATION

See ingredients list from Morcon Bento (left), replace 1 cup fried rice; frozen mixed vegetables; 3 asparagus spears; fresh plum tomato with 1 sweet potato; 1/2 red onion; 2 lettuce leaves; salad dressing; 1 tbsp olive oil. 1-tier bento box.

Cook Morcon as in Morcon Bento recipe. Cut sweet potato into wedges, season, drizzle with olive oil; roast in oven until crispy. Pack next to morcon. Chop lettuce and red onion, dress and place in side compartment.

OMELETTE BENTO

1 egg; 1 tbsp chopped chives; 1 tbsp milk; 5 green beans; handful of cress or rocket; 1 tsp sesame oil; 1 dsp maple syrup; 1 tsp roasted sesame seeds; 1 kiwi fruit; green grapes; strawberries, hulled; sprouted seeds; 2 tier bento box.

Beat egg, milk and chives together; season with salt and pepper. Put well-greased cookie cutters in heated omelette pan. Fill almost to top with omelette mix. Cook until underside is brown and top almost cooked through. Flip over using spatula; gently brown top then remove from pan.

Boil green beans for six mins. Drain and add to larger bento box tier. Dress beans with little sesame oil and maple syrup; sprinkle with sesame seeds. Remove omelette from cookie cutter; place on bed of cress or rocket.

In second tier arrange sliced kiwi, alternate slices of strawberry and grape, and sprouting seeds as shown.

ORECCHIETTE BENTO

1 serving orecchiette pasta; 1 small onion; 1 clove garlic; 1 spear green asparagus; 1/2 small chili, seeds removed; 1/2 red pepper; 2 tbsp low fat cream cheese; olive oil; juice of half lemon; strawberries; green grapes; mixed fruit and nuts; biscuits. 2-tier bento box.

Cook pasta. Add asparagus to pasta water. Cook for five mins.

Fry chopped onion and red pepper in olive oil until soft, add garlic. Fry for further two mins.

Drain pasta and asparagus, add all other ingredients and stir gently, seasoning to taste.

Place in larger bento box tier. Save one asparagus spear to place on top of pasta.

In second tier place dessert: hulled strawberries, cut into slices, grapes, biscuits and mixed fruit and nuts.

LITTLE STARS BENTO

I serving 'little stars' pasta; 5 green beans, chopped lengthways; 2 cherry tomatoes; 1 tbsp corn; 1 small carrot, diced; 2 tsp capers; 3 walnuts, broken up; selection finely-chopped vegetables; olive-oil base wine vinegar dressing; 1 clove garlic; 2 tsp maple syrup; gherkin; nuts and raisins; sliced strawberries; roasted sesame seeds. 2-tier bento box.

Cook pasta. Steam beans (approx seven mins). Make wine vinegar dressing by shaking wine vinegar, garlic, olive oil, mustard in a jam jar with the lid screwed tightly on.

Drain pasta. Add three green beans, chopped into 1/2 ins pieces. Add a little dressing. Allow pasta and beans to cool. Add rest of ingredients shown and and stir; check for seasoning. Add a little more dressing as required. Fill larger bento tier with mix.

In second tier, add gherkins (sliced); beans, sesame seeds, fruit and nuts and hulled strawberries as shown.

CALI MAKI BENTO

Tiger maki sushi (1 cup sushi rice; 1 sheet nori; julienned cucumber; avocado; imitation crab; shrimp); edamame; cucumber kim chee; spinach salad; almond slices; strawberries; grape tomato; soy sauce. 1-tier bento with divider.

Use leftover sushi from restaurant or make sushi as follows: Place sheet of nori on plastic wrap. Spread cooled sushi rice evenly across nori then flip sheet over. Place crab, cucumber and avocado in line 1/2" from edge of nori. Fold edge over; roll nori sheet around ingredients. Use plastic wrap to prevent rice from sticking to fingers. Lay shrimp on top. Slice and place desired amount into bento box. Slide divider over so sushi is snugly packed. Add cucumber kim chee to small food cup and tuck in. Add edamame, flavored or plain. Add grape tomato. In opposite side, add spinach salad and fresh strawberries, sliced almonds. Add dressing in bottle.

WRAP BENTO

1 cup leftover rotisserie chicken, diced; 2 bell pepper, 1 diced, 1 cut into hearts; 1 tbsp fat-free mayonnaise; 3 romaine lettuce leaves; grape tomatoes; kiwi fruit; fresh blueberries; fresh raspberries; carrot flowers. 1-tier bento.

Mix chicken, chooped bell pepper, and mayo together in small bowl. De-stem lettuce leaves, so you have a top cup area with two flaps at bottom.

Spoon some of chicken mixture into the cup of leaf. Wrap sides around and twirl the flaps around base, tearing off any excess leaf.

Place lettuce wraps carefully into corner of bento box. Tuck grape tomatoes into adjacent corner.

Layer sliced kiwi next to grape tomatoes. Arrange raspberries in lower left corner.

Drop a handful of fresh blueberries into remaining space.

SHRIMP BENTO

8 shrimp, cooked and cooled; cocktail sauce; 3 turkey slices; carrot sticks; cucumber kim chee; kim chee crab; 1/2 avocado; 1 boiled egg; grape tomatoes; 1 mini Babybell cheese; parsley. 1-tier bento box.

Arrange shrimp nicely on one side of bento box. Add cocktail sauce in a small container; garnish with parsley, roll the carrot sticks in the sliced turkey and cut into small pieces. Add to bento box. Cut cucumber kim chee into small pieces and place in small food cup.

Place small amount of kim chee crab next to turkey rolls. Add slices of avocado on top.

Place slices of boiled egg on top of avocado.

Tuck in grape tomatoes and add mini Babybell cheese wheel.

SAUSAGE BENTO

See ingredients list from Shrimp Bento (left), replace 8 shrimp; cocktail sauce with 8 mini sausages; 1 tsp honey; 1 tsp wholegrain mustard. 1-tier bento box.

Cook sausages; mix honey and mustard together. Coat sausages in mix then cook for a further five mins. Assemble bento as left, replacing shrimp with sausages. Add mustard in food cup.

PRETZEL BENTO

Glutten-free mini pretzels; 1 victoria plum; 1 pear; serving of polenta; carrot slice; tbsp black tapioca; leftover home-made gazpacho; chunks of red and yellow tomatoes, red and green peppers, red onion, cucumber and 1 clove garlic; 6 black olives, stoned; edible geranium flowers. 2-tier bento box.

Cook polenta and allow to cool. Place in left-half of larger bento box. Edge with 'grass' strip.

Fill right-hand half of bento with rough gazpacho, adding extra chunks of peppers, onions, cucmbers and garlic, as necessary. Decorate polenta with olives. Use cookie-cutter to create flower shape from carrot slice.

In second tier, place pretzels to left, on bed of edible geranium flowers.

Using cookie-cutter take out star shape from plum halves, and swap insides so mirror star image is achieved. Pack spaces with sliced pear.

SUNBURST BENTO

Tomatoes; olives; onions; green, orange, purple and yellow pepper; tofu chunks; cucumber; green beans; coconut rice pudding; cinnamon; victoria plums; pumpkin ginger compote (store-bought); cherry tomatoes; baby carrots; 1/2 cup cooked rice; 1 sheet nori; olive oil. 3-tier bento box.

Dice yellow and purple bell peppers, tomatoes and onions; sautée. Add olives; heat through then cool. Pan-fry tofu chunks. Cook green beans until al dente; cut to fit first tier bento. Lay sautéed vegetables to left, use green beans as divider and base for tofu to right.

Slice cucumber and add. In second tier place rice pudding topped with cinnamon-dusted pumpkin compote, surround with quartered plums. Add tomatoes and baby carrots to right.

In third tier, place rice, slice nori and strips of pepper to create 'sunburst' effect around cherry tomato.

MIDNIGHT BENTO

1 nectarine; 1 peach; 3 avocado sushi rolls; 3 sushi nigiri, with mango or similar; 1 boiled egg; 1 Hawaiian purple sweet potato; 1 carrrot; 1 yellow pepper; strawberry daifuku; 2 tbsp pomagrante seeds; 1/4 orange pepper; 1/4 yellow pepper; broccoli florets. 3-tier bento box.

Slice nectarine and peach. Using cookie-cutter, cut out ten star shapes from each. Place in small tier of bento, alternating shapes. Cook sweet potato and mash. Place, flattened, in one half of larger bento tier. Edge with 'grass' strip. Boil egg in star-shaped egg mold and place as shown. Use cookie-cutter to create smaller stars from carrot and yellow pepper. Place sushi in area beyond 'grass' strip. Arrange strawberry daifuku in third tier and fill with pomegranate seeds; slice yellow and orange peppers and broccolli to fit width of bento and place.

SUNRISE VARIATION

See ingredients list from Midnight Bento (above), replace 1 Hawaiian purple sweet potato with 1 sweet potato. 3-tier bento box.

Assemble bento as in Midnight Bento recipe. Cook sweet potato and mash, place, flattened in one half of larger bento tier.

Boil egg in sun (or circular) -shaped egg mold. Cut 'sun rays' from carrot and yellow pepper. Place.

LENTIL CURRY BENTO

1/2 cup cooked rice; lentil curry (store-bought); 1 red pear; 2 cherry tomatoes; broccoli florets; bean sprouts; 1 carrot. 2-tier bento box.

Pack rice and curry in first bento tier.

In second tier, place sliced pear, cherry tomatoes, broccoli florets (par boiled) and beansprouts as shown.

Cut carrot into star pattern, using cookie cutter. Scatter in patterns on both tiers.

PORK PIE BENTO

4 potatoes; 1 carrot; 1 onion; 2 radishes; 1 tbsp sweetcorn kernels; 1 cucumber; 4 tbsp Japanese mayonnaise; 1 tsp Japanese mustard paste; 1 mini pork pie; portion deli chicken; 6 cherry tomatoes; 1 mini hot dog; 1 slice cheese; sweetcorn; lettuce; parsley; 1/2 cup cooked rice; purple shiso leaf furikake; 2 radishes. 2-tier bento box.

Line both tiers with lettuce. Mix rice with furikake to make speckled pattern. Press into heart-shaped mold. Place on lettuce in top tier. Fill gaps with parsley and cherry tomatoes. Make potato salad: peel potato and carrot and boil together for 20 mins. Thinly slice onion and radishes into circular pieces; cut cucumber in half lengthways; scoop out seeds. Slice thinly, salt; leave to soften for three mins. Slice carrot thinly. Mix mayo in large bowl with mustard, add potato whilst still hot, crushing gently. Place potato salad in cup at one end of bento. Place pork pie at other end. Slice chicken into fan; skewer with toothpick into flower-cut sliced cheese. Slice hot dog to create flower; insert sweetcorn kernel in middle. Fill gaps with parsley and cherry tomatoes.

VISAYAN BENTO

Portion Chicken Inasal (Visayan-style grilled chicken); Japanese vinegar; 5 pieces calamansi (or lemon or lime); splash soy sauce; 1 clove garlic; 1/2 cup cooked rice; 1 dragon fruit; 1/2 mango; cherry tomatoes; chili dip; fresh mint. 2-tier bento.

Mix calamansi, soy, chopped garlic. Soak chicken pieces overnight then grill. Place rice in one tier and lay chicken on bed. Add chili dip bottle. In second tier place sliced mango; calamansi slices; and cherry tomatoes.

DAIKON BENTO

6 strawberries; pickled daikon; leftover fried chicken; green onions; teriyaki sauce; 1/2 apple; 4 quails' eggs, hard boiled; store-bought gyoza; 1 carrot; broccoli florets. 1-tier round bento box, 4 sections.

Place pickled daikon in cupcake cup in one of the sections. Add strawberries whole or hulled, so they squeeze against cup. Use leftover chicken, or fry boneless chicken thigh in chunks, dusted in flour, in hot oil until cooked and brown. Allow to cool.

Par boil broccoli florets. Fry green onion and toss in teriyaki sauce.

Place chicken and broccoli in second section. Scatter onion and sauce on chicken.

Cut apple half in half again and excise skin from flesh to suggest rabbit ears. Fill remaining space in third section with decorated quails' eggs.

Place dumplings in fourth section. Slice carrots into circles and cut flower shapes using cookie cutters.

Decorate as necessary with pink 'grass' trim.

MUFFIN BENTO

1/2 cup Japanese cooked rice; 1 tbsp red shiso furikake; daikon pickles; nori sheet cut in a fun shape like maple leaves; 1 red bell pepper; cucumber; strawberries; 12 mini muffins (1 3/4 cups flour; 4 tbsp cocoa powder; 3/4 teaspoon salt; 1/4 cup sugar; 2 tsp baking powder; 5 oz dark chocolate; 2 eggs; 4 tbsp melted butter; 3/4 cup soy milk; 12 peppermints; silicon muffin liner. 2-tier bento box.

First bake mini muffins. Pre heat oven. Grease mini muffin tray with a little butter. Put dry ingredients in large bowl and mix well. Whisk eggs with milk and butter. Pour into bowl with dry ingredients and mix quickly, with as few stirs as possible. Fill tray with batter; put a peppermint inside each muffin. Bake for 20 mins, until volume has nearly doubled and muffins are slightly browned. Cook rice, allow to cool. Mix with furikake. Put into lower part of bento box, and top with nori leaves and pickles. Cut bell pepper and cucumber into bite-sized pieces. Put in second bento, with a muffin. Fill muffin liner with strawberries.

COW BENTO

3 sugar-snap peas; 1/2 cup leftover shrimp-fried rice; packet of store-bought wasabi; nori strips; 1 packet of laughing cow cheese; 1/2 plum tomato; baby carrots; sugar-snap pea pods. 1-tier round bento bowl.

Place rice in one third of bento box. Add cheese packet to hold in place. Steam sugar-snap peas, create star shape as shown; place on rice. Cut plum tomato into flower pattern. Lean against cheese. Chop raw sugar snap pea pods and pack with baby carrots.

COUSCOUS BENTO

2 oz couscous; 1 tsp vegetable bouillon;
1 oz dried sultanas; 3 oz cooked chick
peas; 1 small onion; 1 zucchini; garlic
clove; olive oil; grapes; strawberries;
cucumber; beansprouts; pear. 2-tier
bento box.

Soak couscous in bouillon and water in
bowl with sultanas and butter. Gently
fry onion, add diced zucchini and
chopped garlic. Fry until soft. Separate
couscous with fork and fluff up. Add
vegetables and olive oil. In separate tier
add cucumber, pear, beansprouts.

CHICKPEA BENTO

7 florets cooked broccoli; handful
rocket; 2 oz chickpeas; 3 cherry
tomatoes; 1 tbsp roasted pine nuts;
olive oil; white wine vinegar; 1 tsp
whole grain mustard; squeeze of lemon
juice; dash of maple syrup. 1-tier bento
box.

Mix rocket, broccoli, chickpeas and
tomatoes; dress with oil, vinegar,
mustard, lemon, syrup and pine nuts.

168

TOFU SOBA BENTO

2 oz tofu; fresh grated ginger; garlic clove; juice half a lemon or lime; soya sauce; 3 small mushrooms; olive oil; 1/2 orange or red pepper; scallion; 2 parsley stalks or lemon grass to use as skewer; 3 oz soba noodles; green steamed beans; sesame seeds; 1 tomato; nuts and raisins; carrot sticks. 2-tier bento box.

Chop tofu into small cubes and marinate for half an hour (or longer) in mix of soya sauce, grated ginger and garlic and lemon/lime juice. Heat grill pan on medium heat with a little oil. Cook noodles (three mins) in a separate pan with boiling water. Thread tofu, mushrooms, pepper and onion onto skewer and cook in grill pan until marked with pattern and cooked through (five to seven mins) turning regularly. Splash noodles with soy and add to larger bento box. Add the kebabs and additional cooked vegetables.

In separate tier add carrot sticks, tomatoes, beans sprinkled with sesame seeds, and fruit and nuts.

169

FRITTATA BENTO

2 eggs; 2 small new potatoes, boiled 1/2 small chili, chopped; 1 small onion; 2 tomatoes; handful of rocket; 1 small carrot; handful mixed aduki and mung bean sprouts; olive oil; white wine vinegar; whole grain mustard; squeeze of lemon juice; hummus; green grapes, strawberries.

Beat eggs.

Add cooked potatoes, chili, one of the chopped tomatoes and cooked onion.

Season to taste.

Add mix to lightly oiled frying pan.

Allow to cook a little before gently moving with a spatula.

The texture should be a mix between an omelette and scrambled eggs.

Once cooked, add to bento box.

Make a dressing with the oil, vinegar, mustard, lemon juice, salt and pepper.

Mix the remaining salad ingredients and dress with the salad dressing.

Add to bento box.

In separate tier add hummus with parsley leaf.

Fill one section with peeled and julienned carrots.

Slice grapes and hull strawberries and add to fill the remaining spaces.

CANELLINI BENTO

Handful rocket; 2 oz cannellini beans; small chunk feta cheese; 3 cherry tomatoes; 1 tsp capers; olive oil; white wine vinegar; 1 tsp whole grain mustard; squeeze lemon juice; dash of maple syrup; hulled strawberries; pickled onion; 2 corn or rice crackers; peanut butter; sprig flat leaf parsley. 2-tier bento box.

Mix oil with vinegar. Add mustard, lemon juice and maple syrup to make dressing. Season with salt and pepper. Shake in watertight jar.

Mix salad ingredients together, crumbling feta with your fingers.

Add dressing and gently toss salad. Place in left of main tier of bento box.

On the right place your strawberries. In smaller tier place corn crackers with peanut butter and quartered pickled onion.

Add parsley to garnish.

ROCKET BENTO

1 serving spaghetti; 1 small onion; 5 mushrooms; 4 walnuts; large handful rocket; 2 tbsp cream cheese; 1 clove garlic; olive oil; green grapes, strawberries, hulled; slice parmesan; watercress. 2-tier bento box.

Cook pasta.

Heat olive oil in pan, cook onions gently until soft.

Add garlic and mushrooms. Cook for four mins.

Mix with pasta and rocket.

Season and stir in cream cheese and walnuts; arrange in bottom tier.

Top tier: grapes, strawberries, parmesan and watercress.

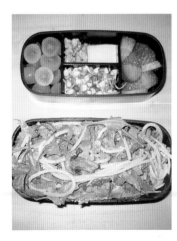

COWPOT BENTO

Whole wheat bread; sliced cheddar cheese; pepperoni slices; pineapple; red grapes; leftover cowpot quinoa; 3 eggs; serving cooked ham; 1 cherry tomato; salad greens. 2-tier bento, round shape.

Make cheese and bread sandwiches, then use cookie cutter, to cut into flowers to make little sandwiches.

Separate sandwiches with slices of pepperoni. and arrange these to one side of smaller bento tier. In remaining space place pineapple and grapes.

Cook quinoa as per box instructions. Scramble eggs. Dice cucumber, tomatoes and cooked ham.

In a large skillet or wok, stir-fry diced ham with a little oil. Add quinoa and eggs. Add cucumbers and tomatoes just long enough to heat. Season with soy sauce and black pepper. Place in larger bento tier.

Cut cherry tomato into two so that it makes flower shapes. Tuck salad greens and tomato flowers beside quinoa.

RAINBOW BENTO

Fresh mixed salad; 2 red bell peppers; 1 yellow bell pepper; shredded cheddar mix; 3 baby carrots; cooked quinoa; leftover ginger chicken; serving cooked black beans; scallion greens; 1 mini carrot. 2-tier bento box.

In smaller bento tier, arrange salad greens to one side. Place cheese and carrots on other side. Using a pairing knife, cut bell peppers into fan shapes for garnish.

Divide larger bento tier into thirds. Fill left third with leftover chicken and the right third with quinoa. Fill middle third with black beans.

Garnish chicken with diced scallion greens. Stick a carrot upright into quinoa. Cut away a small triangle of red bell pepper and place next to carrot.

To cook ginger chicken: marinate sliced chicken breast in soy sauce, fresh minced ginger and a dash of sesame oil for one hour. Grill until cooked through.

RAINBOW VARIATION

Handful rocket leaves; 2 red bell peppers; 1 yellow bell pepper; shredded cheddar mix; 3 baby carrots; cooked quinoa; thin beef sirloin; serving cooked french beans; scallion greens; 1 mini carrot. 2-tier bento box.

Substitute beef for chicken. The secret is to cook soy-marinated thinly sliced sirloin for two mins each side for a delicious rare serving.

GARDEN BENTO

Slice of mango; 1 fruit bar; green pepper; red pepper; 2 purple string beans; small serving polenta; 4 straw mushrooms; 1 hard-boiled egg; tea marinade (soy sauce, chai tea, cinnamon, allspice, black pepper, nutmeg); sugar snap peas; 1 carrot; umeboshi; 1 banana; 1 asian pear. 3-tier bento box.

Using a cookie-cutter, cut flower shapes from mango and fruit bar. Place on 'grass' trim in one bento tier, alternating colors. Cut more flower shapes from halved green pepper. Lay these stars along bottom of second bento tier. Marinade hard-boiled egg in tea marinade for one hour. Cut zig zag shape to suggest hatching. Place in cupcake cup. Lightly fry straw mushrooms. Place in middle of bento. Cut larger star shapes from slice of polenta and place next to muhrooms. In third tier, placed steamed sugar-snap peas and star-shaped carrot slices and umeboshi. Continue star theme with bananas and asian pear slices. Place these in cupcake cups as shown.

Portion French goats cheese; 2 slices smoked salmon; cherry tomatoes; blueberries; dates; 2 romaine lettuce leaves; store-bought pasta salad; furikake: dried fruit or guava roll (shown). 1-tier bento box.

Place goats cheese and smoked salmon in lieu of gouda. Add a 'grass' skirt between the salmon and the cherry tomatoes and dates.

MISS MUFFET BENTO

Serving cottage cheese; raspberries: blueberries: watercress; kumquats; dried fruit (e.g. uncrystallized candied ginger). 1-tier bento box.

Spread cottage cheese over 2/3 of bento. Place raspberries and blueberries in a pattern on top. Create a bed of watercress leaves in empty space. Place cupcake cup to side on the bed of watercress . Fill with kumquats and dried fruit.

NOT JUST FRUIT BENTO

Portion smoked gouda cheese; 2 slices prosciutto; green seedless grapes; raspberries; kumquats; 2 romaine lettuce leaves; store-bought pasta salad; furikake: dried fruit or guava roll (shown). 1-tier bento box.

Line bottom of bento with two large romaine lettuce leaves. Cut 2"x 4" block of smoked gouda into quarters.

Take prosciutto slices and cut lengthwise. Wrap gouda inside prosciutto; leave one end open so gouda peeks out. Place along left wall of bento. Add spoonful of pasta salad in a cup to opposite side.

Fill center of bento with fruits arranged in curved lines. Grapes and kumquats provide support to hold things in place.

Piled raspberries, as contents settle, will give added pressure to keep things from spilling.

Take a pinch of furikake and gently press into gouda and sprinkle the remainder over the pasta salad.

174

Green seedless grapes; grape tomatoes; carrot; pickled ginger; 2 oz. cooked chicken; 1/2 cup cooked sushi rice (koshihikari); umeboshi; scallions; teriyaki sauce. 1-tier bento box.

Press cold rice into side of bento. Top with teriyaki sauce, matchstick-cut carrots and umeboshi. Place three strips of cooked chicken topped with teriyaki sauce and scallions. To left add, in sequence, grape tomatoes, carrot chunks, grapes. Tuck pickled ginger rosette (tightly rolled strips of ginger) or two in gaps.

HAPPY GARDEN BENTO

Kumquat; blueberries; strawberry; sugar snap peas; frozen barbecued pork bun (cha siu bao); wasabi almonds. 1-tier bento box.

Place frozen pork bun in cupcake cup.

Slice ends off kumquats and place in center of bento.

Use small cup to hold almonds.

Clip tips off sugar snap peas at an angle to create 'grass'.

Fill top of bento with pods and save a few for filling in empty spaces later.

Place hulled strawberry upside down in your bento.

Fill spaces with blueberries and tuck in sugar snap pea pods into any remaining gaps.

175

SWEET'N'SOUR BENTO

1/2 cup Japanese rice; 1 tbsp seaweed furikake; nori sheet; 31 rocket leaves; 1 cake tofu; 6 green beans; 1/2 can peeled tomatoes; sweet Indonesian bumbu; 3 tbsp ginger syrup; 1 gold kiwi; seedless red grapes. 2-tier bento box.

Cook rice. Cut tofu in cubes. Wash green beans; cut off tips. Heat a little oil in a pan. Add bumbu and stir-fry for one min. Add tofu; fry for two mins. Add tomatoes and green beans, mix, cover and lower heat. Simmer for ten mins until beans are done, but not too tender. Take off heat, add ginger syrup, mix well. Mix rice with furikake. Put into lower part of bento, flatten surface, top with rocket leaves. Use nori cookie-cutter stars to make 'flowers'. Fill half of upper part of bento with grapes and a half kiwi. Include a spoon to eat kiwi. Put tofu in separate container to prevent spilling sauce on fruit.

TACO BENTO

1 cup cooked taco-seasoned meat; 2 tsp sour cream; 1 cup salsa; pinch shredded taco-seasoned cheese; 4 slices black olive; 1 cup shredded iceberg lettuce; handful tortilla chips; handful prepackaged tortilla strips; 1 clementine. 2-tier bento box.

Place paper éclair cup filled with taco meat, half of salsa and cheese. Top with sour cream and olive slices.

Fill gap with shredded lettuce and remaining salsa. Fill second tier with tortilla chips and tortilla strips.

heat. Pour remaining marinade over diced carrots and zucchini and chopped onion, soak for ten mins. Transfer to hot pan and simmer for further ten mins, until carrots are cooked through. Cook couscous; fill bottom tier of bento. Place vegetables around rim. Add raisins. In upper tier, use peeler to cut long strips of carrot; wrap around tofu bites. Place tofu triangles and fill space with tomatoes.

AUTUMN VARIATION

1 serving leftover lamb leg or shoulder; 3 stoned dates, chopped; cup toasted almonds; six kumquats. 2-tier bento box.

Use ingredients above to replace the vegetable stew. Shred lamb into pan and heat with raisins and chopped onion, adding a dash of cummin. Add to lower tier with chopped dates.Replace cherry tomatoes in upper tier with kumquats, halved across their middles.

AUTUMN BENTO

Roasted garlic; serving olive oil couscous; 1 baby tomato; 1 cup all-purpose flour; 4 oz extra-firm tofu; 2 carrots; 1 zucchini; 1/4 onion; 1 tbsp garlic powder; 2 tsp ground cummin; 3 tsp cilantro; Panko bread crumbs; vegetable oil; 3 bay tomatoes; 1 cup raisins; 3 tbsp soy sauce; 1 tbsp sesame oil; 2 tsp brown sugar; 1 cup vegetable stock. 2-tier bento box.

First make tofu bites: In a mixing bowl, stir tofu until well crumbled. Add water, grated carrot and finely-chopped onion, stir well. Stir in spices: one tbsp garlic powder, one tsp cumin, two tsp cilantro. Mix in flour, one cup at a time. Dip fingers into a bowl of water. Scoop up portion of mixture and shape into a ball or cylinder. Roll ball in Panko crumbs, covering all the outside. Gently lower into hot oil for deep frying. Microwave on high for 30 secs. Next make tofu triangles: Cut tofu into thick triangles. Mix marinade ingredients (three tbsp soy sauce, one tbsp sesame oil; one tbsp cumin; two tsp brown sugar; one tsp black pepper; stock) and sit for 20 mins. Melt knob butter in pan. Put in tofu. Cook each side until golden brown. Remove from

FRIED RICE BENTO

1 cabbage Bao; Japanese wheat cookies; teriyaki sauce; 1 packet silken tofu; 2 onions; 1 can corn; 20 black olives; 6 baby tomatoes; 1 cup all-purpose flour; 1 tbsp garlic powder; 2 dashes turmeric; 1 dash parsley; 1 cup rice; handful frozen peas; 1 carrot; 1 packet eggless omelette mix; 5 tbsp soy sauce; 1 packet Panko bread crumbs. 2-tier bento box.

Mash tofu until it is liquid, add water, spices (garlic powder, turmeric, parsley, pepper) and mix. Mix in flour 1/3 cup

at a time. Melt one slice butter in hot pan, add 1/3 mix to pan. It will make a thick pancake that will turn bright yellow as it cooks. Cook until browning occurs. Cook rice: use one day-old cold rice. Pour three tsp vegetable oil over rice. Mix well, heat oil in a skillet. Sautée omelette mix. Remove from pan. Sautée vegetables until onions are clear. Remove from pan; add rice, stir to release clumps. Cook five mins. Pour in three tbsp soy sauce and cook for five mins. Add vegetables, omelette and two tbsp soy sauce, cook for five more mins. Assemble.

SAUSAGE ROLL BENTO

1 serving plain fried rice; steamed broccoli; cherry tomato; sausage roll slices; store-bought vegetable gyoza; omelette; carrot flower. 1-tier bento box.

Fill half the bento with fried rice, make a line along the edge of fried rice with the steamed broccoli all the way across the bento. Take a small slice of omelette and curl it up on itself. Place at one end of the remaining space. Next add gyoza, sausage roll, a raw carrot flower and a quarter of tomato.

179

STAR BENTO

1 cup sushi rice; 1 sheet nori; julienned cucumber; 1 avocado; imitation crab; tobiko; edamame; lettuce leaf; soy sauce. 1-tier bento box.

Cook rice; cool.

Lay some plastic food wrap on a sushi mat. Place sheet of nori on plastic wrap.

Spread rice out evenly across nori then flip sheet over.

Place crab, cucumber, and sliced avocado in a line one inch from edge of nori.

Fold edge over and begin to roll sheet of nori around ingredients, using plastic wrap to keep rice from sticking to your fingers.

Once you have finished rolling sushi, you can roll it in the tobiko, adding color to your sushi and your bento as a whole. Slice the sushi.

Line bento box with lettuce leaf. Place sushi into bento in neat rows. Stand end pieces from roll at back edge of bento box, so avocado, cab and cucumber pieces stand up on edge. This adds variation to the bento box.

Tuck as many edamame seed pods as will fit into remaining place.

Add a small sauce bottle filled with soy sauce for sushi. Pick a bottle with a bright and attractive color, like the tomato shaped bottle here. This adds interest and contrast to the bento.

SPINACH BENTO

1/2 cup Japanese rice; 1 tbsp red shiso furikake; sheet nori; 4ozs spinach; 1 egg; 1 tbsp sesame oil; 1 tbsp soy sauce; 1 tbsp mirin; 1 red bell pepper; bunch seedless grapes. 2-tier bento.

Cook rice. Allow to cool. Mix rice with furikake. Place in 2/3 of lower bento tier. Mold in pattern if required. Use papercutter to cut star pattern from nori.

Heat sesame oil in a wok or skillet; stir-fry spinach for five mins until tender. Add soy sauce and stir to mix. Add to bento box, next to rice; use a plastic divider. In a bowl, whisk egg with mirin and soy sauce.

Heat a little oil in a skillet, put on low heat and add one third of egg mixture.

Take care egg is evenly distributed. Let thicken for a moment, then roll tightly to back. Add second third of egg and repeat: now start rolling at back with first part and roll back to the front. Repeat with last bit.

Cut egg roll into neat slices and add to bento. Add sliced bell pepper and muffin liner filled with grapes.

SANDWICH BENTO

Deviled egg mix; 2 slices brown bread; lettuce leaves; 10-12 baby carrots; 1 d'anjou pear; cucumber kim chee; 2 jell-o eggs. 1-tier bento box.

Make sandwiches with deviled eggs mix, pepper to taste and two lettuce leaves. Slice in half. Place in bento, support with baby carrots. Chop pear; pack next to cucumber kim chee. Fill remaining space with jell-o-eggs.

HAMBURGER BENTO

1 beef hamburger patty; round onigiri; 1 red bell pepper; cherry tomatoes; 5 baby carrots; lettuce leaf; parsley. 1-tier circular bento box.

Line bento box with lettuce leaf. Make round onigiri and place in bento. Slice hamburger patty into pie-slice shapes. Arrange with sliced bell pepper next to onigiri. Place tomatoes and baby carrot sticks in gaps and add a parsley garnish.

BEANBURGER VARIATION

1 beanburger patty; round onigiri; 1 red bell pepper; apple; 5 kumquats; 3 dates; lettuce leaf; parsley. 1-tier circular bento box.

The vegetarian method is the same; kumquats take the place of carrots and a chopped apple is used instead of tomatoes. Stone three dates and chop roughly before sprinkling over the burger and peppers for garnish.

PLAIN PASTA BENTO

Serving of penne; 10 cherry tomatoes: grated cheese; olive oil; pepper; parsley. 1-tier bento box.

Boil the pasta until al dente. Cool. Grate mature cheddar, parmesan or other hard cheese. Place in bento box. Scatter with cherry tomatoes and several sprigs of parsley.

BREAKFAST BENTO

1 strip bacon; 1 large egg; 1 small baked potato; 1 red bell pepper; blueberries; 1 strawberry; plain yoghurt. 1-tier bento box.

Cook bacon in a small pan until crispy; drain on paper towel. Remove excess grease, return to burner and add diced bell pepper; cook until colors brighten. Remove from pan to cool.

Return pan to burner and crack egg into the pan. Add dash of pepper, scramble evenly, fold cooked bell pepper into mix, crumble bacon strip on top. Remove from heat to cool.

Spoon mixture into a paper cupcake cup and place in bento. Cut baked potato into bite-sized pieces and use to fill top of bento.

Place silicone cup in bento and spoon in yoghurt inside. Shore up sides of both cups with blueberries. Slice a bit off strawberry and snip a few leaves to create mini strawberry decor on top of yoghurt.

SWEET CHILI BENTO

Extra firm tofu; sugar snap peas; grape tomatoes; sweet chili sauce; vegetable oil; olive oil; sesame seeds; dessert (e.g. green tea mochi and guava paste roll). 1-tier bento box.

Place tofu on plate.

Top it with a cutting board, weighing it down with a large can, allowing it to drain, for about 20 mins.

Slice tofu into thick pieces and place in a bowl. Pour some marinade over tofu; reserve rest for basting.

Allow to marinate for 30 mins or more. Oil grill with vegetable oil.

Place marinated tofu on grill (medium hot). Cook about eight mins on first side. If necessary, baste with reserved marinade.

Cook other side for eight mins. Remove from heat and allow to cool.

Cut grilled tofu so fits into bento.

Blanche sugar snap peas until they turn bright green. Remove from heat and douse in cold water.

Drizzle with olive oil and place in bento.

Add sesame seeds for decoration.

Squeeze a few tomatoes in empty space to echo the sweet chili sauce used on tofu.

Add a piece of fruit or a sweet for dessert.

SUMMER GRILL BENTO

Sugar snap peas; edamame; green beans; grape tomatoes; ramen noodles; 2 oz. grilled beef; red chili pepper. 2-tier bento box.

Cook ramen noodles as per package. Drain, allow to cool. Toss in olive oil to prevent sticking and place in bento.

Blanche green beans; let boil until they turn bright green. Remove from heat, douse in cold water. Thinly slice grilled beef and fan over noodles. Lightly sprinkle crushed red chili pepper over meat and noodles.

Place a whole chili pod, single green bean and tomatoes on top of meat for decoration.

In second tier, begin with a bunch of green beans and place in center.

Pile shelled edamame on either side and shore them up with tomatoes on both ends. Top bento off with snap peas, cut into slices and placed to fill empty spots.

Kumquats; pickling cucumber (or small cucumber); mini pear; watercress; grape tomatoes; 1/2 cup sushi rice (koshihikari); soy sauce. 1-tier bento box.

Cook rice. Remove from heat and let sit covered for ten mins.

Shape into balls or press in an onigiri maker.

Heat grill on low; use a vegetable/seafood grill pan or a grill that has bars close together. Place onigiri on grill.

After four minutes, carefully turn over when the edges start to turn brown.

Turn over again if necessary until both sides are light brown.

Brush one side lightly with soy sauce; place back on the grill, soy sauce-side down, for about 30 seconds. Repeat on the other side.

Place cooled onigiri in bento.

Peel skin from a small cucumber, slice into medallions and place in bento.

Put single slice of cucumber and cucumber skin as decoration on onigiri.

Fill empty spaces with watercress leaves.

Add fruit on top.

Place tomatoes around edges to offset golden color of onigiri.

HYACINTH BENTO

Kumquats; blackberries; sugar snap peas; frozen barbecued pork bun (cha siu bao); chocolate dessert item (e.g. chocolate pastry mochi shown). 1-tier bento box.

Place frozen pork bun in cupcake cup. Place blackberries hull side down in bento. Slice the ends off kumquats and place beside blackberries. Clip tips of the sugar snap peas at an angle to create 'grass' and use to fill empty spots. Add a bit of chocolate for dessert. Once bento is ready to be eaten, remove frozen pork bun with paper beneath it. Cover with a damp paper towel and heat in microwave for 30-50 secs.

HYACINTH VARIATION

See ingredients list from Hyacinth Bento (above), replace frozen pork bun with 1/2 cup sushi rice; 1 portion crab; 1 tsp mayo. 1-tier bento box.

Cook rice. Mix crab and mayonnaise together. Fill half of onigiri mold with rice, add crab mix filling, fill rest of mold. Place onigiri where pork bun sits.

CHICK BERRY BENTO

2 red bell peppers; 1 tsp lemon juice;
1 tsp olive oil; pinch salt; 1 lb trimmed
chicken tenderloins; 1 egg, beaten;
flour; dried coconut; 6 spears of
steamed asparagus; 1 strip orange
peel, long enough to tie around the
asparagus bunch; handful frozen
cranberries; 1 tbsp prepared mashed
potatoes; 1 tsp pomegranate seeds.
2-tier bento box.

Bake or boil chicken. Roll in flour, dip
in egg and roll again in dried coconut.
Fry until coconut crust is golden brown.
Purée bell peppers; mix with lemon
juice, olive oil and salt. Cover chicken
with sauce. Tie bundle of asparagus
together loosely with orange peel.
Fit into bottom of one tier; fill rest of
space with frozen cranberries. Spoon
mashed potatoes into right side of
other tier, place chicken alongside it;
spoon red pepper sauce over both.
Sprinkle with pomegranate seeds.

ADVENTURE BENTO

Serving of fettuccine noodles (spinach
and green onion shown); 1 cherry
tomato; handful sugar snap peas;
strawberry; kiwano (horned melon);
mango; sesame seed. 1-tier bento box.

Prepare noodles according to package;
allow to cool. Slice fruit and place in
one half of bento. In other half, place
cupcake cup; fill with noodles. Sprinkle
with sesame seeds and top with
tomato. Surround with sugar snaps.

Squeeze strawberry into empty space.

189

HUMMUS BENTO

Tin of chickpeas; 1 clove garlic; juice of half lemon; 2 tbsp tahini; 2 tbsp olive oil; salt and pepper; handful salad leaves; tomato; 1 in of cucumber; half a pink grapefruit, segments; salad dressing; 4 oz green beans; 2 broccoli florets; sesame oil; roasted sesame seeds. 2-tier bento box.

To make hummus, put chickpeas, garlic, lemon juice and tahini into a blender.

Mix until you get required consistency.

Some people prefer a rougher and others a smoother consistency.

Boil broccoli in salted water for four-seven mins ensuring it retains its bite.

At same time, steam green beans above broccoli until tender but also retaining their bite.

Mix all salad ingredients together and dress with salad dressing.

Mix cooked beans and broccoli together and dress with sesame oil.

Sprinkle both with roasted sesame seeds. Arrange ingredients in bento box as shown above, placing hummus in silicone cupcake cups to keep other ingredients dry.

STAR BENTO

1 cup rice; onigiri filling; 1 strip very thin beef; 2 frozen gyoza; 2 stalks asparagus; 3 strips red pepper; 1 strip green pepper; 1 tbsp avocado; 1 tbsp chick peas; 2 slices each yellow and green zucchini; 2 broccoli florets; 3 snow peas; 6 flowers cut from carrot slices (use vegetable punch); 1 flower cut from thin slice of daikon; 3 strawberries; 5 blueberries; 3 stars cut from nori with a nori punch; pinch fresh parsley, mint and basil; 1 tbsp small jelly beans; soy sauce and garlic marinade for beef; 1 tsp lemon juice; 1 tbsp canola oil. 1-tier bento box.

Cook rice. Marinade beef for 20 mins. Fry gyoza in canola; place in top left corner of bento box.

Steam asparagus, zucchini and broccoli together for two mins.

Add snow peas and carrot and steam for additional minute.

For chick pea salad, chop one strip each of red and green peppers into small pieces.

Mix with avocado, chick peas, basil, mint, parsley, olive oil and lemon juice. Place in an oval wax paper cup.

By now, rice should be finished. Form three onigiri stars using a mold while rice is still hot, and add filling inside.

Sprinkle onigiri with salt and place a nori star in the middle of each one.

Pack remaining ingredients as shown, chopping as necessary.

Take beef slice and place asparagus and remaining red pepper strips near one end, and roll (like maki sushi).

Attach the end with toothpicks. Fry over medium heat until beef is cooked. Allow to cool and remove toothpicks.

Slice into three pieces. Place beef roll slices in a vertical column about a third of the way from the left side of the bento box.

Place onigiri on either side of the beef.

Place gyoza on left and right of the onigiri. Place chick pea salad against the top side of the bento box.

Put jelly beans in a small foil cup; place in the bottom right corner of the bento.

Place strawberries in the top right corner.

Fill gaps around strawberries with blueberries.

Fill any other gaps in the bento with broccoli, snow peas and zucchini.

Place carrot and daikon flowers on top of the vegetables, rice and beef, wherever the bento needs a bit of color.

TULIP BENTO

1 small triangle onigiri; 1 stuffed turkey breast; 1 cup mashed sweet potato; 3 slices green and yellow zucchini, halved; 4 broccoli florets; 4 snow peas; 1/2 cup sliced Chinese cabbage; 3 slices of cucumber; 1/2 tangerine, wedges; 2 strawberries; 5 blueberries; mozzarella cheese; chives; date; 2 tsp apple sauce; 1 tbsp maple syrup; 1 tbsp balsamic vinegar; 1 tsp crushed walnut; 1/4 tsp cinnamon; 1 clove garlic; 1 tbsp dried cranberries; black sesame seeds; 1 piece nori, 1" x 2"; olive oil. 1-tier bento box.

Bake turkey breast covered with foil for 35 mins. Remove foil; bake for an additional 15 mins. Allow to cool, and slice. Microwave onigiri for 30 secs. Fold nori strip over bottom; sprinkle with black sesame seeds. Combine sweet potato, cinnamon, maple syrup and apple sauce. Fill muffin cup with mixture. Place in top left corner of bento. Cut chive to create stem and 'grass' for mozzarella 'tulip'. Fry garlic and cabbage until garlic has browned slightly and cabbage is wilted. Add balsamic vinegar, cranberries and

EGGPLANT BENTO

1 large red onion; 1 red pepper; 1 small eggplant; 1 medium zucchini; 1 tin chopped tomatoes; 5 oz easy soak couscous; vegetable bouillon or stock cube; tomato purée; harissa; lemon slices. 2-tier bento box.

Heat two tbsp olive oil in a large pan. Add chopped onion and chopped peppers. Cook for five mins. Add chunked eggplant and one tbsp of oil. Cook for a further ten mins.

Meanwhile, cook couscous as directed; add one tbsp of tomato purée to stock.

Remember not to touch couscous while it's soaking. Leave until you are ready to fluff it up with a fork.

Add zucchinis and cook everything together for a further five mins or until eggplant and zucchini are cooked.

Add tomatoes and cook for a further five mins, medium heat, stirring occasionally.

Add 1 tbsp of tomato purée and allow to thicken for a few mins. Fluff up couscous with a fork and add to bento, either with ratatouille or separately. Garnish with slice of lemon.

walnuts; mix well. Fill a wax paper oval cup with the mixture.

Steam broccoli and zucchini for two mins. Add snow peas and steam for two more mins. Take four slices of turkey breast; position diagonally in center of box. Place cabbage salad in bottom right corner, date square in top right corner and onigiri in the top middle. Fill gaps with broccoli florets, snow peas, zucchini, orange wedges, cucumber slices, strawberries and blueberries.

WALNUT BENTO

Serving macaroni (or other pasta shapes); 2 oz cream cheese; 2 cos lettuce leaves; 5 walnuts; 3 cherry tomatoes; 1 in piece cucumber; salad dressing; 2 fine slices of lemon. 1-tier bento box.

Cook macaroni. Drain and mix with cream cheese, tomatoes, cucumber. Dress with salad dressing, walnuts, lemon. Fill top tier with fruit/dessert.

PINE NUT BENTO

Serving penne pasta; 2 tbsp pesto; handful pine nuts; 3 cherry tomatoes; 5 broccoli florets; parmesan cheese. 2-tier bento box.

Cook pasta. Steam broccoli, add tomatoes for last two minutes to soften. Drain pasta and mix with pesto, tomatoes and broccoli. Roast pine nuts and sprinkle over pasta, grate parmesan accross top. Pack top tier.

PARMIGIANO BENTO

1 cup cooked egg noodles; leftover chicken parmigiana; 1 diced avocado; fresh blueberries; 1 pickled cucumber; fresh parsley. 1-tier bento box.

Lay egg noodles across middle of box. Place pieces of chicken parmigiana in opposing corners, garnish with parsley. Place fresh blueberries and cucumber into silicone cups in corners. Drop diced avocado into the middle.

CHICKEN POPCORN BENTO

1 small potato; 1 tbsp butter; 1 tbsp milk; frozen chicken popcorn; frozen corn and carrots; 3 grapes; carrot; mini jello cup. 1-tier bento box.

Mash boiled potatoes with butter and milk. Bake chicken popcorn. Add corn, carrots and grapes in cups. Cut carrot slices into flowers. Add jello cup.

SHRIMP BENTO

Boiled shrimp; 1 avocado; kiwi fruit; grape tomatoes; boiled egg; orange slice; shrimp cocktail sauce; lettuce leaf. 1-tier bento box.

Line box with lettuce leaf. Skewer shrimps on food picks; place in bento. Fan out avocado slices and lay over half of shrimp. Peel and slice kiwi fruit. Lay on top of avocado. Peel boiled egg; cut jagged edges to resemble 'cracked' eggshell. Add cocktail sauce to a food cup and place above egg. Add orange slice and tomatoes to middle of box.

FETA BENTO

2 oz penne; 1 scallion; 2 small tomatoes; 1 oz feta cheese; olive oil; black sesame seeds; salt; pepper; 2 mini peppers; grapes; strawberries; stuffed olives; cream cheese. 2-tier bento box.

Boil water in pan and cook pasta until al dente.

Drain and mix with chopped scallion, chopped tomatoes, cubed feta,

Dress with a little olive oil and season to taste.

Garnish with black sesame seeds.

Remove centers of mini peppers, roast and stuff with cream cheese. Add to top tier of bento box.

Chop grapes and strawberries and add to left and right sections of top tier.

Add stuffed olives to remaining section of top tier.

PASTA BENTO

2 oz mini pasta shapes; handful of rocket; 1 oz corn; 2 oz green beans; 3 black olives; 1 tbsp capers; 1 small carrot; 2 cherry tomatoes; 2 walnuts; parmesan cheese; olive oil; sesame oil; gherkin; strawberry; mixed nuts and raisins. 2-tier bento box.

Cook pasta. Boil green beans until cooked but still retain their bite. Set half aside for top tier of bento.

Chop remaining beans, tomatoes, carrot, walnut. When pasta is cooked,

drain and mix with chopped vegetables, olives, capers, corn and rocket. Add one dessert spoon of olive oil as a dressing.

Add Parmesan cheese, cut into a small flower shape or grated.

In top tier, place green beans dressed with sesame oil and sprinkled with sesame seeds.

Slice strawberry, place in right hand section of top tier. Pack mixed nuts and raisins into top section of tier.

Slice gherkin and place into silicon cupcake cup, season to taste.

ROMAINE BENTO

2 or 3 romaine lettuce leaves; 2 oz mozzarella cheese; 2 oz kidney beans, cooked, drained and washed (tinned are fine too); 2 small tomatoes; 1 tsp fresh, sliced red chili; basil leaves; lime-juice base salad dressing; 5 green beans; maple syrup; sesame seeds; 2 slices of really good rye bread; wasabi peas. 2-tier bento box.

Mix all salad ingredients (lettuce, diced mozzarella, kidney beans, chopped tomatoes) together in larger tier.

Scatter with chili and rip a few basil leaves to scatter also. Add dressing.

In second tier add steamed green beans.

Dress with maple syrup and sesame seeds.

Slice bread to fit two compartments in bento. In silicone cup place wasabi peas.

LENTILS BENTO

6 oz red lentils; 1 oz butter; 1 onion; 4 tsp mild curry powder; 1/2 tsp chili powder; paprika; pomegranate seeds; 6 oz couscous; 1 small cooked beetroot; 2 oz feta cheese; scallions, 1 small carrot; handful sprouted mung beans; strawberries; grapes; chocolate raisins; nuts. 2-tier bento.

Wash lentils thoroughly; boil for twelve mins until cooked through. Drain. Heat butter in frying pan; cook the onions until translucent. Add curry and chili powder: cook for a further two mins, stirring. Add onion and curry mix to lentils, mash and season to taste. Set aside.

Soak couscous. Add chopped beetroot and stir into couscous together with onion, chopped carrot, and mung beans. Add feta cheese and garnish with pomegranate seeds. Scatter pomegranate seeds over lentils also.

In second tier place chopped strawberries, grapes, raisins and nuts.

ROCKET BENTO

3 small new potatoes: handful of rocket; 2 oz cooked, drained, washed kidney beans (or other beans of your choice); 2 oz feta cheese; 1 in piece cucumber; 1 small tomato; 4 black olives; salad dressing; mung beans; strawberries; kiwi fruit; pomegranate seeds. 2-tier bento box.

Boil potatoes in salted water for ten mins until cooked through.

Wash and dry salad leaves.

Mix chopped tomatoes, kidney beans, chopped cucumber, quartered potatoes and feta cheese together.

Place in first bento tier and add dressing.

In the second tier add mung beans, chopped strawberries, sliced kiwi and pomegranate seeds.

KIM CHEE BENTO

1 cup broccoli florets; 4 cherry tomatoes (2 red, 2 yellow); 1 leek; 1/2 cup kim chee (pickled cabbage); 3 oz flour; 1 egg; 1/2 pint soy milk; okonomiyaki sauce. 2-tier bento.

Cook broccoli florets for three mins. Drain and flush with cold water.

Make pancake batter by mixing flour, egg and soy milk.

Add very thinly sliced leek and kim chee.

Heat oil in a skillet. Make 5 little pancakes by pouring a little batter into skillet each time.

Fry, medium heat, until brown. Turn and repeat. Keep going until all batter is used.

Fill bento with pancakes.

Fill other section of bento with broccoli and add muffin liner filled with tomatoes.

Fill food cup with okonomiyaki sauce to dip the pancakes in. Carry this separately to bento box.

KIM CHEE VARIATION

1 cup broccoli florets; 4 cherry tomatoes (2 red, 2 yellow); 2 slices salami; 1/2 onion; 1/2 cup kim chee (pickled cabbage); 2 eggs; 1/2 pint soy milk. 2-tier bento.

Cook broccoli florets for three mins. Drain and flush with cold water. Whisk eggs, add milk, season. Chop onion, salami and add to mix with kim chee. Cook as omelette and cut into quarters. Fill bento with stacked omelette. Fill other section of bento with broccoli and add tomatoes.

198

TOFU SCRAMBLE BENTO

Extra firm tofu; 4 large eggs; scallions; 1 bell pepper; mushrooms; banana; strawberry; cottage cheese (low-fat); baked potato; French bread; vegetable oil; soy sauce. 2-tier bento box.

Place tofu on a plate, top with a cutting board, weigh down with a large can, allow to drain (about 20 mins). Slice tofu into one-inch thick blocks and place in a bowl.

Heat oil in a pan (medium hot); add mushrooms, bell peppers and baked potato. Cook until mushrooms are soft. Add soy sauce, scallions and tofu and cook for about 4 mins. Transfer into a bowl. Crack eggs into pan and lightly scramble. Add contents of bowl to pan and finish cooking, lightly stirring. Remove from heat and allow to cool.

Cut French bread and place a few pieces in one tier. Spoon cooled tofu scramble beside bread. In second tier, place thick layer of cottage cheese; top with sliced banana and strawberry.

TWO MUFFIN BENTO

2 zucchini and basil mini muffins (shop bought); 2 oz feta cheese; 2 small ripe tomatoes; 2 ins chunk of cucumber; 1/2 orange pepper; 2 tsp parsley; small handful of mung bean sprouts; olive oil; white wine; cream cheese (to serve with muffins); strawberries; grapes; wasabi peas; mini biscuits. 2-tier bento box.

Mix diced feta, chopped tomatoes, chopped cucumber, diced orange pepper, mung beans together. Place in one half of larger bento tier. Dress with olive oil, white vinegar, salt and pepper. Slice muffins; spread with cream cheese to create a sandwich. Place in second half of bottom tier. Fill spaces with salad. In top tier, place strawberries, sliced grapes, wasabi peas; mini biscuits and cream cheese.

TWO EGGS VARIATION

See ingredients list from Two Muffin Bento (above), replace 2 zucchini and basil mini muffins with 2 boiled eggs.

Prepare bento as above but add boiled eggs for a lighter lunch.

VEGGIE BENTO

Hummus; carrots; handful sugar snaps; yellow bell pepper; cherry tomatoes; radishes; flat parsley; tortilla chips. 3-tier bento box.

Put as much hummus as you think you will need for dipping in a container that will fit into your bento.

Garnish with parsley.

Steam sugar snaps for five mins. Flush with cold water to stop cooking process.

Cut carrots and bell pepper into bite-sized pieces.

Place all vegetables in bento and arrange in a colorful fashion, separating vegetables into bands of color.

Fill remaining tier with tortilla chips.

PANCAKES BENTO

5 small buttermilk pancakes; molasses, or favorite pancake topping; 1 orange; 1 tea bag (e.g. green tea); 1 serving scrambled eggs; 1 shake of cayenne pepper flakes. 2-tier bento box.

Arrange pancakes in row in one tier of bento box. Using a squeeze bottle, drizzle topping over pancakes. Line up silicone cups in second tier of bento box. Put tea bag in middle cup and eggs and orange (halved and cut into slices) on either side. Sprinkle pepper flakes over eggs.

®

Tropical
Green Tea

CANDY BENTO

Starburst candy; gluten-free mini-pretzels; strawberry daifuku; cup of glutino brown rice pasta; 1 clove garlic; handful mushrooms; 1 onions; mustard greens; 5 string beans; 2 cooked shrimp; 6 sugar snap pea pods; apple slices; pickled mango slices; umeboshi 3 white baby carrots. 3-tier bento box.

In smallest tier, arrange pretzels and starburst candy, or other sweets of your choice.

Cook pasta according to instructions.

Finely chop garlic and fry in vegetable oil with chopped onion in small pan.

Steam beans, chop three string beans into two in sections and add to garlic and onion.

Steam sugar snaps for four mins. Add to onion, garlic and beans.

When pasta is cooked toss into onion, garlic and bean mix.

Fill the largest bento tier with the pasta.

Sizzle cooked shrimp in garlic oil and add to top of pasta.

In third tier of bento box, arrange remaining string beans (cut to fit), apple slices, mango slices, peeled and steamed baby white carrots.

Arrange to create stripes of color that mirror eachother.

Place umoboshi in center of section.

SPAM BENTO

2 slices Spam luncheon meat; 1 cup cooked Japanese rice; 2 strips nori; 3 tsp butter; 5 asparagus spears; half a small carrot; 1 egg; 1 tsp milk; pineapple slices, chunked or tinned pineapple chunks. 1-tier bento box.

Lightly fry Spam in oil. Wet your hands then lightly dust with salt; using your salted, wet hands, mold half the rice into a thick rectangle. Top with Spam; bind with a nori strip.

Melt butter in pan. Lightly sauté asparagus spears cut into thirds with chopped carrot; vegetables should be brighly colored but sill crisp. Garnish with cracked pepper.

Make scrambled eggs: beat together egg, milk, salt and pepper. Melt butter in a non-stick pan. Sauté egg mixture vigorously. Cook until egg sets.

Place egg in cupcake cup in one corner of bento. Border with pineapple chunks in triangular food cup.

Use a cookie cutter to cut carrots into star shapes and place with asparagus in a second cupcake cup.

BIRD'S NEST BENTO

Vietnamese bean cake (storebought); 6 yellow and red grape tomatoes; 9 yellow and orange baby carrots; 7 snow pea pods; 1 quail's egg; chai tea; soy sauce; anise; pinch cinnamon; shirataki (yam flour) noodles; bottled pad thai sauce; 1 sheet nori; 1 onion; 1 mushroom; handful bean sprouts; 1 broccoli floret. 2-tier bento box.

Place bean cake into one tier of bento. Arrange yellow and orange baby carrots in 'frame' shape in remaining space. Place yellow and red baby tomatoes in center. Cut mini stars from slices using cookie cutter. Take one snow pea pod and cut more stars. Sprinkle over bento.

Boil quail's egg in chai tea, soy sauce, anise, and cinnamon. Cook shirataki noodles, toss in pad thai sauce and cool. Arrange in nest shape and place egg in center. Decorate with nori leaves. Stir-fry onions, snow pea pods, mushrooms, and bean sprouts, place in remaining space. Top with par boiled broccoli 'tree'.

MISO STEW BENTO

1/2 cup Japanese rice; 1 tbsp nori flakes; 1 eggplant; 1/2 chili pepper; 1 tbsp miso; 1 scallion; 1 egg; 2 tbsp mirin; 1 cucumber; Japanese seaweed salad with sesame and chili pepper. 2-tier bento box.

Cook rice. Cut eggplant into small cubes. Heat a little oil in a pan and stir-fry eggplant and chili pepper for a few mins.

Cover with lid and stew for ten mins, until tender. Add miso, one tbsp mirin, and a few tbsp water.

Bake for a few more mins. Add chopped scallions, mix; remove from heat.

In a bowl, whisk egg with mirin and one tsp soy sauce to taste.

For baking, you will need a Japanese omelette pan or a rectangular skillet. Heat a little oil, put on low heat and add 1/3 egg mixture. Ensure egg is evenly distributed. Let thicken for a moment, then roll tightly to back. Add second third of egg and repeat: now start rolling at back with first part and roll back to front.

Repeat with last bit. Put rice into lower part of bento box; top with nori flakes.

Put miso stew next to rice, with plastic divider in between.

Cut egg roll into neat slices and add to second bento tier, together with seaweed salad.

Add cucumber slices to salad.

MISO STEW VARIATION

See ingredients list for Miso Stew Bento (left), add 1 chicken breast. 2-tier bento box.

Prepare ingredients as in Miso Stew Bento. Dice chicken breast, heat a little oil in a pan and stir-fry chicken until cooked through, then add eggplant and chili pepper and stir-fry for a few more mins. Continue with recipe and pack bento as left.

SAKURA DENBA BENTO

1/2 cup Japanese rice; 1 tbsp sakura denba; 1 egg; 3 cherry tomatoes; 2 carrots; 1 snack cucumber; 1 big strawberry; mochi candy with sweet bean filling. 2-tier bento box.

Cook rice. Mix with sakura denba. Put into larger bento tier. Boil egg. Peel and place in bento box. Add tomatoes. Fill smaller tier with bite-sized carrot, cucumber, strawberry and mochi.

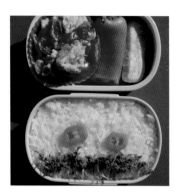

FLOWERS BENTO

1/2 cup Japanese rice; garden cress; 1 small orange bell pepper; 1 egg; 4 cherry tomatoes; 1 clove of garlic; 1 tsp soy sauce; mochi candy with sweet bean filling. 2-tier bento box.

Cook rice. Put rice in larger tier of bento box. Make a flat surface with a rice spoon. Make 'grass' by placing garden cress on lower part of rice. Cut two slices off tip of bell pepper and place 'grass' to make orange 'flowers'.

Break egg in a small bowl, add soy sauce and mix. Heat a little oil in a skillet. Add choped garlic and tomatoes, stir-fry for two mins, then add egg mix and make scrambled eggs by stirring slowly.

Put in a silicon muffin liner and place in bento. Place rest of bell pepper and mochi next to it.

If you like your rice with more flavor, add a small soy sauce container to your bento.

MUFFIN BENTO

1/2 cup Japanese rice; Japanese seaweed salad with sesame and chili pepper; nori, cut in maple leaves; daikon pickles; 1 red, 1 yellow bell pepper; seedless grapes; 2 cups oatmeal; 3/4 tsp salt; 1/4 cup sugar; 2 tsp baking powder; 4 oz white chocolate; 2 eggs; 4 tbsp butter; 3/4 cup soy milk; 3 oz raspberries. 2-tier bento box.

Make muffins first: Preheat oven.

Grease a mini muffin tray with a little butter.

Put oatmeal, salt, sugar, baking powder, chocolate in bowl and mix. Whisk eggs with milk and butter.

Pour into bowl; mix quickly (batter mustn't get homogenous, some lumps are ok).

Fill tray with batter.

Bake for 20 mins until the volume has nearly doubled and muffins are browned.

Cook rice according to recipe.

Put into the lower part of bento.

Make 'grass' with seaweed, place nori leaves above it.

Cut bell pepper into bite sized pieces and lay in bento, together with pickles.

Use a separate container for grapes and one muffin.

GYOZA BENTO

8 ready made gyoza; 1 cup frozen edamame; 3 tomatoes; 3 dates; 1 cucumber; soy sauce. 2-tier bento box.

Fill a pot with water and bring to a boil. Add edamame and cook for six mins. Drain, and add to bento. Sprinkle on a little salt. Leave a few beans apart.

Heat a little oil in a pan. Add gyozas and fry for one min. Add a glass of water and cover pan. Let steam on low heat until the water is absorbed (about five mins).

Uncover and fry for five more mins until bottoms are nicely brown. Arrange gyoza on top of edamame.

In other bento tier, arrange cucumber in sequence: one slice with skin side up, the next skin side down, etc. Arrange dates in row next to cucumber.

Fill open space with tomatoes and upright standing edamame. Include soy sauce container.

ANTIPASTI BENTO

1 tomato; serving red cabbage; garbanzo beans (canned); artichoke hearts; pepperoni; 1 carrot; black olives; 1 roasted red pepper; salami; mozzarella; romaine lettuce; Italian salad dressing. 1-tier bento box.

Line bed of bento with large romaine leaves. Chop all ingredients into 1/2" pieces, keeping each item in a separate pile. Move piles into bento to create loose bands of color. Drizzle with salad dressing garnish with pepperoni.

RED POTATO BENTO

4 oz. Chicken; 1 clove garlic; 1 lb baby potatoes; parsley; parmesan; key lime; tequila; olive oil; whole wheat bread. 1-tier bento box.

Heat grill to medium heat. Place minced garlic, olive oil and tequila into a bowl.

Coat chicken with mixture and place on grill. Grill eight mins per side, or until no pink remains in center. Remove from heat and let cool. Arrange potatoes in a shallow baking dish and lightly coat with olive oil.

Bake, uncovered on a high heat for 30 mins, or until potatoes are tender.

Remove from oven, grate fresh parmesan cheese over top and sprinkle with finely chopped parsley.

Begin with cooled parmesan parsley potatoes arranged neatly at one end of the bento. Take chicken and slice evenly.

Place in center, allowing room for a halved key lime.

Finish with a thick slice of wheat bread and a sprig of parsley.

SALMON BENTO

1 large handful fusilli; 1-2 tbsp pesto; freshly grated parmesan cheese; thinly sliced smoked salmon; romaine lettuce; cream cheese; scallions; fresh pineapple; several butter cookies; mini cheese. 2-tier bento box.

Cook pasta, drain and toss with pesto sauce. Take half a leaf of romaine lettuce, splitting it along center. Remove center. Spread some cream cheese on lettuce leaf. Add a layer of smoked salmon. Roll, then tie with a scallion stalk.

Fill one tier bento with pasta. Top with grated parmesan. Place three cream cheese, salmon and lettuce rolls on one side of second tier. Place butter cookies in muffin cup at opposite end.

Place bento cup of pineapple, covered with cling wrap, between rolls and cookies. Plug empty space on top of cup with a mini cheese.

SALMON VARIATION

See ingredients list for Salmon Bento (left), replace 1 large handful fusilli with 6 new potatoes; 2 tbsp mayonnaise. 2-tier bento box.

Boil potatoes; once cooked, drain and press with back of spoon to smash. Chop one slice smoked salmon into strips and one scallion. Mix with potatoes and mayonnaise. Pack in one tier; prepare rest of bento as left.

BUN BENTO

3 Chinese buns, filled with sweet pumpkin and lotus paste; garden cress; cucumber; 1 orange bell pepper; red and yellow cherry tomatoes; 1 tsp honey; 2 tbsp rice vinegar; 1 tbsp mirin; 1 tsp soy sauce. 2-tier bento, small square shape.

Steam buns for nine mins in a steam pan, or heat in microwave.

Cut into quarters and put in one tier of bento box.

Sprinkle with some garden cress.

Make dressing of honey, rice vinegar, mirin and soy sauce.

Chop tomatoes, cucumber and bell pepper. The variety of colors brightens up the bento and provides good contrast to the Chinese buns.

Mix the salad and place in second bento tier. Pour dressing over them or keep in small sauce container to pour over just before eating.

MEATBALL BENTO

1/2 cup Japanese rice; 1 tsp nori flakes; 4 oz minced meat; 4 tbsp coconut milk; 2 tbsp grated coconut; 1 egg; 1 tbsp soy sauce; 1 tbsp bread crumbs; 1 eggplant; 1/4 orange bell pepper; cherry tomatoes; juice of 1/2 lime; 3-5 leaves of basil; 1 1/2 tbsp ginger syrup; 1 1/2 tbsp sesame oil. 2-tier bento box.

Cook rice. Preheat oven to medium high. Cut eggplant into small cubes. Mix with a little olive oil; place on baking sheet. Bake in oven for 20 mins. Make dressing of lime juice, ginger syrup, sesame oil and basil. Add baked eggplant and mix. Add halved tomatoes and chopped bell pepper.

In a large bowl, mix minced meat with coconut milk, grated coconut, one egg, soy sauce and bread crumbs.

Knead and form small balls. Heat a little oil in a pot. Add meat balls, fry on medium heat until slightly browned on each side. Cover with lid; bake for eight mins on low heat until done and brown. Put rice into lower part of bento box. Make dots with nori flakes. Place meat balls next to rice, with a plastic divider in between. Put cooked vegetables in second tier of bento.

HARVEST BENTO

Kumquats; dried fruit (cranberries and dragon fruit are pictured); green seedless grapes; baby zucchini; baby squash; grape tomatoes; baby carrots; 1 /2 cup sushi rice (koshihikari); 1/2 cup forbidden rice (black rice); whole wheat pita bread; double cream brie; dried or fresh chopped parsley. 2-tier bento box.

Soak rice overnight (one cup rice, two cups water). Drain soaked rice.

In a small saucepan, combine rice, fresh water and bring to boil over high heat.

Stir well, reduce heat to low, cover and cook for 25 mins. Remove from heat and set aside, covered, for ten mins.

Black rice will turn a deep purple once cooked.

Create double rice onigiri with sushi rice on outside and forbidden rice on the inside.

Place in bento and use some black rice grains to decorate.

Add baby squash and carrot on one side of onigiri; place tomatoes, more carrot and baby zucchini on the other – arrange these in stripes and use the ends of baby zucchini for a highlighting pattern.

In second tier, slice brie and pita bread and place in middle as shown.

Place kumquats and dragon fruit on one side and grapes and dried fruit on the other.

VIETNAMESE BENTO

Red and green pepper strips; purple string beans; Vietnamese bean cake; 1 peach; petite Brussels sprouts; mini plums; salmon onigiri; soy sauce; ginger; 2 sheets nori; edamame beans. 3-tier bento box.

In top tier, alternate red and green pepper strips and steamed purple string beans.

Add Vietnamese bean cake to middle tier. Halve the peach, remove stone, and place on either side. Add sprouts to cupcake cup. Halve plums and add to right of bento.

For the bottom tier prepare two onigiri, filled with flaked salmon, soy sauce and thinly-cut ginger. Decorate with nori as shown.

Accent the onigiri with red pepper strips on each side, and fill any remaining gaps with edamame.

STAR BENTO

White nectarine; mango pieces; spinach; onigiri; chopped red cabbage; ginger; soy sauce; smoked salmon; shredded umeboshi; mashed sweet potato; petite brussels sprouts; red and yellow pepper strips; cucumber; purple pole beans. 3-tier bento box.

Use a cookie cutter to cut star shape in nectarine slice and mango. Swap pieces out as shown to fill star shape with mango. Place in top tier, with small pieces mango in between.

In second tier line bed of bento with steamed spinach. Layer over with cooked red cabbage.

Create star onigiri with sweet mashed potato with flaked salmon, soy and ginger at center.

In third tier place steamed sprouts, red and yellow peppers cut into strips and star shapes.

Add a chunk of cucumber, shredded umeboshi and purple pole beans.

Blackberries; mini plums; strawberries; cucumber; natural fruit bars; 1/2 cup jasmine rice; yellow, orange, and red bell peppers; black sesame seeds; scrambled egg; green pepper; 1 sheet nori. 3-tier bento, plus side-dish.

Place blackberries, plums, sliced strawberries and sliced cucumber in top tier. In second tier, use cookie cutter to create star shapes from fruit bars as shown. In bottom tier, cover base with steamed jasmine rice, and create a shooting star from red, yellow and orange bell pepper.

Layer side tier with more rice. Sprinkle with sesame seeds to create night sky.

Scramble an egg, chop finely and arrange in moon and galaxy shape using cookie cutters. Make stars from orange bell pepper. Cut a green pepper into alien shape and add nori for eyes and detail.

1 pod of edamame; 1 carrot; red cabbage; scallions; 4 oz. cooked chicken; 1 cup cooked sushi rice (koshihikari); teriyaki sauce; sesame seeds. 1-tier bento.

Place rice at one side. Add cooked chicken in teriyaki sauce. Garnish with sliced carrot and a few scallions, sesame seeds, red cabbage. Fill space with boiled and salted edamame.

In bottom tier, place bean sprouts, par-boiled broccoli florets, tomatoes.

Chop red and black plums and place as shown.

Add rice pudding in remaining space.

FRIED RICE BENTO

1 can pink salmon; 1 onion; 3 eggs; day-old fried rice; garlic; flaked dried fish; soy sauce; sweet chili sauce; frozen cooked corn; 1 carrot; frozen shrimp dumplings. 2-tier bento box.

Drain liquid from salmon tin. Mix salmon, onion and two eggs in bowl.

Mold into two inch patties. Pan fry until golden brown. Turn over; fry until both sides are done. Serve with sweet chili sauce.

Sauté together day-old fried rice, garlic, flaked dried fish and an egg. Season with soy sauce. Defrost corn, steam chopped carrots.

Steam frozen dumplings until cooked.

Fill lower tier with fried rice and garnish with carrots: use a cookie-cutter to make star shapes.

In second tier place the shrimp dumpling; use a 'grass' divider to separate this from the salmon patties.

Fill a muffin cup with corn and cooked carrots.

STRIPED BENTO

Purple, orange, yellow, and green peppers; tomatoes; grilled shrimp; mango; leftover tofu chunks; thick rice noodles; honey; balsamic vinegar sauce; bean sprouts; broccoli florets; cherry tomatoes; red and black plums; coconut rice pudding. 3-tier bento box.

In top tier of bento box create a rainbow of alternate strips of finely-chopped pepper of different colors and tomatoes. Cook rice noodles according to instructions (or use leftovers).

Place at bottom of middle bento tier.

Make a sauce of balsamic vinegar, honey and cumin.

Brush the shrimp with this and grill until well cooked.

Place shrimp on noodles and flank with tofu and mango.

MIXED BENTO

3/4 cup rice; 3 oz lean ground chicken; 2 tsp corn starch; 2 tsp flour; 1 tsp beaten egg; 1/8 cup minced green onions; 2 eggs; avocado; broccoli; 4 snow peas; 1 asparagus spear; green and yellow zucchini; 1 carrot; 1 red pepper; 1 green pepper; 3 pieces fresh pineapple; 2 strawberries; 4 blueberries; 1 chocolate truffle; nori; soy sauce; 2 tbsp sushi vinegar; black sesame seeds; 1 tbsp canola oil. 1-tier bento box.

MEAT LOAF BENTO

Leftover meat loaf; 1/2 cup rice; broccoli; 1 carrot; takuan; pickled eggplant; cucumber kim chee; toasted sesame seeds; ketchup. 1-tier bento box.

Break apart meat loaf into small pieces and mix together with rice and finely chopped steamed broccoli.

Place in bento box and top with ketchup.

Using a vegetable cutter, cut three carrot flowers and add to top of ketchup.

Cut takuan into bite-size strips. Top with sesame seeds.

Add pickled eggplant alongside takuan.

Add cucumber kim chee, cutting into small pieces if needed.

Scatter bento with toasted sesame seeds for garnish.

QUAILS' EGGS BENTO

Yakitori chicken breasts; green onions; 2/3 cup soy sauce; 1/2 cup sugar; 5 tsp sake; 1 tbsp flour; 6 quails' eggs; eggplant; 1/2 cup rice. 2-tier bento box.

Cook rice. Soak some wooden skewers in water. Cut chicken into bite-sized chunks. Mix soy, sugar, sake and flour. Heat over a low flame, allow yakitori sauce to thicken. Skewer chicken and green onions alternately; four chunks per skewer. Baste chicken with sauce, then grill over medium heat until cooked but not dry. Baste chicken with the sauce while grilling for extra flavor.

Hard boil quails' eggs. Peel, then roll in yakitori sauce. Grill, basting with yakitori sauce on both sides. Fill half of one tier of bento with rice. Fill the rest with quails' eggs.

Garnish rice with carrot flower and parsley. Remove chicken from skewers, then fill half of second tier with yakitori. Add a 'grass' divider, then fill the remainder with eggplant.

Cook rice, add vinegar when cool. In a bowl, combine chicken, corn starch, flour, beaten egg and green onions. Divide into six and shape into patties. Wrap a nori strip around and fry in canola oil until cooked through. Steam asparagus, zucchini and broccoli together for three mins. Add snow peas and steam for one min. Fry omelette with asparagus. When cool, cut the ends off the roll and slice the rest of the omelette into four pieces. Make sushi with chicken and avocado. Arrange other ingredients, including steamed broccoli florets, as shown.

CUTE EGG BENTO

Red pear; green plum; shelled edamame; orange pepper; hard boiled egg; sweet potato, leftover rice pasta shells tossed in marinara sauce. 2-tier bento box.

Slice pear and plum and arrange in top half of first bento tier.

Place edamame beans in rest of space. With a cookie cutter, make flower shapes from pepper. Arrange flowers and scraps decoratively.

Boil sweet potato and mash with a little butter and salt. Cook egg using pig-shaped egg mold.

Fill one side of second bento tier with mashed sweet potato, placing pig-shaped egg in the center and smoothing sweet potato around it.

Add decorative 'grass' along free edge of sweet potato.

In second half of tier, place pasta shells.

STEAM CHICKEN BENTO

Strawberry daifuku; 1 white nectarine; serving white rice; leftover steamed chicken; leftover broccoli in white sauce; green and purple string beans; cucumber slices; plum; red and yellow grape tomatoes; gluten-free mini-pretzels. 3-tier bento box.

Slice nectarine and place with daifuku in top bento tier (not shown).

Cook rice. Once cooled, place in 1/3 of main bento tier. In remaining space place leftover chicken (diced) and broccoli in white sauce.

If you don't have the latter, steam broccoli florets for five mins and add to chicken.

Steam beans for five mins. Cut into two in pieces.

Cut five cucumber slices. Place in third bento tier as shown.

Add grape tomatoes, plum and pretzels in paper cupcake cup.

LIBERTY BENTO

Star fruit; sugar snaps; leftover rice pasta; marinara sauce; mushrooms; onions; 1 chicken sausage; 2 plums; 1 yellow plum tomato; green and red bell peppers; 1 cream cheese triangle, tiny potato starch cookies. 3-tier bento box.

Thinly slice yellow tomato.

Halve and stone plums and place in second bento tier as shown.

Slice green and red bell peppers and place by plums.

Add 'grass' divider and fill bottom of remaining space with shop-bought potato starch cookies.

Add cheese on top.

Take cooked pasta and sauté in marinara sauce, sliced onion and sliced mushroom.

Fill bottom of main bento tier with mix, half-way up.

Cook chicken sausage and halve lengthways.

Cut out two tower shapes as shown and place on pasta.

Create a liberty bell from mushroom and small piece of sausage.

In third tier add star fruit, sugar snap pods.

Cookie-cut snap pea stars and place in centre of star fruit pieces.

221

COBB BENTO

Strawberry daifuku; mango; plum; romaine lettuce; leftover chicken; tomato; olives; cheddar cheese; blue cheese; black olives; 3 tomatoes; 2 baby carrots, white and orange; umeboshi; broccoli florets; snow pea pods. 3-tier bento box.

In top tier place strawberry daifuku; make sun rays from thin mango triangles.

Use a cookie-cutter to make stars from plum. Alternate skin-side up and skin-side down.

Make a cobb salad from leftover chicken (shredded), romaine lettuce, chopped tomatoes, sliced olives, and short strips of cheddar and blue cheese.

Add your dressing of choice.

Fill the middle tier with salad.

In bottom tier add diced tomatoes in a cupcake cup.

Cut a flower-shape from mango using cookie-cutter.

Cut coins from boiled carrots and add as shown.

Create a barrier from steamed pea pod shells and fill space with steamed broccoli.

Cut a flower from halved tomato.

Add cookie-cut mango flower on top.

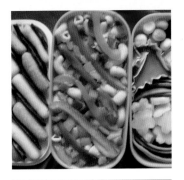

COLORS BENTO

Purple pole beans; white and orange baby carrots; rice pasta; peppers; onions; garlic clove; cucumber; tomato; dolphin-free tinned tuna fish; red, yellow, and green bell peppers; sugar snap peas; mango; Asian pear flowers; laughing cow cheese; peanut butter; potato-starch cookies; natural fruit bar. 3-tier bento box.

In top tier, alternate steamed peas, and white and orange baby carrots to create pattern as shown. Cook pasta. In pan toss crushed garlic, sliced onion and diced tomatoes in a little olive oil. Add to pasta, together with a healthy serving of tuna. Mix and add to bottom of second tier, about 2/3 of the way up. Cut strips of bell peppers and decorate as shown, alternating colors. Cut flower-shapes using a cookie-cutter from mango ad pear slices. Place as shown, encased in sugar snap pods. Place in bottom bento tier. Fill cupcake cup with peanut butter and place against sugar snaps. Fill gaps with starch cookies and slice of fruit bar cut into flower-shapes.

TRADITIONAL BENTO

4 eggs; 2 tbsp sugar; 2 tsp soy sauce Handful spinach leaves,; frozen vegetarian gyozas; 1/2 cup cooked rice; umeboshi; 1 radish; sesame seeds; tomberries; 2 lettuce leaves. 2-tier bento box.

To make the omelette, beat eggs, add sugar and soy sauce and beat again. Gently heat some oil in a large non stick pan, pour in one third of the mixture. Cover egg completely with a layer of spinach leaves. When base of egg is cooked, roll up using a spatula and push roll to edge of pan. Pour in another third of the egg, lifting up roll to allow it to flow underneath. Repeat process, rolling egg up each time, until you run out of egg. Take a bamboo mat (the kind you use to make sushi rolls) and line with cling film. Place egg roll inside while still warm and roll up tightly. You can place a heavy object on top to give the roll its distinctive shape.

Leave to cool – this will ensure the egg continues to cook with the residual heat. When it's cool, unwrap and cut into slices. If you use a round frying pan, you may want to trim the edges.

Prepare vegetarian gyozas. Thinly slice radish and top with black sesame seeds, place in a side dish container. Pour dipping sauce into your soy sauce bottle. Fill bottom bento with rice and place umeboshi in the middle. Line top bento with lettuce and place rolled omelette slices together at one end. In the other half, place gyozas slightly on a diagonal, then place sliced radishes and dipping sauce bottle in the middle. Fill any empty spaces with tomberries.

HEART SUSHI BENTO

1 sheet white mamenori (soy paper); 1 1/4 cups prepared sushi rice; 1/4 avocado; 1/4 boiled sweet potato; nonstick cooking spray; 1/4 sheet green mamenori; 1/4 sheet orange mamenori; very small dab of light corn syrup in a lidded condiment cup; 1 prepared omelette (plain). 1-tier bento box.

For sushi filling, cut sweet potato and avocado into long strips, brush avocado with lemon juice. Take a heart-shaped sushi mold; drape white mamenori inside the mold, pack in hot sushi rice half way. Add filling the length of the mold, packing in more rice, crisscrossing the mamenori over on top, and pressing the top part of the mold down firmly to create the shape. Cut into slices and let cool.

Spray hands with nonstick cooking spray and mold remaining rice into oblong nigiri pieces for the base of the egg-sushi. Let cool. Cut omelette into rectangles to fit onto nigiri. Use strips cut from the green mamenori to form bands (if they don't stick on their own, use a tiny dab of corn syrup). Decorate the top of each with a blossom punched from the orange mamenori. Arrange in bento box and keep chilled.

227

CHICKEN WING BENTO

1 chicken wing; 1/2 tbsp soy sauce; 1/2 tbsp sake; aonori; shichimi togarashi (Japanese chili pepper); 1 red lettuce leaf; 1/2 cup cooked rice; 1 slice ham; 1 slice cheese; 1 tomato; 1 blanched broccoli floret; 1 blanched cauliflower floret; Japanese potato salad; 1/2 green pepper. 1-tier bento box.

Joint chicken wing by popping apart the bone, then cutting through the skin and flesh in the middle joint.

This creates two pieces. Remove wing tip.

Pierce in several places; marinate in soy sauce and sake for an hour.

Bake in a medium hot oven for 20 mins, or until juices run clear.

Sprinkle one chicken wing with the aonori, and the other with the chili pepper.

Fill base of bento with cooked rice, top with cuts from ham and cheese.

Line half of bento with red lettuce, lay two chicken wings on the top.

Fill a bento cup with blanched cauliflower and broccoli.

Add a cherry tomato and thinly sliced green pepper, fried in oil for a few minutes.

Slot in a bento cup full of Japanese potato salad.

MAKI SUSHI BENTO

Sushi ingredients: 3 1/2 oz sushi rice; 1/2 cup water (plus extra to soak and wash); 1 tbsp rice wine vinegar; 2 tsp sugar; 1/2 teaspoon salt; 3 nori sheets; wasabi; soy sauce. Sushi mat. For filling: 1/3 avocado, cut into long thin slices; 1/2 red pepper, cut into long thin slices. 2 lettuce leaves; cucumber; 3 strawberries; 6 grapes. 2-tier bento box.

Wash the rice thoroughly turning it over with your fingers until water runs clear. Cover (just cover– don't use lots of water) with cold water and leave to soak for one hour. Use a timer to help. Prepare sushi vinegar by mixing the rice vinegar, sugar and salt in a small jar or glass. Set aside for later use, stirring occasionally to ensure everything has dissolved.

After rice has soaked for one hour, rinse once more then add to small pan with airtight lid; add 1/4 pt cold water. Bring to the boil gently. As soon as rice has boiled turn on to a very low heat and simmer very gently for 15 minutes. Do not open lid. After 15 minutes is up, remove rice from heat and leave to sit with lid on for a further 15 minutes. Prepare the sushi fillings at this time and get your sushi mat ready for rolling. Don't be tempted to do anything to the rice until the time is up.

Now you can start to work with the rice. Remove lid and work quickly to spread the rice on a large flat plate or tray. Use a rice paddle or wooden spatula. You now need to cool the rice as quickly as possible. Add the sushi vinegar mix little by little and gently turn the rice with the paddle until it is covered in the mix but not wet. You may not need to use all the mix.

Now place a Nori sheet on your sushi mat about 1/4 inch from the edge nearest you. Place shiny side down and the small lines lying vertically (these are markers to cut the sushi roll later).

Using the cool rice and wet fingers, gently spread a very thin but even layer of rice over the sheet, taking it to the nearest bottom edge and the right and left edges, but leaving a 1/4 inch gap across the top. Keep your hands wet and clean using cold water with a splash of rice vinegar.

Your sheet is now covered with rice. About 1/2 inch in from the edge nearest you, add wasabi to taste. Use your finger to add a little from left to right.

Add a row of avocado on top of the wasabi and then a row of red pepper next to it (or whatever filling you want to use).

Using the sushi mat to help, gently roll the first edge of nori over, and then continue to roll tightly away from you making sure sushi mat remains on the outside. Leave rolled sushi to rest on a chopping board for a few minutes before cutting. Wash and clean the knife after every couple of cuts.

Line one tier of bento with lettuce leaves and then pack in sushi and soy sauce in small container with lid. In top tier, pack sliced cucumber, sliced strawberries, halved grapes and pudding or omelette.

AVOCADO BENTO

Sushi ingredients from Maki Sushi Bento (left). For filling: 1/3 avocado, cut into long slices 1 cm wide; sesame seeds. 2-tier bento box.

Prepare sushi as in Maki Sushi Bento recipe, using avocado as filling. Pack in one tier of bento box and sprinkle with sesame seeds.

Fill second tier with cherries, sliced plums, sliced cucumber and soy sauce.

INSIDE OUT BENTO

Sushi ingredients from Maki Sushi Bento (left). For filling: 1/2 avocado; 1/2 carrot; 1/2 red pepper sliced; black sesame seeds; wasabi; soy sauce; wasabi nuts; mini biscuits; grapes; strawberries. 2-tier bento box.

Prepare sushi as in Maki Sushi Bento recipe. If you have become practiced at rolling maki sushi rolls, you are ready to try the inside out or California roll.

This time cover the whole of the nori sheet with cooked sushi rice.

If rice sticks to your fingers, wash your hands and work with the rice with slightly wet hands (but don't touch the nori with wet hands).

When the nori is covered, pick up the whole piece and flip it over on the sushi mat so the rice is underneath and the nori is on top.

Add a little wasabi and then add your fillings on top of the nori, as usual.

Roll in the same way as you would for maki sushi and you will end up with the filling and nori inside and the rice on the outside.

Roll the sushi roll in sprinkled sesame seeds on a board. Allow to sit for a few minutes, then cut.

Pack sushi in one tier of bento box with wasabi in cupcake cup.

In top tier pack wasabi nuts, mini biscuits, sliced grapes and whole strawberries.

Add container with lid containing soy sauce for dipping.

CARROT SUSHI BENTO

Sushi ingredients from Maki Sushi Bento (left). For filling: 1/2 avocado; 1/2 carrot; wasabi nuts; Japanese rice crackers; soy sauce. 2-tier bento box.

Prepare sushi as in Maki Sushi Bento recipe. Chop avocado and carrot into long thin slices for filling. Once prepared and sliced, pack in one tier of box, pack wasabi nuts, rice crackers and soy sauce in other tier.

TERIYAKI CHICKEN BENTO

1 chicken thigh; 1 tbsp oil; 2 tsp sugar; 2 tsp dark soy sauce; 2 tsp mirin; 2 tsp sake; 1/2 cup rice; 1 broccoli floret; 1 cauliflower floret; 1 lettuce leaf; 1 carrot; 1/2 onion; 1 slice cheese. 1/2 cup corn; 4 baby tomatoes. 1-tier bento box.

Cook rice. Dice onion and half of carrot and stir-fry.

Mix with rice and corn, allow to cool and pack in 1/2 of bento.

Cut star shapes from remaining carrot and cheese slice for decoration.

Place on rice, alongside skewered baby tomatoes.

Sauté the chicken thigh on both sides in a frying pan.

When browned, add sugar, dark soy sauce, mirin and sake and simmer until cooked and glazed.

In the other half of the bento, pack some blanched broccoli at the top.

Lay teriyaki chicken at the bottom, on top of some lettuce.

In the remaining space, pack some blanched cauliflower and baby tomatoes.

Add a food pick for decoration.

SEAWEED SALAD BENTO

1/2 cup rice; 1 tsp furikake; 1 handful rocket leaves; 1/2 red bell pepper; 1/4 aweed; Japanese sesame dressing. 2 bento boxes.

Cook rice. Soak the wakame in cold water for approximately 20 minutes. Mix half of rice with furikake. Make plain and furikake onigiri shapes using rice onigiri mold (or shape by hand). Put in a container.

Mix the wakame and with chopped bell pepper, sliced cucumber and rocket leaves. Store the sesame dressing in a separate container.

You can save time by making a whole bunch of onigiris at once and store them in the freezer. To defrost, microwave on high for a minute or so.

FIG BENTO

1/2 cup rice; 2 tbsp soy sauce; Japanese seaweed salad with sesame and chili pepper; 1/2 tablespoon seaweed furikake; 1 fresh fig; 2 cherry tomatoes; seedless grapes; portion cucumber. 2-tier bento box.

Cook rice. Take one half and mix with furikake. Make separate onigiri shapes from plain and furikake-mixed rice by placing the rice in a triangle mold or shaping by hand. Fill plain rice onigiris with seaweed for extra taste.

Grill the plain onigiris in an oven until slightly browned, then turn and put back under grill.

As soon as both sides are brown, dab soy sauce on top with a brush and return to grill for 2 more minutes. Turn again and repeat.

Fill bento with plain and furikake onigiris. Use the space that is left empty for seaweed salad, with a plastic divider in between.

Fill other part of bento with halved figs, grapes, tomatoes, and bite-sized cucumber.

YAKI ONIGIRI BENTO

1/2 cup Japanese rice; 2 tbsp soy sauce; 1 egg; portion cucumber; red grapes; Japanese daikon pickles. 2-tier bento box.

Cook rice. Make onigiri shapes using triangle onigiri mold or shape by hand.

Grill the onigiris in an oven until slightly browned; turn and put back under grill. As soon as both sides are brown, put a little soy sauce on top with a brush and put back for 2 more minutes. Turn again and repeat.

Boil egg. Peel and place in bento box. Season to taste.

Add grapes, chopped cucumber, yaki onigiris, pickles and cherry tomatoes.

Yaki onigiris are also suitable for freezing.

YAKI ONIGIRI VARIATION

1/2 cup Japanese rice; 1 /2 tuna steak; 1 tbsp mayonnaise; 2 tbsp soy sauce; 1 egg; portion cucumber; red grapes; Japanese daikon pickles. 2-tier bento box.

Slice tuna steak into cubes, pan fry until cooked. Mix with mayonnaise. Cook rice and make onigiri, fill with tuna mix. Prepare bento as in Yaki Onigiri Bento recipe (left).

SALTED SALMON BENTO

1 portion salmon; 2 tsp salt; 1/2 cup rice; 1/2 Japanese cucumber; 3 baby tomatoes; tea marbled boiled egg; 1 peppadew pepper; 1 tbsp cream cheese; 1 sprig parsley; 2 lettuce leaves; 2 blanched asparagus spears; pre-prepared pasta salad. 1-tier bento box with lid space for onigiri.

Cook rice and shape onigiri and place them inside the lid of the box.

Sprinkle 1 tsp salt on salmon; leave to stand for 30 mins.

Grill until golden brown on all sides.

Cut cucumber in half lengthways and scoop out seeds with a spoon.

Thinly slice and sprinkle with 1 tsp salt.

Squeeze, and leave to rest for three minutes. Squeeze again to remove bitter liquid.

Line box base with green sushi grass and lettuce.

Fill one bento cup with salted cucumber topped with tomatoes and the other with pasta salad.

Place tea-marbled egg in center. Add salmon, and asparagus spears.

In the last remaining space, place the Peppadew pepper, stuffed with cream cheese.

Fill any gaps with parsley.

SCATTERED SUSHI BENTO

Teriyaki chicken; edamame beans; 1 hard-boiled egg; 1 cupcake. For summer sushi: 1 cup rice; small piece konbu; splash of sake; 3 tbsp liquid sushi seasoning; packet mange tout; packet cherry tomatoes; 1 tbsp white sesame seeds, toasted. 2-tier bento box.

This style of sushi, with ingredients laid over the top of the rice, is called scattered sushi.

Place raw rice in your rice cooker, and add the konbu and sake, along with the required amount of water.

When rice is done, allow it to steam for 10 minutes, then remove and place in a dampened, flat container.

Sprinkle with sushi vinegar, then fold and fan the rice (using a wet spatula) until no more steam rises from it.

Cover with a damp towel and leave to sit until cool. Blanch the mange tout and slice thinly on the diagonal. Deseed the cherry tomatoes and chop into wedges.

Fill the bottom layer of your bento with sushi rice. Spread a mixture of the mange tout and tomatoes over the top of the rice, then sprinkle on the sesame seeds.

In the bottom layer, place the teriyaki chicken at one end and the boiled and salted edamame beans next to it.

Fill the remaining space with the hard-boiled eggs.

STUFFED CHILI BENTO

1/2 cup rice; 2 baby pickled beetroot; 1 hard-boiled egg; 2 lettuce leaves; 6 cherry tomatoes. For stuffed chilis: 1 clove garlic; 1/2 shallot; small piece ginger; small handful basil, mint and cilantro leaves; 10 oz pork mince; 2 tbsp fish sauce; 1 tbsp soy sauce; 1 tsp sesame seed oil; juice 1 lime; 4 shredded lime leaves; 5 medium-sized mild chilies; 1 red chili, sliced. 2-tier bento box.

Make stuffed chilis. Place garlic, peeled shallot, ginger and herbs in a food processor; mince finely. Add pork mince and process until smooth. Add liquids and lime and mix again. Cut chilies in half and deseed, stuff with pork mince. Leftovers can be formed into burgers. Bake on baking tray in a medium high preheated oven for 20 minutes. Add pickled beetroot to rice cooker when cooking rice. When finished, allow to steam for a few minutes, then remove beetroot and mix well. Shape the onigiri with a flower shaped mold, and top with finely chopped chives. Cut egg into zig zag pattern, then pull apart. Line boxes with lettuce before packing.

MAYO PRAWNS BENTO

3 raw prawns; 4 tbsp soy sauce; 1 tbsp Japanese mayonnaise; oil for frying; 1/2 red pepper; 1/2 green pepper; sesame seeds; 1 carrot; 2 tbsp mirin; 1 tsp miso; tea marbled boiled egg; 2 lettuce leaves; 1 eggplant; 1 tbsp vegetable oil; 1 tbsp sesame seed oil; 1 tbsp sugar; 1 1/2 tbsp rice vinegar; 1/2 cup cooked rice. 2-tier bento box.

Mix mayonnaise and prawns with 1 tbsp soy sauce; marinate in fridge for two hours.

Fry in hot oil for a minute or so each side.

Cut eggplant into small pieces; fry in oil until slightly browned.

Add sugar, rice vinegar, vegetable and sesame seed oil, 1 tbsp mirin and 2 tbsp soy sauce, and simmer for a few seconds, until sugar is dissolved.

Cool, chill until needed.

Sauté thin strips of red and green pepper in oil and sprinkle with sesame seeds.

Peel carrot, fry for a few minutes.

Add 1 tbsp mirin, miso and 1 tbsp soy sauce to pan.

Pack bottom tier with cooked rice.

Line top tier with lettuce.

Pack ingredients and tea marbled egg as illustrated.

RICE BALL BENTO

1/2 cup short grain rice; toasted white sesame seeds; leftover meat; pinch salt; red grapes. 1-tier bento box.

Cook rice and allow to cool. Mix with sesame seeds. Reheat meat in microwave. Mold rice into triangular shape with leftover fillings in the middle. Sprinkle a dash of salt over each rice ball. Pack alongside grapes.

RICE BALL VARIATION

1/2 cup short grain rice; toasted white sesame seeds; 1/2 eggplant; 1/2 zucchini; pinch salt; red grapes. 1-tier bento box.

Cook rice and allow to cool. Mix with sesame seeds. Dice eggplant and zucchini, pan fry until soft. Use as filling for rice balls, filling half of mold with rice, then packing vegetables into center and closing with more rice. Add salt. Pack alongside grapes.

GOLDEN RICE BENTO

1/2 cup short grain rice; cooking oil; soy sauce; 1 sheet nori; 1 frozen gyoza; red grapes; 1 cherry tomato. 1-tier bento box.

Cook rice. Mold cooked rice into two triangular shapes. Heat cooking oil in a frying pan over medium heat.

Sear all sides of the rice balls until the outside is crispy. Brush rice balls with soy sauce and cook until all sides are golden brown.

Cut nori into two long strips. Wrap bottom of rice balls with nori strips.

Heat cooking oil in a frying pan over medium high heat. Add frozen gyoza to pan and cook until the bottom is golden brown. Add water to pan, cover, and cook until water is absorbed. -Arrange rice balls, gyoza, red grapes, and cherry tomato in bento box.

Heat oil in a frying pan over medium high heat.

Add chopped onion to pan and cook for 30 seconds. Add chicken pieces to pan. Add vinegar mixture to pan. Remove from heat when sauce has thickened.

Cook frozen vegetables in a pot of boiling water.

Fill remaining space in bento box with chicken, vegetables and grapes.

SEAWEED STRIP BENTO

1/2 cup short grain rice; sakura denbu; toasted white sesame seeds; wakame furkikake; 1 sheet nori; 1 chicken thigh; 1/4 small onion; 1 tbsp rice vinegar; 1 tsp sugar; 1 tsp soy sauce; cayenne pepper; corn starch; cooking oil; frozen vegetables; red grapes. 1-tier bento box

Cook rice. Divide into 2 equal portions. Mix one half with sakura denbu and sesame seeds.

Mix other half with wakame furikake. Form rice into small oval-shaped balls.

Cut nori into thin strips. Wrap each rice ball with a strip.

Arrange rice balls in alternating colors in bento box.

Cut chicken thigh into bite-size pieces. Coat each piece of chicken lightly with cornstarch.

Mix rice vinegar, sugar, soy sauce, and cayenne pepper in a small bowl.

PATTERN BENTO

1 cup rice; shiso furikake; 1 sheet nori; 2 eggs; scallions, dashi stock; pinch sugar; 3 weiners; cooking oil; shichimi powder; portion pickled cucumbers; sesame seeds; 1 apple; lemon juice. 1-tier bento box.

Cook rice. Mix with shiso furikake.Mold into triangular shapes.

Wrap the bottom of the rice balls with strips of roasted seaweed. Arrange rice balls in an alternate fashion. Beat eggs with chopped scallions, dashi stock, and sugar.

Heat oil in a non-stick frying pan, or a rectangular tamagoyaki pan, over medium heat.

Spread a thin layer of egg in pan and roll it up carefully. Continue to build up egg roll by rolling it in additional layers of egg.

Slice egg rolls into thin pieces.

Make checker cuts at the end of wieners. Heat oil in a frying pan over medium high heat.

Stir-fry wieners and season with shichimi powder.

Fill a small plastic divider with pickled cucumbers.

Slice apple and coat with lemon juice to prevent browning.

Fill remaining spaces in bento box with egg slices, wieners, pickled cucumber, and apple slices.

INARI SUSHI BENTO

2 cups hot, cooked rice; 3 tbsp liquid sushi seasoning; 1 tbsp black sesame seeds; 6 inari skins; 3 slices eggplant; 3 slices cucumber; 1 chicken breast; 1 tbsp soy sauce; 1 tbsp balsamic vinegar; sprig parsley. 1-tier bento box.

Pour sushi seasoning over rice; turn and fan until cool and no longer steaming.

When cold, stir in black sesame seeds.

Take inari skins and slit open along the longer side.

Carefully pull the edges apart to make a pocket. Fill with rice.

Line the bento with lettuce.

Place the two pieces of inari sushi at one end, rice side up.

Place a divider next to them.

Put a food cup with the eggplant and cucumber in it on the other side.

Alternate the pan-fried eggplant and cucumber, skin side up, for a nice contrast in colors.

Marinade chicken in soy sauce and vinegar then grill.

Slice chicken and pack next to tomato wedge.

Fill remaining spaces with parsley.

TSUKUNE BENTO

1/2 cup rice; 1/2 carrot; 6 stalks green beans; 1 tbsp konnyaku; 1/2 cup dashi stock; 1 tbsp soy sauce; 1 sprig parsley. For tsukune: 8 1/2 oz ground chicken meat; 1 egg; 1 onion; 1 1/2 tsp sugar; 1 1/2 tsp soy sauce; 1 tbsp oil. For teriyaki glaze: 2 tbsp soy sauce; 2 tbsp sake; 2 tbsp mirin; 2 tbsp sugar. 1-tier bento box.

Cook rice. Slice carrot, green beans and konnyaku. Boil together with dashi stock and soy sauce. Simmer together until done but not overcooked.

Make tskune. Mix together chicken, chopped onion, egg, sugar, and soy sauce. Spread the oil evenly on a flat frying pan, preferably non-stick. Drop balls of batter on the frying pan, not letting them stick to each other. Let fry gently for three minutes, then flip over and fry the other side for another three minutes.

While the chicken is frying, mix together ingredients for the teriyaki glaze. When both sides of the chicken are well done, pour the glaze over and let the chicken continue cooking over low heat, flipping over until both sides have been glazed sufficiently and the remaining sauce has thickened.

Cut flower shapes from carrot slices, using a stainless steel cutter.

In a segregated box, or using dividers to create sections, fill separate compartments with vegetables, tsukune and rice.

Garnish with carrot slices and parsley.

HALF MOON BENTO

1/2 cup rice; black sesame seeds; 1 chicken breast; 1 scallion; teriyaki sauce; store-bought potato salad; 3 strawberries; handful blueberries; 1 satsuma. 2-tier bento box, half-moon shaped.

Arrange rice in half of one of the tiers, sprinkle with black sesame seeds. Place a grass divider beside the rice. Fry chicken and scallion with teriyaki sauce, place in other half of the box. Fill half of upper tier with potato salad and the other with fresh fruit.

HALF MOON VARIATION

1/2 cup rice; black sesame seeds; 3 broccoli florets; 1/2 red pepper; 1/2 yellow pepper; 1/2 red onion; 6 sugar snap peas; teriyaki sauce; store-bought potato salad; 3 strawberries; handful blueberries; 1 satsuma. 2-tier bento box, half-moon shaped.

Create bento as in Half Moon Bento recipe (left), but replace chicken teriyaki stir-fry with fresh vegetable main. Heat oil in wok, dice onion, chop broccoli, peppers and peas and add to wok. Stir-fry with teriyaki sauce.

TONKATSU PORK BENTO

Tonkatsu pork cutlet; 1/2 cup rice; tonkatsu sauce; leftover portion honey ginger pork with green beans; shredded cabbage; 1 slice apple; 3 gyoza. 2-tier bento box.

Steam rice. Place in lower tier of bento box, filling a third of the base.

Arrange a grilled tonkatsu pork cutlet on the rice.

Pour a little tonkatsu sauce over this.

In the remaining space in this tier, place a small foil cup and fill it with leftover honey ginger pork.

Divide the top tier of the box in half.

In the left half place a layer of shredded cabbage topped with an apple slice cut to represent a rabbit.

Cook 3 gyoza and place in the right half of box.

HOT CUCUMBER BENTO

1/2 cucumber; 1/4 tsp salt; 1 tsp mirin; 2 tbsp soy sauce; 1 tsp English mustard; 2 frozen gyozas; 1 egg; 1/2 cup rice;. 1-tier bento box.

Halve cucumber and scoop out the seeds.

Cut into half moon chunks, salt and leave to stand for 20 minutes in a covered bowl.

Take a plastic bag and add salt, mirin, soy sauce and mustard, mixing well so that mustard is dissolved.

Add cucumber and mix well.

Refrigerate until needed – leaving for at least 10 minutes.

Drain well before adding to bento.

Cook rice and use mold to make two bear shaped onigiri; sprinkle with furikake.

Hard boil egg in star-shaped mold, cut in half.

Line bento with the sushi grass, and place the onigiri to one side.

Put some sushi grass next to them, and rest gyozas in the middle.

Place a bento cup of cucumber

in other side of the bento, fill the remaining space with egg and dipping sauce.

Pack with soy sauce bottle.

TRIANGLE BENTO

1 cup rice; 4 two-potato gyoza; 3 steamed broccoli florets; 3 slices carrot; 2 Morningstar Farms Chik'n Nuggets; 4 baby tomatoes; 2 slices lemon. 2-tier bento box.

Steam rice, make two onigiri. Pack one in each tier, top with lemon. In top tier pack gyoza and steamed broccoli. In the bottom tier pack nuggets, broccoli, carrot, tomatoes, lemon.

BALSAMIC CHICKEN BENTO

1 sweet potato; 2 baby tomatoes, 1/2 cup rice. For spicy green beans: 5 oz green beans; 2 1/2 oz minced pork; 1 tbsp garlic oil; pinch dried chili powder; 1 1/2 tbsp soy sauce; 1/2 tsp sugar. For soy and balsamic vinegar chicken: 6 chicken thighs; 4 tbsp dark soy sauce; 2 tbsp balsamic vinegar; 2 tbsp sugar; 1 tbsp oil. 2-tier bento box.

Trim green beans into halves. Boil for four minutes, drain and refresh quickly in cold water to retain color. Drain again. Heat garlic oil in pan and add pork, stirring to break up. Add chili pepper and stir well to coat; add the soy sauce and sugar. Mix well, ensuring sugar has dissolved, serve beans with mince on top.

To make balsamic chicken, mix soy sauce, balsamic vinegar and sugar in pan, then simmer. Cook for several minutes, reduce sauce until thick and glossy. Wash and dry chicken thighs, place in a hot pan with oil; allow to brown on one side. Turn them over and pour over the sauce; cover and cook

for five minutes, taking care not to let the sauce burn. Remove chicken and test it's cooked by slicing a piece in half. Return to heat if it needs longer. Allow to cool before slicing, save leftovers for another bento.

Roast peeled sweet potato wedges in the oven until golden brown; dress with lime juice and honey to taste. Cook rice and mold into onigiri.

In bottom tier, arrange onigiri; fill space with sweet potatoes. In top tier, place bento cups with chicken and green beans and pork at either end of the container. Fill gaps with two cherry tomatoes.

OMELETTE VARIATION

See ingredients list as left, replace spicy green beans with Japanese omelette: 1 egg; 1 1/2 tbsp dashi; 1 tsp mirin; 1/2 tsp sugar; pinch of salt; dash of light soya sauce. 2-tier bento box.

Break up egg; mix with ingredients. Heat pan, add a quarter of mixture. Cook through. Use spatula to roll thin omelette to back of pan. Add another quarter of mix. Lift existing layer up so this layer can go underneath. Cook layer as above then repeat. Wrap layers in sushi mat; shape into oblong. Slice.

MODERN ART BENTO

2 baby carrots; portion roasted corn; portion edamame beans; 3 baby tomatoes; 2 lettuce leaves; lemon grass; 1/2 cup sushi rice (koshihikari); umeboshi. 1-tier bento box.

The clean surface of an onigiri can be transformed simply into something beautiful. This bento has a recurring theme of triangles.

Cook rice and use mold to create onigiri stuffed with umeboshi. Rest on a romaine lettuce leaf in left side of bento box.

Using a clean paper punch, create geometric punch-outs from a piece of romaine lettuce.

Using a peeler, remove a few thin wisps from one of the carrots.

Arrange these geometric punch-outs and wisps on the onigiri.

Fill a small cup with cooked corn kernels (fresh or frozen) and place in a larger cup. Fill in the larger cup with cooked edamame (fresh or frozen).

Slice carrots and place upright underneath cups.

Add three tomatoes to provide support for the cup and fill in the empty spaces.

Slice a two inch piece of lemon grass at a deep angle and arrange the two pieces at the top of the bento.

MODERN ART VARIATION

4 asparagus tips; 4 baby tomatoes; 1 salmon steak; 1 slice lemon; 1/2 cup sushi rice (koshihikari); umeboshi. 1-tier bento box.

Cook rice; use mold to create umeboshi-stuffed onigiri, place in box. Par boil asparagus and tomatoes, grill salmon. Stack asparagus tips and tomatoes in box base. Rest salmon on top. Decorate onigiri with lemon slice.

HAIKU BENTO

! handful watercress; 8 baby tomatoes; 1 oz. smoked turkey; 1/2 cup sushi rice (koshihikari); umeboshi; furikake. 1-tier bento box.

Perfect for a snack or a light lunch, two simple onigiri make up the bulk of this bento.

Cook rice, use mold to make two onigiri, one with a center of thinly sliced turkey and the other with a pitted umeboshi.

Place in the center of the bento, slightly parted with one nearly touching the top and the other, the bottom.

Divide tomatoes equally and flank the onigiri. Think of a ying/yang shape when arranging.

Place rinsed and dried watercress in the void between the two onigiri.

Carefully sprinkle the furikake in a line across the onigiri.

TAKEAWAY BENTO

Leftover takeaway (teriyaki chicken); 1/2 cup rice; steamed edamame; 2 kumquats; 3 blackberries; 1 strawberry; 1 scallion; carrot; cabbage; sesame seeds. 1-tier bento box.

Use leftover rice, chicken and edamame from takeaway dinner. Also pick a few bits of garnish from leftover salad to decorate with. Prepare bento as soon as possible so that the onigiri can be molded before the rice gets too cold. Pack the bento box with onigiri, teriyaki chicken and edemame. Place fresh fruit in remaining space.

TAKEAWAY VARIATION

Leftover takeaway (teriyaki chicken); 1/2 cup rice; 2 carrots; 1 sweet potato; 1 red pepper; 1 tbsp olive oil; 1 tsp tumeric; 1 tsp cumin; 1 tsp cilantro. 1-tier bento box.

Peel carrots, cut 3 matchsticks to garnish onigiri then quarter remaining carrots. Cut sweet potato wedges. Halve pepper, cut 3 thin strips for garnish. Sprinkle vegetables with oil and spices, roast in oven until crisp. Place chicken and onigiri (garnished with pepper and carrot strips) in bento box. Fill space with roasted vegetables.

HEFTY MISO BENTO

3 shiitake mushrooms; 6 sugar snap peas; portion red cabbage; 2 scallions 1 daikon; packet ramen noodles; packet instant miso soup; furikake. 2-tier bento box.

All ingredients are prepared so that you just need to add hot water.

Cook ramen noodles according to package, but skip the seasoning. Cut shiitake, cabbage, scallions and daikon into thin slices and cut tops off pea pods; place into separate piles in bento.

Take a large cabbage leaf and place cooked noodles inside. Sprinkle with furikake.

When bento is ready to be eaten, begin by dissolving instant miso soup in hot water.

Add vegetables and then noodles. Stir gently, cover and allow to sit for 1 minute. This will allow the shiitake and daikon to soften in the miso.

PORK AND EGG BENTO

Portion mange tout; 1 egg; 1/2 cup rice; 1 baby tomato. For sweet simmered mince: 15 oz minced pork, turkey or chicken; 6 tbsp soy sauce; 2 ½ tbsp sugar; 3 tbsp mirin. 1-tier bento box.

First, prepare sweet simmered mince. In a large pan, mix ingredients over a medium heat. Stir and break up the mince in the liquid until most of the moisture has gone and the mince has darkened in color. Once the mince is cooked you can check for seasoning. This will make enough mince for four generous bento sized portions.

Boil egg for ten minutes. Cool under running water, peel and chop finely. Cook mange tout in boiling hot water for one minute, remove and refresh under cold running water; slice on the diagonal. Cut flower from baby tomato. Cook rice, lay it in the bottom of the bento, then cover half of it with the mince and half with the egg. Arrange the mange tout around cherry tomato, in the center.

HIJIKI BENTO

Portion sesame soy noodles; 1/2 cup brown rice; leftover teriyaki chicken; dumpling dipping sauce, 3 frozen gyozas; 1/2 red pepper; 1/2 yellow pepper. For simmered hijiki and carrot: 3 tbsp hijiki; 1 large carrot; cooking oil; 1/3 pt dashi stock; 6 tsp soy sauce; 1 1/2 tsp sugar. 2-tier bento box.

Soak hijiki in warm water for 25 mins, then drain. Sauté hijiki and julienned carrot in a pan with the oil for a few minutes, add remaining ingredients and simmer for three to four minutes.

Pack one tier with sesame soy noodles, cooked brown rice and teriyaki chicken laid over the top. To decorate the teriyaki chicken, add stars cut from red and yellow peppers.

Fry gyozas and put dumpling dipping sauce in cherry soy sauce bottles.

Add simmered hijiki and carrot to a bento cup and slot into corner of other bento tier. Pack gyozas and soy sauce bottles in remaining space.

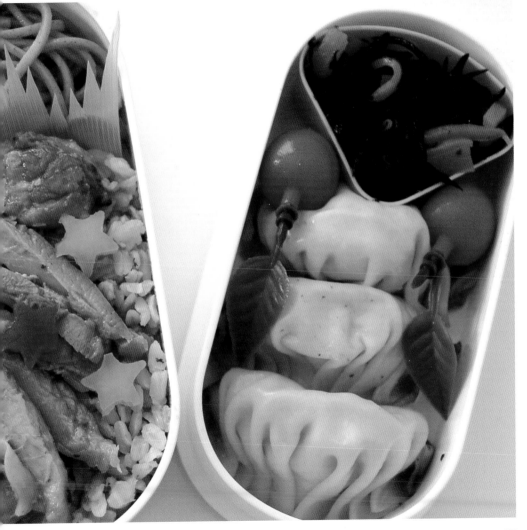

MISO CHICKEN BENTO

2 peppadew peppers; 3 tsp cream cheese; 1 small piece carrot; portion Japanese potato salad; sprig parsley; 1 green pepper; 1 mini hot dog 1 slice cheese; 1 baby tomato. For miso relish chicken: 2 boned chicken thighs; 1 tbsp miso relish; 1 tsp mirin; 1 tsp soy sauce. 1-tier bento box.

To make the chicken, mix the miso relish, mirin and soy sauce together in a plastic bag.

Flatten the thighs down, and place inside the bag.

Squash together well; marinate in the fridge for at least an hour, or overnight.

Remove marinade and pat dry.

Grill for five minutes on both sides, until browned and cooked through.

Cut carrot into thin strips.

Using a food cutter, create stars for the top of the pepper.

Fill pepper with cream cheese and top with stars.

Fill a large bento cup with potato salad, lay stir-fried green pepper along one edge.

Create a flower with hot dog using cutter, tuck inside the cup.

Place in the bento box, with stuffed peppers, miso chicken and parsley garnish.

GOLDEN CHICKEN BENTO

Premade tomato salad; 1 tea marbled boiled egg; 1 hot dog; 2 lettuce leaves; 1/2 cup rice; black sesame seeds 3 baby tomatoes. For golden chicken: 2 chicken breast steaks; 1 tsp salt; 1 egg; pinch turmeric; plain flour; oil; soy sauce, to serve. 1-tier bento box.

Use a rolling pin or meat hammer to flatten chicken, cut into bite sized pieces.

Sprinkle on some salt, then pat dry.

Beat egg with the salt and turmeric.

Coat chicken sparingly with flour, then dip into the beaten egg mixture.

Fry chicken in oil over low temperature until it is no longer pink.

Dip chicken in the egg again, then cook until the egg is set and slightly golden.

Line bento box with lettuce.

Prepare rice with onigiri mold to make a line of mini onigiri along one side.

Top each one with black sesame seeds.

Fill a bento cup with premade tomato salad and push to one side of bento.

Against it, rest tea marbled egg, hot dog (cut into a flower shape) and a soy sauce bottle.

Nestle two pieces of golden chicken in remaining space, alongside tomatoes.

GINGER PORK BENTO

Portion white cabbage; 3 baby tomatoes; 1/2 cup rice, 2 lettuce leaves; apple, tuna and avocado salad; salad dressing; bean sprouts; pepperoni slices. For ginger pork: 2 pieces pork loin steak; 2 tbsp dark soy sauce; 2 tbsp mirin; 3 tsp sugar; 2 tsp ginger juice. 2-tier bento box.

Make the ginger pork. Add the liquids and sugar to a bowl, then add pork. Leave to marinade for ten minutes. Remove pork from marinade and pat dry, reserving the liquid. Fry until browned on both sides. Add liquid, allow to bubble and reduce until it sticks to the pork.

If the pork is already cooked, you may want to remove it from the pan when you do this to prevent it becoming tough. Slice into strips.

Chop white cabbage finely and sauté. Use cabbage in bottom layer as a bed for pork to lay on. Cook rice, mold into onigiri and place with baby tomatoes.

In top layer, make bed of lettuce and lay a cup with dressed salad, sautéed bean sprouts, skewer of mini pepperoni slices.

PRAWN BALL BENTO

2 lettuce leaves; 1/2 cup short grain rice; 2 prawns; 1 egg; 1/4 cup flour; 1/4 cup Japanese bread crumbs; oil for frying; 1 sheet nori. 1-tier bento box.

Line box with lettuce. Cook rice. Shell prawns. Coat with egg, flour, and bread crumbs. Heat oil in a small pan. Deep-fry prawns until coating turns crispy and golden. Shape with rice into two balls. Wrap with nori strips.

FURIKAKE BENTO

8 sugar snap peas; portion edamame beans; 3 baby tomatoes; 1 carrot; 2 oz. cooked chicken; 1/2 cup sushi rice (koshihikari); umeboshi; teriyaki sauce; Various furikake. 1-tier bento box.

Cook rice, place in mold to create plain onigiri. Place in bento. Slice carrot into thin sticks about the size of matchsticks.

Arrange carrot pieces in a fan shape leaving some white space between each piece. Shake some furikake into a napkin or folded piece of paper and use this to control the flow of the furikake as you fill the white spaces.

Place a single edamame in the center of your design. Lightly coat the cooked chicken in enough teriyaki sauce to make it slightly shine. Sprinkle a little more furikake on the chicken.

Cut tips off sugar snap peas and place lying in the same direction as chicken strips. Fill empty area with tomatoes and add a few edamame.

Snuggle a umeboshi beside the chicken to add color.

TUNA STRIP BENTO

2 lettuce leaves; 1/2 cup short grain rice; 1/2 tuna steak; 1 tsp olive oil; 1 clove garlic; 1 tsp lemon juice; 1 chili; 1 sheet nori. 1-tier bento box.

Line box with lettuce. Crush garlic and chop chili and mix with olive oil and lemon juice. Slice tuna steak into two strips and marinate in mix. Cook rice. Place tuna in pan and sear. Shape with rice into balls. Wrap with nori strips.

PEPPER BALL BENTO

2 lettuce leaves; 1/2 cup short grain rice; 1/2 pepper; 1 egg; 1/4 cup flour; 1/4 cup Japanese bread crumbs; oil for frying; 1 sheet nori. 1-tier bento box.

Line box with lettuce. Cook rice. Chop pepper into strips. Coat with egg, flour, and bread crumbs. Heat oil and deep-fry until coating turns crispy. Shape with rice into two balls. Wrap with nori strips.

SALMON FILLET BENTO

1 cup short grain rice; 1/2 salmon fillet; 1 scallion; 1 tbsp mayonnaise; pinch salt; pinch cayenne pepper; 1 tsp sesame oil; 1 sheet nori. 1-tier bento box.

Cook rice and let cool to room temperature.

Cook salmon fillet in a frying pan over medium high heat.

Flake cooked salmon with a fork.

Mix salmon with chopped scallion, mayonnaise, salt, cayenne pepper, and sesame oil.

Divide rice and salmon filling into three equal portions.

Cut nori into three long strips.

Mold rice into a triangular shape with salmon filling in the middle.

Wrap bottom of each rice ball with a strip of nori.

261

THAI OMELETTE VARIATION

See ingredients list from Thai omelette Bento, replace Swedish meatballs with spinach balls: 8 cups chopped spinach, 3 tsp butter, wedge parmesan cheese, 1/2 onion, 1 egg. 2-tier bento box.

To make spinach balls, steam spinach, grate parmesan cheese and whisk egg. Finely chop onion, melt butter in pan.

Mix ingredients together, shape into 3 balls and bake in oven until browned.

THAI OMELETTE BENTO

Shiso furikake; 1/2 cup rice; portion edamame beans; 1 red chili; 1 tbsp sesame seed oil; pinch sea salt; 1 wedge lime; Swedish meatballs. For Thai flavored omelettes: 1 red chili; small bunch cilantro; 1/2 clove garlic; 1 tsp soy sauce; 1 tsp fish sauce; pinch sugar; 3 large eggs; oil for frying; lime juice and soy sauce, to serve. 2-tier bento box.

To make Thai omelettes, put the peeled garlic clove, red chili and cilantro in a food processor.

Process until finely chopped.

Add soy sauce, fish sauce, sugar and eggs and mix, taking care not to make too bubbly.

In a large, non-stick frying pan, pour a layer of oil and a third of mixture.

Heat on a low heat until set but not browned; roll up and remove from the pan.

Repeat for the rest of the mixture.

Slice rolled omelettes diagonally when cool.

To prepare the edamame beans, boil, then toss them in a hot wok for a few minutes along with a deseeded, chopped red chili and some sesame seed oil.

Once cooked, sprinkle with a little sea salt.

Cook rice and mold into onigiri.

To assemble, pack omelette slices in a row on the top layer of bento.

Tuck a lime wedge behind them, and add the soy sauce and lime dressing in a bottle.

Fill remaining space with Swedish meatballs, topped with food picks.

For the bottom layer, roll onigiri in the shiso furikake, and place at one end.

Fill remaining space with chili spiced edamame beans.

SPICY THAI BENTO

Furikake; 3 strawberries; 2 lettuce leaves; 1 lime; 2 shallots; 1 cup rice; . For spicy Thai mince: 1/2 inch piece of ginger; 3 cloves garlic; 2 red chilies; 15 oz turkey mince; 1 tsp light brown sugar; 2 tbsp fish sauce; juice of 1 lime; 2 lime leaves; 1 tbsp chopped cilantro leaves. 2-tier bento box.

Prepare spicy Thai mince. Heat a little cooking oil in a pan and fry chopped ginger, crushed garlic and half the julienned chilies for one minute, or until they become fragrant. Add the mince. Sprinkle over the sugar, and add the fish sauce, lime juice, the shredded lime leaves and remaining chili. Cook until the sugar has dissolved and made a sticky sauce. Using lettuce, create a base to lay your mince inside. Place strawberries behind divider, and top mince with sliced shallot, herbs and a slice of lime. Using an onigiri mold, shape cooked rice into triangles, then roll them in three different kinds of furikake.

CARROT RICE BENTO

Teriyaki burgers; rolled omelette; serving edamame beans; 1/2 carrot; 2 lettuce leaves; 4 baby tomatoes. For carrot and onion rice: 2 cups rice; 1 carrot; 1/2 onion; 1 tsp butter; splash soy sauce; seasoning. 1-tier bento box.

Make carrot and onion rice. Process onion and carrot until they are finely chopped, then sauté in butter until softened but not browned.

This will take around five minutes.

Season and add soy sauce. Add to a rice cooker with washed rice and an equal amount of water; cook as normal.

Cut shapes in the carrot rounds. Centralise them, in order to use the outside of the carrot as an additional decoration.

Thread edamame beans onto a skewer, broad side down.

Line bento box with the carrot and onion rice so that it fills a diagonal space. Top with the carrot decorations.

Place a bento cup in the remaining space, and line with some lettuce.

Push teriyaki burgers to one side.

Place a slice of rolled omelette in the other side.

Fill the gap in between with baby tomatoes, then top with edamame skewers.

SAUSAGE RICE VARIATION

See ingredients list from Carrot Rice Bento, replace carrot and onion rice with Italian sausage and pea rice: 2 cups rice; 1 Italian sausage; 1/2 onion; 1 tsp butter; 1/2 cup frozen peas; seasoning. 1-tier bento box.

Cook rice, finely chop onion and fry in butter until transparent. Grill sausage and dice. Boil peas, add peas, sausage and onion to rice. Assemble bento.

NIKUJAGA BENTO

Serving nikujaga (beef and potatoes stewed in soy); 1 small omelette; 1 slice cake; 4 grapes; 1 strawberry; 5 blueberries. For egg fried rice and peppers: 2 cups cold, cooked Japanese rice; 1/2 green pepper; 2 scallions; 1 egg; 1 1/2 tbsp soy sauce; 1 tsp sake; pinch pepper.

Make egg fried rice. Chop pepper into small squares, and cut scallions on a diagonal. Beat egg. Fry pepper and onions until slightly soft, and remove from pan. Scramble egg, then add rice to the pan, along with the vegetables, and stir until mixed and fried. Add the rest of the seasonings.

To assemble, fill one tier with nikujaga. Fill a bento cup with egg fried rice. Place in another tier, with a piece of omelette at the back. In the remaining layer, place a quarter of a piece of cake, surrounded by fruit. Nikujaga can be heated in a microwave before eating.

SUSHI ROLL BENTO

Sushi ingredients from Maki Sushi Bento (page 190). For filling: 1 carrot; 5 mushrooms. Sesame seeds; 1 radish; 1 piece watermelon; soy sauce; wasabi; 2 pak choi leaves; handful cress. 2-tier bento box.

Slice raw carrot into matchsticks. Stir-fry mushrooms and slice into long thin strips.

Prepare sushi as in Maki Sushi Bento recipe, using carrot and mushrooms as filling. Place pak choi leaves and cress into base of bento. Pack sushi in both tiers of bento box and sprinkle with sesame seeds.

Cut small triangles into the side of the radish before slicing, to make flower shapes. Slice watermelon into bite-sized chunks. Pour soy sauce into a cup with a lid. Squeeze wasabi into paper cup.

Pack radish, watermelon, soy sauce and wasabi into remaining space in top tier.

FROGGY BENTO

1 cup rice; portion leftover cooked salmon; 2 broccoli florets; 1 clove garlic; a few toasted, slivered almonds; 1 sheet nori. 1-tier bento box.

Cook rice and cool to room temperature. Use rice mold to create onigiri or make by hand, using a small bowl of salt water to keep hands moist so the rice sticks to itself.

If making by hand take a small handful of cooked rice. Pat a little so it sticks together. Poke a small well in the center and fill with cooked salmon.

Take another handful of rice and pat the two together. Gently shape into a triangle. The rice balls will stick together if they touch, so separate them with a piece of sushi grass.

Decorate onigiri with cut nori; use exotic frog craft-punch. Craft punches work just fine with nori. For side dish, mince garlic and stir-fry with broccoli in a little oil. Sprinkle with toasted almonds.

GINGER BALL BENTO

1 cup rice; 1 chicken breast; 2 slices ginger; dash sesame oil; 1 tbsp soy sauce; 7 snap peas; 2 mini bell peppers; 1 cherry tomato; 1 nori sheet. 1-tier bento box.

Marinate sliced chicken breast in soy sauce, fresh minced ginger and a dash of sesame oil for one hour. Grill. Cook rice and cool to room temperature. Create onigiri filled with chopped ginger chicken. Decorate rice balls with nori. Cut cherry tomato into a flower and place in front of the rice balls. Arrange fresh snap peas with sliced bell peppers, for side dish.

CHILI PRAWN BALL VARIATION

See ingredients list from Ginger Ball Bento, replace chicken filling with chili prawns: 4 raw prawns; 1 chili; dash oil.

Marinate prawns in oil and finely chopped chili for one hour. Grill. Fill onigiri with cooked prawn mixture.

SIMPLE BENTO

Sushi ingredients from Maki Sushi Bento (page 190). For filling: 1 carrot; 1 red pepper. Black grapes; black sesame seeds; handful rice crackers; wasabi; soy sauce. 2-tier bento box.

Prepare sushi as in Maki Sushi Bento recipe (page 190), using sliced carrot and pepper as filling. Pack in bottom tier. Sprinkle with sesame seeds. Cut grapes in half and pack with rice crackers, soy sauce and wasabi.

SIMPLE VARIATION

Sushi ingredients from Maki Sushi Bento (page 190). For filling: 1/2 mango. Black grapes; black sesame seeds; handful rice crackers; wasabi; soy sauce. 2-tier bento box.

Prepare sushi as in Maki Sushi Bento recipe (page 190), using sliced mango as filling. Pack in bottom tier. Sprinkle with sesame seeds. Pack remaining ingredients in top tier of bento box.

YAKI UDON BENTO

2 inari sushi pockets (see page 192); 1 hot dog; 1 piece sweetcorn; 1/2 red pepper; 1 quail's egg; 2 tomberries; 2 edemame beans; 2 lettuce leaves; 1/2 yellow pepper; 1 slice cheese; 1 thin slice carrot; 1 broccoli floret; 1 cauliflower floret. For yaki udon: 2 portions cooked udon noodles; 2 oz thinly sliced chicken thigh; 4 scallions; 2 leaves white cabbage; 2 shiitake mushrooms; 1/2 green pepper; 1 tbsp soy sauce; 1 tsp Worcestershire sauce. For grilled tuna skewers: 7 oz tuna; 1 1/2 tbsp soy sauce; 1/2 tbsp mirin. 2-tier bento box.

Yaki udon is a meal in itself, but with snacks this is really a bento for day trip somewhere. Prepare yaki udon. Cut chicken into small pieces. Cut scallions diagonally in small pieces. Thinly slice mushrooms. Chop cabbage roughly and julienne pepper. Stir-fry chicken, add scallions, cabbage, mushrooms and pepper and fry until tender. Add cooked noodles and fry for a minute, then add seasoning, soy sauce and Worcestershire sauce.

Prepare tuna skewers. Marinate cubed tuna for one hour in mixture of mirin and soy sauce. Place tuna on wooden skewers which have been soaked in water. Drain tuna, grill briefly on all sides until slightly browned. The center will be slightly raw in the middle; if you're not eating the tuna on the same day be sure to cook it more thoroughly. Rethread the chunks onto food picks for a cute look.

Prepare inari sushi pockets (see page 192 for recipe) and a hot dog flower (slice a cold hot dog into sixths along the base, then insert a piece of sweetcorn in the middle). Make a pepper egg by slicing red pepper, placing one slice into frying pan and breaking quail's egg into the space in center of slice. Fry and the egg will cook and attach to the pepper. Blanch broccoli and cauliflower, and make an edamame and tomberry skewer.

Line the bottom of top tier with sushi grass and fill with yaki udon. Cut off the base of a yellow pepper, top with a flower cut-out of cheese, and cut a star shape out of a thin slice of carrot. Place on top of yaki udon for decoration, add a soy sauce bottle filled with any leftover liquid from the noodles.

Line the bottom tier with lettuce, and place the inari sushi at one end. In the remaining space, place the tuna skewers at the top, then fit pepper egg between them.

Fill remaining spaces with cauliflower and broccoli, the edamame and tomberry skewer, and the hot dog flower. Other gaps can be filled with tomberries or small sprigs of broccoli.

NIKUJAGA BENTO

2 quails' eggs; 1 carrot; 1 baby tomato; portion edamame beans; piece of rolled omelette; 1/2 cup rice, soy sauce; furikake. For nikujaga: 10 oz thinly sliced beef brisket; 25 oz potatoes; 2 small white onions; 1 tbsp oil; 1 1/4 pt dashi; 4 tbsp sugar; 5 tbsp light soy sauce; 2 tbsp mirin; 1 tbsp sake; chives; seven-spice. 2-tier bento box.

Nikujaga is Japanese comfort food – the sort of thing cooked by mothers for their children in winter.

It's not usually served in bentos, but you can always reheat it the next day for lunch or eat it cold.

About an hour before you make the bento, prepare the quails' eggs by hard boiling, peeling and soaking in soy sauce.

Cook rice, shape into onigiri using mold.

Peel potatoes; cut into small chunks.

Peel onions and cut into small wedges.

Cut beef into small pieces. Heat oil and cook potatoes for two minutes.

Add meat and onions, stir well and cook for another two minutes.

Add dashi, sugar, soy sauce, mirin and sake and simmer the mixture with a drop-lid on top until the potatoes are cooked through.

Portion leftover spicy green beans; portion soy sauce and balsamic vinegar chicken; slice rolled omelette; 1 tea marbled boiled egg; 1 gyoza; 1 tomato. For green pea rice: 2 cups rice; large handful frozen peas; 1 tbsp mirin; 2 tbsp soy sauce; 1 egg, scrambled. For sweet simmered green beans: 1 1/2 oz green beans; 5 tbsp dashi; 1/2 tsp mirin; 1/2 tsp sugar; 2 tsp soy sauce. 2-tier bento box.

Make green pea rice. Add rice, peas, mirin, soy sauce and egg to a rice cooker, along with water. Put on lid and cook as usual. Once finished, mix well. Prepare sweet simmered green beans. Cut beans into short lengths, then add to a saucepan and simmer for six minutes. Fill two thirds of bottom tier with the green pea rice. Put the green beans in bento cup, fill remaining space with chicken. In the top, add two sweet rolled omelettes and a deep fried gyoza, then place a bento cup of spicy green beans in the middle. Place a marbled tea egg and tomato wedges in the remaining space.

This should take about 15 minutes.

Strain off most of the liquid and place in your bento. When eating, you can have it cold or reheat it.

Place a small amount of drained nikujaga in a bento dish on the bottom layer of your bento box.

Fill the remaining space with the onigiri rolled in furikake.

On the top layer, place rolled omelette in a small bento cup.

Cut carrots into patterns using cutter and place alongside omelette.

Alternate soy sauce eggs with tomatoes.

Fill remaining space with boiled edamame beans, sprinkled with a little salt.

269

TEA MARBLED EGG BENTO

Pre-bought korokke; 1 Thai spring roll; 1 inch cucumber slice; 1 slice red pepper; 1 slice yellow pepper; hoisin bun; 3 cherry tomatoes; chili dipping sauce. For tea marbled egg: 1 egg; 2 tbsp tamari; 2 tbsp loose leaf tea; 2 tsp sugar. For sesame and soy soba noodles: 3 1/2 oz soba noodles; water to boil; 2 tbsp light soy sauce; 2 tbsp sesame oil; 2 tsp sugar, dissolved in 1 tbsp hot water; 1 tbsp sesame seeds. 2-tier bento box.

Prepare tea marbled egg. Ensure that pan isn't too big as egg should fit snugly in the bottom.

Don't leave too much empty space here as it will dilute the soaking liquid

Put the egg into cold water and bring to the boil.

After boiling for ten minutes, remove from the heat and allow to cool slightly.

To create the spider web pattern, tap egg gently with a spoon.

Don't hit it too hard or you'll break the membrane between the egg and the egg shell, which will dye the whole egg brown.

Once you've done this, return egg to the saucepan and add tamari, loose leaf tea and sugar.

Now bring mixture to the boil, then allow to simmer for around an hour and a half.

Once you've done that, drain away the liquid, rinse the eggs and allow to cool so you can peel them.

To make noodles, boil soba noodles in water until done, then drain.

Combine all other liquid ingredients and add to a bowl, tossing well to coat. Top with sesame seeds.

Fry korokke in the hot oil according to the instructions on the packet, and drain. Cut cucumber and peppers into star shapes and squares.

Cut korokke in half diagonally and place in bottom tier of bento.

Slice the Thai spring roll diagonally as well, and lay each half on top of the other with the cut side exposed.

Fill the space with the chopped vegetables.

In the top tier, nestle the noodles at one end, place the egg at the other end, and fill the remaining spaces with baby tomatoes.

YAKITORI BENTO

1 cup rice; furikake; 3 carrot slices; 1 egg; 2 baby tomatoes; 2 sprigs parsley; 2 lettuce leaves; 1/4 tsp curry powder; 2 tsp mayonnaise. For yakitori chicken: 6 boneless chicken thighs; 1 young leek; 1/2 pt light soy sauce; 1/4 pt mirin; 7 tbsp sake; 3 1/2 oz sugar; Japanese seven spice powder. 2-tier bento box.

Make yakitori chicken. Simmer sauce ingredients until sauce thickens. Cut chicken and leek into small cubes, skewer the chicken and leek onto

soaked bamboo skewers. Grill and allow chicken to cook on both sides. Now brush on yakitori sauce and grill until the chicken is glossy, basting as you go along. Sprinkle with Japanese seven spice powder.

Hard boil an egg, slice in half and remove yolks. Mix yolks with curry powder, mayonnaise and 1 sprig chopped parsley. Return the filling to gap where yolk was; top with more parsley. Fill bottom layer of bento with rice; add a line of furikake.

Line top layer with lettuce, nestle yakitori chicken to one side. Add devilled egg, carrot shapes, tomatoes.

SUSHI BENTO

Salmon nigiri; shrimp nigiri; packet of soy sauce, packet of gari; small chocolate; maki made with salmon and avocado (see recipe on page 190). 2-tier bento box.

Cook rice and mold. Cut slices from a salmon steak. Cut against the grain to see pattern of salmon fat; use any mistakes for maki. Shrimp is pre-made for sushi so simply place on rice balls.

CHICKEN WING BENTO

1 slice rolled omelette; dried seaweed salad mix; cooked Japanese rice; furikake; 2 lettuce leaves. For teriyaki chicken wings: 3 chicken wings; 4 tbsp mirin; 4 tbsp soy sauce; 4 tsp sugar; oil. 2-tier bento box.

Joint chicken wings and remove tips, creating two pieces from each wing. Marinate for at least an hour, or overnight, in mirin, soy sauce and sugar, mixed well. Remove and pat dry. Heat the oil in pan, add wings and cook until browned. Add water and marinade, cover. Allow to simmer until cooked

through. When juices run clear, remove cover and boil marinade until thick and glossy. Allow to cool before adding to bento. This will make enough for two to three bentos. Prepare rolled omelette; line top tier of bento with lettuce. Sit the chicken wings at one side.

Reconstitute seaweed salad according to instructions (usually by soaking, rinsing and squeezing vegetables) and add it to a food cup. Place rolled omelette in front, with a bento divider and food pick to decorate. Fill bottom tier with rice and add a line of furikake down the middle.

VEGGIE SUSHI VARIATION

Egg nigiri; pepper nigiri; packet of soy sauce, packet of gari; small chocolate; maki made with mango and avocado (see recipe on page 190). 2-tier bento box.

Cook rice and mold. Cook thick omelette in small pan and slice into three rectangular pieces. Cut 3 rectangular slices from pepper and grill until soft. Place omelette and pepper slices on 6 rice balls. slice mango and avocado into long thin strips and use to fill maki. Pack sushi in both tiers.

GYOZA BENTO

RIGHT: Three cylinder shaped onigiri wrapped in nori; 2 pork gyoza (frozen); takuan; shelled edamame; umeboshi. 1-tier bento box.

Using a mold, create three cylinder shaped onigiri flavored with furikake or onigiri flavor mix. Fry gyoza and add to box. Slice takuan and arrange in corner. Top with umeboshi. Add shelled edamame to last section.

GYOZA ONI BENTO

1/2 cup rice; drop red food coloring; 2 pork gyoza (frozen); edamame pods; takuan; kim chee crab; umeboshi; 1 lettuce leaf; soy sauce. 1-tier round bento box.

Add red food coloring one drop at a time when cooking white rice. Mix well until you have your desired color.

Line circle bento box with lettuce leaf.

Mold rice into onigiri and add to box.

Fry gyoza in a small pan and add to bento box.

Add kim chee crab to box next to gyoza.

Add salted edamame pods, laying them down in a group.

Slice takuan into bite size strips and tuck in between food.

Add umeboshi as garnish.

EGG SUSHI BENTO

RIGHT: 2 pieces tamago nigiri sushi; 6 pieces ume maki sushi; 4 baby carrot sticks; 2 nori strips; 3 avocado slices. 1-tier bento box.

Using your favorite tamagoyaki recipe, cut two slices for your tamago nigiri. Place on top of small onigiri and wrap with nori strips.Using sushi mat, spread sushi rice on top of a half sheet of nori. Spread mashed ume in a line at the edge. Roll sushi. Cut into pieces to fit bento box. Tuck in baby carrot sticks and avocado slices in spaces.

HAPPY BENTO

LEFT: 1 cup rice; leftover pork loin; 4 slices cucumber; 3 cherry tomatoes; 1 sheet nori. 1-tier bento box.

Create onigiri filled with chopped pork loin. Decorate rice balls with nori cut into a happy face. Arrange sliced fresh cherry tomatoes and cucumber slices as a side dish.

STYLISH BENTO

ASPARAGUS BENTO

1/2 cup rice; sprinkling furikake; 1 salmon fillet; 1/4 cup chopped scallions; dash lemon juice; 1 tbsp plain yoghurt; 2 tbsp flour; pinch baking powder; pinch salt; pinch pepper; cooking oil; 1 sheet nori; 2 slices ham; 9 asparagus spears; 1 apple; dash lemon juice; 1 golden cherry tomato. 1-tier bento box.

Cook rice. Place in one half of bento box and season with furikake.

Dice salmon fillet. Mix salmon cubes with chopped scallions, lemon juice, yoghurt, flour, baking powder, salt, and pepper.

Heat oil in a non-stick frying pan over medium heat. Spoon salmon mixture into pan and form small fritters.

Cook fritters until batter is set and both sides are golden. Cut nori into thin strips. Wrap fritters with nori strips.

Chop asparagus spears into halves of equal length. Blanch and divide asparagus into bunches of 6 pieces. Wrap asparagus pieces with ham.

Slice apple and toss with lemon juice to prevent browning.

Arrange apple slices and cherry tomato in top half of remaining space in bento box.

Fill the middle section with ham-asparagus rolls. Fill the bottom section with salmon fritters, arranged neatly in a row with loose ends of nori strips facing down into box.

POLKA DOT BENTO

1/2 cup rice; frozen edamame beans, shelled; 1 salmon steak; pinch salt; cooking oil; 1 egg; 1 tsp mirin; 1 tbsp dashi stock; 1/4 cup milk; 1 sheet nori; 1 tsp gochujang; 1 tsp sesame oil; handful red grapes. 1-tier bento box.

Cook rice and edamame beans in rice cooker. Fill one half of bento box with edamame rice, arranging beans in a polka dot pattern on top of rice.

Season salmon with salt. Heat oil in a frying pan over medium high heat.

Sear salmon on both sides and cook through. Mix egg with mirin, dashi, and milk. Brush seaweed with gochujang.

Heat oil in a non-stick frying pan over medium heat. Spread a thin layer of egg into the pan and place seaweed on top.

Allow to cook; roll egg and seaweed up. Brush the outside of the egg roll with sesame oil. Cut into thick slices.

Place salmon next to rice, and red grapes into a small divider cup in the top right corner of bento box.

Fill remaining space with slices of egg roll.

PINK NOODLE BENTO

Serving 'sakura' noodles tinted pink with umeboshi; 1 daikon radish; 1 scallion; 1 quail's egg; 10 edamame beans; 1 portion seaweed salad. For tamagoyaki: 2 eggs; 1 tbsp water; 1 tsp soy sauce; 1 small pinch of dashi granules; cooking spray or oil. 2-tier bento box.

Make tamagoyaki. Mix the ingredients in a small bowl. Use a mini hand mixer to blend well, ensure texture is consistent and smooth. Turn stove to medium. Oil pan liberally. When pan is heated, pour in enough egg mixture to cover the surface of the pan. Allow to set.

Using a spatula, pry up the egg 'pancake' which will have formed from the edge closest to you. Fold over repeatedly to make a tight roll. Move the roll from the back of the pan to the front.

Add more egg again to cover pan base, and repeat. The new egg mixture will bond with the roll and make the second and third rolling much easier.

Do not let the heat get too high or egg will brown. Repeat until egg mixture is used up, remove roll from the pan and set aside to cool. Slice and serve.

Cook pink noodles, place in one tier of box. Cut radish into flower shapes using cookie cutter.

Slice scallion diagonally and place with radish on noodles to create shooting star decoration.

Boil quail's egg and shell. Place seaweed salad in food cup, add to second tier. Place quail's egg on top. Fill remaining space with tamagoyaki.

Spear edamame beans on two food picks and place on top of tamagoyaki.

BONBON BENTO

ABOVE: 2 ready-to-eat meatballs;
3 carrots; 1/2 cup rice; sprinkling
furikake; serving edamame beans; 1
sprig parsley. 1-tier bento box.

Heat two ready-to-eat meatballs, place
in box. Cook rice and using a mold or
your hands, shape with furikake into a
triangle. Add to box. Julienne carrots
and tuck next to the meatballs and
onigiri. Add edamame pods in cupcake
cup. Garnish with parsley.

PATTY BENTO

BELOW: 1 corned beef hash patty;
takuan; ketchup in sauce bottle; 1/4
cup brown rice; 1/4 cup white rice;
sprinkling toasted sesame seeds;
umeboshi. 1-tier bento box.

Cook rice and mix. Place in one half of
bento box; sprinkle with sesame seeds,
add umeboshi to center. Wrap bottom
of takuan slices in tin foil to keep juices
separate. Cut hash patty into two
pieces. Add ketchup bottle.

SASHIMI BENTO

1/2 cup rice; 1 grape tomato; 1
Okinawan sweet potato; serving
pickled eggplant; serving pickled
cucumber; 4 pieces firm tofu; 1/2 cup
finely chopped lettuce; 4 pieces sliced
raw ahi (sashimi); soy sauce; sprinkling
furikake. For teriyaki beef; 2 pieces
thin sliced beef; 1 tbsp teriyaki sauce; 2
scallions. 1-tier bento box with divider.

Chop scallions and add to teriyaki
sauce. Marinate beef in teriyaki sauce
for 30 minutes or overnight. Fry beef
slices with a small amount of oil or
with leftover sauce. Cut into small bite-
size slices.

Cook rice. Add divider to box. Place
rice into a corner in a triangle shape on
larger side of the box. Sprinkle furikake
onto rice. Add teriyaki beef slices, grape
tomato, pickles, and boiled Okinawan
sweet potato. Line empty section with
lettuce 'bed'. Place tofu and sashimi
onto the lettuce. Add soy sauce bottle.
Pack in ice-packed lunch bag to ensure
sashimi remains cool.

DONBURI VARIATION

RIGHT: 1/4 cup rice; serving shelled edamame; 1 cup mandarin orange slices; handful dried fruit. For Donburi: 3 chicken breasts, cubed; 1 small onion; 1 pink kamaboko (fish cake); 1 tsp chili flakes; 1/2 cup soy sauce; 1/2 cup mirin; 1 tbsp sugar; 5 eggs. 1-tier bento box with 2 sections.

Add chili to donburi to make a spicier variation. Include dried fruit in cup.

DONBURI BENTO

1/4 cup rice; serving shelled edamame; 1 cup mandarin orange slices. For Donburi: 3 chicken breasts, cubed; 1 small onion; 1 pink kamaboko (fish cake); 1/2 cup soy sauce; 1/2 cup mirin; 1 tbsp sugar; 5 eggs. 1-tier bento box with 2 sections.

Make donburi. In a shallow pan, fry cubed chicken breast until half cooked; set aside in bowl.

Fry diced onions and diced kamaboko on medium heat for one minute. Add

soy sauce, mirin, and sugar. Return chicken to pan. Simmer for five minutes.

Scramble eggs and pour over donburi. Let ingredients sit on heat until eggs are cooked.

Cook rice. Add to fill half of one section. Spoon donburi into the other half of the section.

In opposite section, add shelled edamame in a cupcake holder.

Drain mandarin orange slices and place into cupcake holder and tuck into remaining space.

INARIZUSHI BENTO

2 pre-seasoned inarizushi aburaage (fried tofu skins); 1/2 cup sushi rice; serving cucumber kim chee; 1/2 carrot; 3 grape tomatoes. 1-tier bento box.

Cook rice. Cut tofu skins in half. Stuff each half with sushi rice and add to bento box.

In a foil food cup, add cucumber kim chee, chopping into smaller pieces as needed. Fill empty space with grape tomatoes.

PINEAPPLE BENTO

2 Aidell's teriyaki pineapple meatballs; 1 fish cake; 1 pack ready-made yaki soba noodles; 1 sprig parsley. 1-tier bento box.

Cook noodles according to directions. Add a small amount to the bento box. Cut fish cake into bite-size pieces. Add food divider and place two meatballs into box. Garnish with parsley.

PINEAPPLE VARIATION

2 Aidell's teriyaki pineapple meatballs; 1 pack ready-made yaki soba noodles; 1 sprig parsley; 1 fresh pineapple. 1-tier bento box.

Prepare bento as in Pineapple Bento (left). Top and tail fresh pineapple; remove the pineapples hard center. Cut two pineapple rings and slice into chunks. Place in food cup and arrange in bento in place of sliced fish cake.

MARBLED EGG BENTO

2 raw broccoli florets; 3 sugar snap peas; 1/2 lemon; 1 tbsp shredded imitation crab; 1 cilantro leaf; soy sauce; 1 serving soba noodles; 1/2 scallion; 1 tsp fish roe. For 4 marbled tea eggs: 4 eggs; 1/4 cup soy sauce; 1 tbsp five spice; 2 Earl Grey tea bags. 1-tier bento box.

Make marbled eggs.

Medium to hard boil eggs.

Remove from water but leave the heat on the stove.

Hold each egg and roll it gently against a cutting board until the shell cracks all around.

Be careful not to split the white of the eggs.

Return eggs to the water and add soy sauce, five spice and tea bags.

Reduce heat to simmer; cook for at least two hours.

The longer you cook the eggs, the darker the marbling effect and the stronger the flavor.

Peel eggs, place one in corner of box.

Cook noodles, place in half of box, garnish with chopped scallion and fish roe.

Fry sugar snap peas lightly for one minute. Tuck next to egg. Half stuff lemon with crab and cilantro. Place.

DIVIDED BENTO

2 oz soba noodles; pinch white sesame seeds; 1 tbsp toasted sesame oil; 1 scallion. 1 wagashi (Japanese sweet); handful pomegranate seeds; 3 slices salami; 3 sugar snap peas; 1/4 avocado; 7 cuttlefish balls; 1/4 cup unagi sauce; pinch black sesame seeds; handful peanuts and Japanese rice crackers. 1-tier separated tupperware box and 1 standard tupperware box.

Boil and cool noodles, then drizzle with sesame oil and sprinkle with white sesame seeds and diced scallion, cut on the bias. Add to tupperware box.

In divided tupperware box, place wagashi and pomegranate seeds in top section, sliced avocado in bottom section. Wrap salami around sugar snap peas and place in right section.

Add cuttlefish balls to left section, drizzle with unagi sauce and black sesame seeds. Place spicy Japanese rice crackers and peanuts in remaining section.

KITSUNE SOBA BENTO

4 leaves romaine lettuce; 1 daikon radish; 1 carrot; 1 slice lemon. For kitsune soba: serving soba noodles; 4 cups green tea; 6 inarizushi wrappers; 1 scallion. 2-tier bento box.

Cook soba noodles in green tea to give the soba a depth of taste.

Cook until soft and place in one tier of bento.

Cut inarizushi wrappers into thin strips.

Layer on top of soba noodles.

Slice scallion into small pieces and sprinkle on top of inarizushi wrappers.

This adds color and a crisp fresh taste to the noodles.

Fill second tier with salad made of romaine lettuce, and daikon and carrot cut into star shapes using a cookie cutter.

Add slice to lemon to garnish, this can be squeezed onto the salad as a dressing.

Soba noodles are very refreshing in warm months.

When paired with fried tofu the dish is called 'kitsune soba'.

INARIZUSHI BENTO

1 Granny Smith apple; 1 carrot; dash lemon juice; 2 imitation crab legs; 3 broccoli florets; 1 slice lemon; 2 lettuce leaves. For inarizushi with sushi rice: 5 inarizushi wrappers; 1 cup sushi rice; 1 tbsp mirin; 2 tbsp rice vinegar. 2-tier bento box.

Make inarizushi. Inarizushi no moto wrappers are made of tofu, keep sushi rice moist until lunch and are fine prepared the night before. Rinse the rice three times in water to remove extra starch. Place rice in a bowl and cover with water. Swirl with hands until the water becomes cloudy. Drain water and repeat two more times. The water will become less cloudy each time and will hardly become cloudy the third time. This is enough or all the starch will be gone and the rice will not be sticky.

Cook rice in rice cooker. When cooked, add mirin and rice vinegar and mix to coat. Do not allow to cool too much. Remove wrappers from their container and open very carefully. Cradle one wrapper in your left hand and scoop a little rice at a time into the pocket. Press down gently with each small scoop of rice and then add more until pocket is full. Set aside and repeat four more times. Line bottom tier of bento with lettuce. Arrange inarizushi in tier, leaning at an angle. Grate carrot, arrange in nest shape in one side of top tier. Slice apple into rabbit shape, spray with water mixed with lemon juice to prevent browning. Place on carrot nest. Add sliced crab, raw broccoli florets and lemon slice to remaining space.

TURKEY WRAP BENTO

1 pre-made turkey wrap; handful raspberries; 4 grapes; 1 cherry tomato; 1 sprig parsley. 1-tier bento box.

Slice wrap in two.

Place slices into box, filling side up so the colorful ingredients can be seen.

Tuck grapes into the empty spaces.

Place raspberries in a silicone baking cup and tuck into space next to the wraps.

This is an easy way to make store-bought wraps more interesting to eat.

It also allows you to carry a portion of fruit with your lunch.

Experiment by filling tortillas with favorite ingredients to make your own wraps at home.

SEAWEED SALAD BENTO

5 shrimp; 1 slice lemon; sushi rice; umeboshi. For seaweed salad: 1 cup fresh seaweed of any type; 1 tbsp toasted sesame seed oil; 1 tsp dried hot chili pepper; 1/2 tbsp rice vinegar; pinch white sesame seeds for garnish. 2-tier bento box.

Make seaweed salad. Chop chili pepper as finely as possible then add 1 tsp to seaweed.

Toss seaweed in oil, pepper and rice vinegar. Let marinate overnight.

Cook rice. Pack into one tier of bento. Place umeboshi in center of rice.

Place grass divider into second tier of bento box, fill smaller section with seaweed salad.

Sprinkle with sesame seeds and garnish with lemon slice.

Boil shrimp and stack in the remaining section of bento.

TREE BENTO

1 cup rice; 1 nori sheet; 1 portion seaweed salad; 1/4 cup small fish roe. 1-tier circular bento box.

Cook rice and press into bento box, smoothing down with back of spoon or spatula to create flat surface. Nori will shrink a little if moist, so do not use very wet or hot rice.

Use scissors (dedicated to bento use) to cut out the shape of a tree trunk and branches. You can use a pattern, or just make it free form. Layer on top of the rice.

Layer fish roe on top of the rice and nori to create leaves. Layer on small amounts at a time to ensure that design looks delicate.

Place the seaweed salad at the base of the nori tree, lining up against the bottom edge of the bento to create grass.

SOUP BENTO

1 tsp instant dashi granules; 1 serving rice noodles; 2 imitation crab legs; 1 bean curd sheet; 1 scallion; 1 egg; 1 sprig cilantro. 1-tier bowl shaped bento with lid.

In soup it is best to have eggs medium boiled so they retain bright yellow color and are a little under cooked in the middle.

Take egg out of fridge and sit for a few minutes to bring to room temperature. Place pot on the stove and put in plenty of water. Bring to a boil. Place egg in the boiling water and boil for 7 minutes. When the 7 minutes are up, put egg in ice water immediately and allow to cool. Peel, slice into two.

Cook rice noodles. Put dashi granules in base of bento bowl, top with cooked rice noodles. Slice imitation crab leg at an angle and tuck into noodles at back of dish. Place egg pieces in front. Finely chop scallion and place next to egg. Tie bean curd sheet into knots and place at opposite side of dish. Slot fresh cilantro into gap between eggs and imitation crab. Before eating, add hot water and let sit for a few minutes to let flavors mingle.

BONFIRE BENTO

1 cup rice; 1 nori sheet; 1 portion seaweed salad; 1/4 cup small fish roe; 1 tsp toasted white sesame seeds. 1-tier circular bento box.

Cook rice and press into bento box. Arrange seaweed salad at base of bento to create grass. Cut twig shapes from nori sheet. Arrange in a loose triangular pile with base resting on seaweed. Layer fish roe on top of nori and rice in dancing flame shapes. Lightly sprinkle sesame seeds above roe to create smoke trails.

1 daikon radish; 10 -15 pieces dried wakame; soy sauce; red gel food coloring; 1 cup sushi rice. 1-tier bento box.

Put the dried wakame in a bowl with some soy sauce and a little water to help it hydrate. Set aside.

Cut the daikon in half lengthwise. Use a vegetable peeler to shave off a wide thin strip of daikon. Wrap in paper towels and place a book or something flat and heavy on top. The idea is to squeeze out as much moisture as possible.

Cook rice and layer into bento. Top with daikon strip.

Using gel food coloring, dip in a small paintbrush and paint the shading of your painting first. You are doing this painting backwards so you may want to sketch out the design on paper beforehand. Use pictures of Japanese paintings for inspiration. This design features Mount Fuji.

Pick up your hydrated wakame on piece at a time and put it on your daikon as 'brush strokes'. Let sit for about 20 minutes before you finish packing your bento. The design will hold easily till lunch time and you can lift off your daikon painting to reveal moist flavorful rice. You can eat your painting too if you wish. The seasoned seaweed and daikon is very nice.

This would be a good snack or side dish. The daikon keeps the rice moist and ever so slightly flavored.

BEEF ROLL BENTO

1 cup rice; 2 carrot slices; 6 pieces gari; 2 lettuce leaves. For beef and scallion roll ups: 2 tbsp soy sauce; 2 tbsp black vinegar; 1 tsp sugar substitute; gari; 1/2 cup rice wine; 6 very thin slices of lean beef; 3 scallions. 1-tier bento box.

Make beef rolls. Layer the beef into a shallow dish. Add the soy sauce, vinegar, a small piece of gari and sugar substitute. Cover with wine and let marinate for an hour.

When the marinating is done, take beef out and pat dry with a paper towel.

Wrap around the scallion vertically (like a taquito). Squeeze slightly so it sticks. Pan fry with just a touch of oil or put grill until cooked.

Slice the beef on the bias into 2" long pieces so the scallion will show through. Cool.

Cook rice, shape into two onigiri using mold. Line bento box with lettuce and place onigiri at one side. Top with carrot slices cut into star and moon shapes using cookie cutter. Layer into bento. Because this is a strong dish, pair it with more gari. Gather pieces together in a flower shape and tuck in.

SARDINE BENTO

1 leaf lettuce; 2 slices carrot; 2 slices daikon; ginger dressing; serving sliced water chestnuts; serving marinated bamboo shoots; 1/2 cup rice; 1 sardine; soy sauce; few slices gari; 1 tsp marinated wakame. 2 tier bento box.

Cook rice, pan fry sardine and brush with soy sauce, add to one tier with gari wakame. Fill second tier with salad, chestnuts and bamboo shoots.

PEPPER VARIATION

See ingredients list from Sardine Bento, replace 1 sardine with 1 Italian sweet pepper, 1 slice mozzarella; 5 pitted black olives. 2 tier bento box.

Prepare as in Sardine Bento (left). Chop pepper lengthways into two pieces, de-seed. Grill until soft. Chop olives; stuff one pepper piece with olives and cheese, return to grill so cheese melts. Replace pepper lid, place on rice.

SHRIMP AND EGG BENTO

1/2 cup rice; pinch toasted black sesame seeds; 1/2 sweet potato; 2 eggs; 1 tbsp flour; oil for frying; 4 florets broccoli; serving shrimp; pinch ground white pepper; 1 tsp corn starch; 1 scallion; pinch salt. 1-tier bento box.

Cook rice. Place in right third of bento and garnish with sesame seeds.

Cut sweet potato into thin slices. Heat frying oil in a small pot. Beat 1 egg, 1/2 cup iced water, and flour in a bowl. Dip sweet potato slices into egg batter and deep-fry. Remove sweet potato from heat when coating turns crispy.

Blanch broccoli. Shell and clean shrimp, season with white pepper and corn starch. Beat 1 egg and mix with scallions and salt. Heat cooking oil in a frying pan over medium high heat.

Stir-fry shrimp until they turn pink. Pour in egg and diced scallion and stir-fry.

Place shrimp and egg into a triangular divider cup on the left side of box.

Fill remaining gap with sweet potatoes.

TOFU VARIATION

1/2 cup rice; pinch toasted black sesame seeds; 1/2 sweet potato; 2 eggs; 1 tbsp flour; oil for frying; 4 florets broccoli; 1/2 packet tofu; pinch ground white pepper; 1 tsp corn starch; 1 scallion; pinch salt. 1-tier bento box.

Prepare as in Shrimp and Egg Bento (left). Chop tofu into bite-size chunks. Beat 1 egg, mix with scallions and salt. Stir-fry tofu. Pour in egg and diced scallion and stir-fry. Place tofu and egg into a cup on left side of box.

KOREAN BEEF BENTO

1/2 cup rice; 1/2 medium carrot; 1 handful bean sprouts; 2 handfuls spinach; 5 oz beef; 1 tbsp Korean barbecue sauce; sesame oil; pinch salt; 1 tsp gochujang; dash sugar; pinch white sesame seeds; cooking oil. 1-tier bento box.

Cook rice and spread evenly in base of bento box. Bring a small pot of salted water to boil. Blanch julienned carrots, bean sprouts, and spinach. Drain vegetables. Season with a dash of sesame oil and salt.

Marinate thinly sliced beef with Korean barbecue sauce for ten minutes. Heat cooking oil in a frying pan over medium high heat. Stir-fry beef until cooked through. Mix gochujang with a dash of sugar and a few drops of water. Pack top half of bento box with beef. Fill bottom half of bento box with evenly proportioned vegetables.

Spoon gochujang mixture over center. Scatter white sesame seeds over gochujang.

CHECKED BENTO

1/2 cup rice; pinch toasted white sesame seeds; 1 tsp sakura denbu; 1/2 sweet potato; 1 tsp honey; handful asparagus tips; 2 frozen mini burgers; 1 cube cheddar; 1/2 tsp chopped parsley; olive oil; pinch salt; pinch pepper; 1 apple; 1/2 cup lemon Juice. 1-tier bento box with divider.

Cook rice and place in half of box. Sprinkle sesame seeds and sakura denbu over rice. Preheat oven to medium heat. Line a baking tray with tin foil brushed lightly with olive oil.

Cut sweet potato and asparagus into bite-size pieces.

Place sweet potatoes in baking tray. Bake for 35 minutes.

Thaw burgers in microwave. Sprinkle grated cheddar and parsley over burgers.

Remove sweet potatoes and baking tray from oven.

Drizzle honey over sweet potatoes.

Add seasoned asparagus and burgers to baking tray.

Return to oven and bake for 10 more minutes.

Slice apple; coat pieces in lemon juice to prevent browning.

Fill space in bento with burgers, asparagus, sweet potatoes, and apple slices. Alternate sweet potato cubes to show skin and flesh in checked pattern.

DANDELION BENTO

1 eggplant; 3 carrot slices; 2 lychee; serving crushed pineapple; handful grapes; cooked white rice; handful salad greens; 1 sheet nori. For jungle curry: 1/4 cup May Ploy green curry paste; 1 cup coconut milk; 1 lb chicken breast; 1 green bell pepper; 1/2 cup bamboo shoots; 1/2 onion; 1 cup pineapple chunks; 1 cup pineapple juice; 1 tsp corn starch. 2-tier bento box.

Make jungle curry: stir-fry May Ploy green curry paste in 1/2 cup coconut milk until fragrant. Add another 1/2 cup coconut milk and diced chicken breast. Cook until chicken is done.

Add diced green bell pepper, bamboo shoots, diced onion, pineapple chunks and pineapple juice. Cook until bell pepper turns bright green. Thicken with corn starch.

Cook rice, place in left half bottom tier and fill the remaining space with curry.

Cut flower shapes from carrot slices using cookie cutter.

Use salad greens to create a plant stalk in between the rice and curry. Add carrot flowers to make a Dandelion. Decorate the rice with small star shapes cut from nori.

Bake eggplant. Fill one section of top tier with eggplant; garnish with leftover carrot rounds.

Fill top section with pitted lychee and the section below this with pineapple. Fill the last section with halved grapes.

CUTE BENTO

1/2 small cucumber; 1 mini orange bell pepper; 2 cherry tomatoes; handful fresh blueberries; 2 lychees; serving leftover curry; 1/2 cup rice; 3 carrot slices; 1 scallion; 1 sprig celery leaves; pinch black sesame seeds. 2-tier bento box.

Divide the top tier of bento with a side dish container. Slice cucumber, tomatoes and bell pepper, keep cap of bell pepper to one side.

Arrange salad ingredients in bento according to color. In the other half of top tier, place blueberries and lychees; fill the pitted lychees with blueberries.

Fill 2/3 of bottom bento tier with rice and the remaining space with curry. Place a sprig of celery leaves at the division to decorate.

Use a small flower shaped cookie cutter to make carrot flowers. Cut scallion on the diagonal to make leaves for the flowers.

Make a miniature pumpkin out of the bell pepper cap. Use a small paring knife to pierce the pepper skin and insert black sesame seeds to make eyes. Place above flowers in the rice.

CUTE VARIATION

See ingredients list from Cute Bento, replace serving leftover curry with 6 prawns; 1/2 yellow pepper; 1 clove garlic; 1 chili; 1/2 lemon; 1 mini orange bell pepper; 1 celery stalk. 2-tier bento box.

Chop chili, remove seeds. Mix with lemon and crushed garlic. Marinate prawns in mixture for 30 minutes. Stir-fry prawns until pink; add chopped bell pepper and thinly sliced celery stalk. Once cooked, place in bento box next to rice. Use bell pepper cap to make another miniature pumpkin garnish.

BELOW RIGHT: 1/2 cup rice; 1 onion; handful green peas; 1 tsp curry powder; 1 tsp ground cinnamon; 1 tsp ground turmeric; 1/4 can mixed beans; 1 egg; ketchup; 2 cherry tomatoes; olive oil; balsamic vinegar; 1 sprig parsley; pinch salt; pinch pepper; 1 granny smith apple; 1 tbsp lemon juice.

Cook rice and allow to cool.

Heat oil in a large frying pan over medium high heat. Sauté chopped onions until fragrant.

Add rice, green peas, curry powder, cinnamon, and turmeric to pan; stir vigorously.

Place fried rice into bento box, leaving space on the left for beans and apple.

Heat a non-stick frying pan over medium heat. Whisk egg; add to frying pan and spread out into a thin crepe.

Cover fried rice with egg crepe. Write or draw desired message on egg with ketchup.

Cook beans in boiling water. Marinate beans and sliced tomato halves with olive oil, balsamic vinegar, chopped parsley, salt, and pepper.

Fill top left corner of bento box with a small cup of bean-tomato salad.

Slice apple and toss with lemon juice to prevent browning.

Fill bottom left corner of bento box with apple slices.

SEAWEED SQUARE BENTO

1/2 cup rice; 1 sheet nori; 3 chicken thighs; 1 scallion; 1 egg; cooking oil; 1 dried red chili pepper; 1 tsp mirin; dash vinegar; soy sauce; pinch sugar; 1 thick slice cucumber; La-yu (chili oil); sesame oil; 1 cherry tomato. 1-tier bento box.

Cook rice. Fill bento box with cooked rice, leaving a gap on both sides. Place a sheet of nori over rice. Cut chicken thighs and scallion into bite-size pieces.

Heat oil in a frying pan over medium high heat. Stir-fry scallion and chicken briefly until slightly browned.

Place chicken, hard boiled egg, chopped chili pepper, mirin, vinegar, soy sauce, sugar, and water into a small pot. Simmer for 25 minutes, stirring occasionally.

Add scallion to pot and cook for five more minutes. Fill left side of bento box with chicken, scallions, and sliced egg. Break cucumber into bite-size pieces with a rolling pin.

Toss cucumber pieces with la-yu and sesame oil. Place cucumber into a small divider cup in the remaining space in bento box. Fill space with cherry tomato.

CHILI BEAN BENTO

RIGHT: 1/2 cup rice; 1 egg; serving green beans; 1 tsp crushed walnuts; soy sauce; 1 tsp honey; cooking oil; serving ground pork; 1 clove garlic; 1 tsp mirin; 1 tsp miso paste; pinch sugar; 1/4 cup chili bean sauce. 1 tier bento box.

Cook rice; spread out evenly in bento box. Make scrambled egg in a frying pan over medium high heat. Top and tail green beans, cook in a pot of salted boiling water. Toss cooked green beans with crushed walnuts, soy sauce, and honey.

Mix water, mirin, miso paste, sugar, and chili bean sauce. Heat oil in a frying pan over medium high heat. Add ground pork and minced garlic. Add mirin mixture to pan when pork has browned. Continue cooking until pork is done. Arrange scrambled egg, green beans, and ground pork over rice, with each dish taking up a third of the space.

DAIKON BENTO

1/2 cup rice; pink gel food coloring; 1 scallion; 1 daikon; 11 frozen edamame beans; 1/4 cup seaweed salad. 1-tier bento box.

Cook rice, add a few drops gel food coloring to water to dye pink.

Place rice in bento box, smoothing surface with back of spoon or spatula.

Carefully make a slit down one side of scallion, stop cutting 1/2 inch from base.

Ensure that knife cuts through only one layer of scallion.

Pull this top layer away from the rest of scallion to create 'branch' shape. Rest on top of rice.

Cut flower shapes from daikon using cookie-cutter.

Place daikon flowers across scallion 'branch'. Dying the rice pink means that the pale daikon flowers stand out.

Seaweed salad makes beautiful tasty 'grass', place this at the base of the bento box, draping over scallion base.

The seaweed salad can be mixed into the rice when the bento is eaten for a little extra flavor.

Frozen edamame are pre-shelled for convenience. Take out 11 from packet and sit in some warm water until they thaw. Skewer edamame onto toothpicks and place at base of bento.

BBQ CHICKEN BENTO

1/2 cup rice; 1 diced chicken thigh; 1 tbsp barbecue sauce; 3 shrimp; 1 quail's egg; 7 pieces gari; 2 broccoli florets; 1 piece leftover tamagoyaki (omelette); dried wakame; red gel food coloring; pinch black sesame seeds. 2-tier bento box.

Cook chicken in a skillet with barbecue sauce thinned with water.

Boil shrimp; steam broccoli.

Boil quail's egg. Cut top of egg off, scoop out a little yolk and stuff with one piece gari.

Place shrimp, tamagoyaki, broccoli and stuffed egg in a side dish and place in right side of top tier of bento box.

Place barbecue chicken in left side of top tier of bento box.

Cook rice and place in bottom tier of bento, spread out and flatten surface with back of spoon or spatula. Allow to cool.

Take dried wakame and place in a little dish of water.

When wakame is hydrated it will be soft and malleable.

Remove from dish with tweezers and place on rice.

The wakame will look like brush strokes. Arrange in branch shape.

Take wide pieces of gari and press between paper towels with a weight on

top to squeeze out liquid. When the gari has had moisture removed, use flower vegetable cutter to cut into blossom shapes.

Using gel food coloring, tip the edges of the gari to create more contrast.

Place gari flowers next to branches on top of rice and then add black sesame seeds to the center of flowers.

Carry bento carefully and the pattern should remain in place in transport When ready to eat bento, break up the painting and stir the ingredients into the rice to add taste.

BBQ RIBS BENTO

1/2 cup rice; deli-bought barbecued ribs; 3 shrimp; 1 quail's egg; 7 pieces gari; 2 broccoli florets; 1 piece leftover tamagoyaki (omelette); dried wakame; red gel food coloring; pinch black sesame seeds. 2-tier bento box.

Prepare as in BBQ Chicken Bento recipe, replacing barbecued chicken with barbecued ribs.

Cut gari using star-shaped vegetable cutter. Place on rice with wakame tails to create 'shooting star' pattern.

NOODLE BENTO

1 portion leftover peppered sirloin steak; 1 lettuce leaf; serving angel hair pasta; 1 tbsp butter; 1 clove garlic; 1 floret broccoli, 1/2 carrot; 1 floret cauliflower; 2 tbsp Italian salad dressing; 4 slices muenster cheese; 1 mini carrot; dash lemon juice; pinch pepper. 1-tier bento box.

Cook angel hair pasta. Drain. In a large pan, melt butter over medium heat. Add fresh minced garlic. Add pasta. Splash with fresh lemon juice.

Make broccoli slaw. Combine grated broccoli, carrot and cauliflower. Add your favorite Italian dressing. Refrigerate for an hour.

Place two side-dish cups into the main container and fill the remaining space with buttered noodles. Stick a carrot upright into the center. Sprinkle with ground black pepper.

Slice steak and place in left cup, garnish with lettuce. In the right cup, place slaw; layer cheese slices on top.

THREE ONIGIRI BENTO

1 cup rice; sakura denbu coating; 1 strip spicy flavored nori; umeboshi; 1/4 avocado; 1/4 cup fish roe. 1-tier bento box.

Onigiri can be sweet or savory. Wet a rice mold before filling with hot rice. Layer in rice, add a small amount of filling and top with more rice. Squeeze and then remove and let cool. Afterwards you can roll or wrap with various ingredients. In the three flavored onigiri shown here, the pink onigiri is unstuffed because the sakura denbu coating is so flavorful.

Sakura denbu powder is made with ground seasoned codfish, sugar and other sweet and delicate flavors. Sakura is Japanese for cherry blossom and refers to the color of this seasoning.

The white onigiri has an umeboshi (pitted) inside and is wrapped with a small strip of spicy flavored nori. The orange onigiri is filled with avocado and rolled in fish roe.

SOUP AND TOFU BENTO

1 portion leftover beef; 1/2 cup rice noodles; 1 scallion; 1/2 block of tofu (not silken); 1 tbsp instant dashi; 1 tbsp soy sauce; 1 tsp granulated sugar substitute; 1 tbsp water; 1 octodog; 1 serving Japanese style pickled cucumber; 1 slice carrot, 1 lettuce leaf, 1 broccoli floret. 2-tier bento box, with bowl.

Place tofu in a small pot; cover with water. Add dashi granules; simmer for 20 minutes. Remove and pat dry. Pan fry in skillet sprayed with cooking spray on high heat till edges are crispy. Turn with tongs to make sure all edges are crispy. Remove from heat and brush with soy sauce mixed with sugar substitute and one tablespoon water.

Wrap tofu in several paper towels. Place tofu in baking pan. Put a heavy book on top and a few heavy cans of soup or something similar on top. Put in the refrigerator for 4 hours. Remove, change paper towels and repeat.After the process is complete, freeze overnight and then thaw. You will find the texture of the tofu has changed greatly. This sort of tofu is wonderful for stir-fries, to grill, or put in salads.

Put dashi in base of soup bowl, cook rice noodles and place on top. Add leftover beef, chop scallion and sprinkle on top of beef. Before eating, add hot water to bowl and let sit for a few minutes. Line one side of other tier with lettuce, tofu triangles, and broccoli. Top with octodog. Fill remaining space with pickled cucumber. Cut carrot slice into flower shape to garnish.

OCTODOGS VARIATION

See ingredients list from Soup and Tofu Bento. Replace 1 portion leftover beef with 2 octodogs. To create octodog: 1 hot dog; 2 black sesame seeds. 2-tier bento box, with bowl.

Make 2 octodogs. Cut hot dog in half. Take one section at the rounded end and proceed to cut slits in the hot dog lengthwise, leaving a half inch gap at the rounded end.

Cut 4 slits through the hot dog at equal intervals so you have 8 'legs' dangling down.

Boil the hot dog till the legs spread and the hot dog is cooked through. Take out and cool.

With the knife put two very tiny shallow slits in your octodog for eyes. Using tweezers, slide a black sesame seed into each slit.

Octodogs look best in bento slightly reclining against the wall of the bento.

Prepare bento as in Soup and Tofu Bento recipe.

In soup bowl, chop scallion and sprinkle at one edge of bowl. Recline 2 octodogs against wall, resting them on the scallion.

303

GINGER PORK BENTO

1 tbsp grated ginger; 1 piece round pork; pinch white pepper; 1 tsp mirin; soy sauce; cooking oil; 1/2 cup short grain rice; dashi stock; 3 scallions; 1 eggplant; 1 daikon; 1 tbsp chili bean sauce; 1 tsp sugar; dash rice vinegar; 3 broccoli florets; 1 cherry tomato; 1 prune. 1-tier bento box.

Marinate pork with pepper, mirin, soy sauce, and grated ginger for ten

CHIVE PANCAKE BENTO

1/2 cup rice; 1 tsp toasted white sesame seeds; 2 chicken thighs; 1 tsp mirin; pinch salt; pinch ground white pepper; 1 clove garlic; 4 leaves Chinese cabbage; 1 carrot; 1 onion; gochujang; 1 tsp sugar; sesame oil; soy sauce; cooking oil; handful chives; 1 tbsp flour; pinch salt; 1 egg; handful bean sprouts. 1-tier bento box.

Cook rice and place in one half of bento; garnish with sesame seeds. Chop chicken into bite-size pieces. Marinate with mirin, salt, white pepper, and half a clove minced garlic for ten minutes. Mix

chicken with gochujang, sugar, sesame oil, soy sauce, and more minced garlic. Thinly slice carrot and onion. Stir-fry chicken, onion, and carrot until cooked. Add cabbage to pan and cook until wilted. Place in top half of remaining space in bento box.

Chop chives into an even length. Mix flour, water, salt, and egg. Line chives evenly in pan, cover with batter. Turn chive pancake over and cook until it turns golden. Cut into even slices. Blanch bean sprouts; toss with sesame oil and salt. Place into a small divider cup in corner of bento box. Fill space with slices of chive pancake.

minutes. Heat cooking oil in a frying pan over medium high heat. Stir-fry pork until it is thoroughly cooked.

Add one half of pork to rice. Cook rice and pork in rice cooker, substituting water with dashi stock. Mix rice with chopped scallions when it is done.

Fill one half of bento box with rice. Chop eggplant and daikon into bite-size pieces.

Mix chili bean sauce, sugar, vinegar, and soy sauce in a small bowl.

Heat oil in a frying pan over medium high heat.

Stir-fry eggplant and daikon until both turn tender. Stir in sauce mix and cook until it thickens.

Place eggplant and daikon in a triangular divider cup next to the rice. Blanch broccoli.

Cut prune into thin slices.

Fill remaining space in bento with broccoli, tomato, and prune slices.

GROUND PORK BENTO

1/2 cup short grain rice; 2 shallots; 1 clove garlic; portion ground pork; cooking oil; 1 egg; 1 cinnamon stick; 1 star anise; soy sauce; 1 tsp rock sugar; 2 scallions; 1 broccoli floret; 1 cherry tomato; 5 red grapes; 1 apple; dash lemon juice. 1-tier bento box.

Cook rice and place in one section of bento. Finely chop shallots and garlic. Sauté until fragrant. Add ground pork to pan and stir-fry until it browns.

Transfer shallots, garlic, and pork to a pot. Add hard-boiled egg, cinnamon, anise, soy sauce, sugar, and water. Simmer over low heat for 30 minutes.

Spoon pork mixture onto rice. Sprinkle chopped scallions over pork. Slice hard-boiled egg and arrange one half in a divider cup.

Slice apple in rabbit shape and toss with lemon juice to prevent browning. Fill remaining space in bento box with grapes, tomato, and apple.

305

Portion pink soba noodles; wasabi furikake; 3 dill pickles. For Spanish omelette: 3 large potatoes; 7 oz cooked ham; 4 oz frozen peas; 2 oz oak smoked tomatoes; 4 eggs; salt and pepper; slice cheddar cheese. 1-tier bento box.

Prepare omelette. Peel potatoes and slice thinly. Wash to remove starch; fry very lightly in olive oil to ensure potato is slightly sealed. Remove to a microwave dish, cover and cook until tender. Whisk eggs and add the chopped ham, tomatoes and peas. Mix. Add the hot potatoes to the egg, mix again, return to pan. Once bottom of the omelette is well set, grate some cheddar cheese onto it and put in oven on a low temperature until set. Remove, leave to stand for a few minutes and slice. This will make around four large bento portions, pack one into bento. Cook soba noodles; arrange in bento with a sprinkling of wasabi furikake. Add your dill pickles to a food dish and nestle this in the remaining space, adding a food pick.

OMELETTE BENTO

1/2 cup short grain rice; 1 sheet nori; sprinkling shiso furikake; 2 1/2 oz shredded crab meat; 1 egg; 2 scallions; 2 small carrots; pinch ground white pepper; 1/2 tbsp Chinese oyster sauce; 1 tsp sugar; 1/2 tbsp water; 1/2 tsp corn starch; 7 red grapes; 1 apple; dash lemon juice. 1-tier bento box.

Cook rice and place into bento box, leaving space on right for fruits. Sprinkle shiso furikake over rice and place a strip of nori over right side.
Julienne and blanch carrots. Beat egg

lightly in a bowl. Add crab meat, finely chopped scallions, carrots, and ground white pepper. Spoon egg mixture into frying pan and make a 1/2 inch thick patty. Cook omelette until both sides are nicely browned. Remove from heat and quarter.

Mix oyster sauce, sugar, water, and corn starch in a small bowl. Add mixture to the frying pan and heat until thickened. Place two of the omelette slices on top of the rice. Spoon oyster sauce glaze over omelette. Slice apple and toss with lemon juice to prevent browning. Fill remaining space with apple slices and red grapes.

SPAGHETTINI BENTO

RIGHT: 1 portion spaghettini ; 1 small onion; 1/2 green pepper; 2 wieners; cooking oil; pinch salt; pinch pepper; 1 tbsp ketchup; salad greens; 2 cherry tomatoes; 1 wedge orange; sprinkling parmesan cheese; 2 cubes cheese. 1-tier bento box.

Cook spaghettini in a pot of boiling water. Remove spaghettini from heat; drain well. Finely slice onion and green pepper. Slice wieners.

Heat oil in a frying pan over medium heat. Sauté onion and green pepper. Add sliced wieners to pan. Add spaghettini to pan and stir thoroughly. Season with salt, pepper, and ketchup.

Fill bento box with pasta, sprinkle on parmesan. Leave space for salad. Arrange salad greens and tomatoes in a small plastic cup.

Place cup into the top right corner of bento box. Fill remaining space with orange slices and cheese cubes.

SAUSAGES BENTO

LEFT: 1/2 cup short grain rice; pinch toasted black sesame seeds; 2 potatoes; 3 baby carrots; cooking oil; dashi stock; 1 tsp mirin; soy sauce; 1 tsp sugar; sesame oil; 6 sugar snap peas; portion cabbage; 2 Italian sausages; 1 tbsp tomato sauce; pinch pepper. 1-tier bento box.

Cook rice, place in one half of bento; garnish with sesame seeds. Cut potatoes into bite-size pieces. Heat cooking oil in a pot over medium high heat. Sauté potatoes and baby carrots

briefly. Add dashi, mirin, soy sauce, sugar, and sesame oil and bring to boil. Reduce to medium heat and let simmer over low heat until potatoes are tender. Add peas and simmer for 5 minutes. Fill a triangular divider cup with potato, carrots, and peas. Place divider next to rice, leaving space on the left.

Chop and blanch cabbage. Slice Italian sausages. Heat cooking oil in a frying pan over medium high heat.

Stir-fry sausages and season with tomato sauce and pepper. Fill remaining space in bento with cabbage and sausages.

ABURAAGE BENTO

1 leftover stuffed aburaage; 1/4 cup brown; 1/4 cup white rice; 1 stalk asparagus; serving pickled cucumbers; 1 piece takuan; 1 tbsp pickled eggplant; handful fresh raspberries. 1-tier bento box.

Take leftover stuffed aburaage that has been refrigerated, slice into pieces.

Cook brown and white rice, mix. Place in half of one section of bento box.

Place slices of stuffed aburaage next to rice.

Steam asparagus and cut diagonally, tuck next to rice and stuffed aburaage.

Slice takuan into strips; arrange with pickled eggplant.

Wash raspberries and fill separated section of bento box, or keep separate by placing in a paper or silicone cupcake cup.

SALMON BENTO

1 small fillet salmon; 1 tbsp wasabi furikake; 3 romaine lettuce leaves; 1/4 cucumber; 1/4 carrot; French salad dressing. 1-tier bento box.

Grill salmon until cooked, remove from grill and coat with olive oil. Roll in furikake.

Chop lettuce and add to box. Lay salmon filet onto one side of the salad.

Slice cucumber into thin slices.

Carefully layer cucumber slices over lettuce to one side of salmon.

Cut carrot into three thin slices.

Use a veggie cutter to create carrot flowers. Place flowers onto cucumber.

Decant small amount of dressing into mini sauce bottle and pack with bento.

MEAT LOAF VARIATION

1 cooked meat loaf; 1/4 cup brown; 1/4 cup white rice; 1 stalk asparagus; serving pickled cucumbers; 1 piece takuan; 1 tbsp pickled eggplant; handful fresh raspberries. 1-tier bento box.

Take leftover meat loaf that has been refrigerated, slice into pieces. Prepare bento as in Aburaage Bento (above).

YUMMY SHRIMP BENTO

1 portion leftover vegetable stir-fry; portion yaki soba noodles; 4 slices mozzarella; handful salad greens; 2 slices green bell pepper; 1 small piece nori; 1/2 cup rice; 1/2 cup broccoli; 1 mini carrot; sprinkling black sesame seeds; 2 frozen cooked tempura shrimp; 1 tsp crushed sesame seeds; pinch salt; 1 clove garlic. For sauce: 2 tbsp tomato sauce, 2 tbsp Worcestershire sauce, 1 tbsp fish stock, 1 tbsp soy sauce, 1 tbsp honey. 2-tier bento box.

Cook yaki soba noodles and drain. Mix ingredients for sauce. Stir-fry noodles with a little oil, minced garlic and sauce. Fill half top tier with noodles and the other half with vegetable stir-fry. Arrange stir-fry to form fan-like pattern. Line bottom edge of tier with salad greens; place bell pepper slices to make flower stems. Cut mozzarella into flower shapes and place. Use a little cut nori to accent the flowers. Pack rice to one side of bottom tier form a diagonal edge across the box. Arrange shrimp at left. Fill remaining space with broccoli; sprinkle with crushed sesame and salt mix. Insert mini carrot upright into the rice and sprinkle with black sesame seeds.

YUMMY VARIATION

See ingredients list from Yummy Shrimp Bento, replace frozen shrimp with 4 frozen cooked tempura chicken pieces. 2-tier bento box.

Prepare bento as above, arrange chicken on rice in place of prawns.

TACO BENTO

Portion leftover taco meat (ground beef seasoned with taco mix); 1/4 cup salsa; 6 cherry tomatoes; 1/2 cup shredded cheddar; 1/2 cup shredded lettuce; 1 tbsp sour cream; 2 slices provolone cheese; 2 slices deli turkey; 5 cucumber slices; 2-tier bento box.

Roll the provolone and turkey into burrito shapes. Place diagonally in one tier of box.

Fill top left with cucumber slices and place three cherry tomatoes at bottom right.

Place taco meat in bottom third of second tier.

Chop remaining tomatoes and mix with salsa.

Layer salsa with tomatoes, shredded cheddar and lettuce covered with sour cream in remaining space in tier, arranging in strips.

MOZZARELLA STAR BENTO

Leftover pizza; slice mozzarella cheese; 3 black olives; 6 snap peas; 2 black sesame seeds; 2 lychees; handful blueberries; handful spinach; 2 cherry tomatoes; 1 tbsp salad dressing. 2-tier bento box.

Cut pizza into a square and place in box. Garnish with blanched and diced snap peas along one side.

Chop black olives and use to decorate pizza.

Make a star with mozzarella cheese. Use pea to form the nose and black sesame seeds for eyes.

Separate bottom tier into two parts using a divider. In one half arrange the lychee and blueberries.

In the other, arrange spinach and halved tomatoes. Add salad dressing.

TWIRLS BENTO

2 small flour tortillas; 2 ham slices; 2 turkey slices; handful spinach leaves; 1 Laughing Cow light Swiss cheese wedge; 6 black olives; 4 carrot sticks. 1-tier bento box.

Lay tortillas flat.

Spread cheese on.

Layer ham, turkey, spinach leaves on top.

Roll up and cut each tortilla into four even pieces.

Place rolls into bento box, stacking them to show the filling.

Add carrot sticks to end pieces.

Fill center of box with olives.

TWIRLS VARIATION

2 small flour tortillas; 2 smoked salmon slices; 1 scallion; 1 Laughing Cow light Swiss cheese wedge; 6 olives; 1/2 avocado. 1-tier bento box.

Lay tortillas flat. Spread cheese on. Layer smoked salmon and chopped scallion on top.

Roll up and cut each tortilla into four even pieces. Place rolls into bento box.

Add sliced avocado to end pieces. Fill gap with olives.

SHISO BENTO

7 oz cooked rice; 3 Shiso perilla; dried bonito flakes; sesame oil; 2 small tomato; 1 tsp white sesame seeds; 1 oz chicken breast; bread crumbs; 1 oz spinach; 1 tbsp soy sauce; flour; pinch salt; 1/2 egg; pinch pepper; lettuce. 1-tier bento box.

Gently stir cooked rice with dried bonito flakes and soy sauce. Make 3 onigiri. Stir-fry onigiri. Brush top of onigiri with soy sauce; turn. Brush other side with soy sauce. Repeat several times. Wrap shiso perilla around onigiri. Put into bento box. Blanch spinach; cut into bite-size pieces. Season with sesame oil, pepper and salt. Sprinkle with sesame seeds. Put into small bowl and tuck into box. Cut chicken into bite-size pieces, season and coat in flour. Dip in beaten 1/2 egg. Put bread crumbs on chicken and pat well. Fry in hot oil until browned. Cut in half. Add fried chicken, tomato and spinach to box.

SANDWICH BENTO

2 slices sandwich bread; broccoli; 1 slice lettuce; pinch pepper; 1 egg; handful grapes; 1 eggplant; 1 fish sausage; 1/4 small tomato; frozen croquette; mentsuyu; 1/4 cheese slice; mayonnaise. 1-tier bento box.

Dilute mentsuyu with water, cook. Hard boil egg, chop and stir with mayo, season. Place with lettuce in buttered bread and quarter. Boil broccoli. Cut eggplant and deep fry then marinade in mentsuyu. Wrap fish sausage with cheese. Place in box, slot in croquette.

SALMON AVOCADO BENTO

1/2 cup short grain rice; 1 slice nori; 1 egg; 1 piece smoked salmon; 1 avocado; 1 piece pickled daikon; rice vinegara dash salt; lemon juice. 1-tier bento box.

Cook rice in rice cooker. Add a drizzle of vinegar and a dash of salt to rice when it is done.

Stir rice with a spatula and fan vigorously to remove excess moisture.

Spread rice out evenly in bento box. Shred nori; place on top of rice. Heat a non-stick frying pan over medium heat.

Beat egg and add to frying pan; spread out into a thin crepe.

When cooked, cut egg into fine shreds and scatter it over seaweed.

Cut smoked salmon and avocado into bite-sized chunks. Toss avocado with lemon juice to prevent browning.

Cut pickled daikon into diamond-shaped pieces.

Scatter smoked salmon, avocado, and pickled daikon evenly over bed of rice.

ITALIAN VARIATION

See ingredients list from Salmon Avocado Bento (left), replace 1 piece smoked salmon; 1 avocado; 1 piece pickled daikon; lemon juice with 1/2 pepperoni sausage; 1/2 green pepper. 1-tier bento box.

Prepare bento as in Salmon Avocado Bento recipe. Cut pepperoni and pepper into bite-sized chunks. Lightly fry pepper to soften.

Scatter pepperoni and pepper evenly over eggs and nori on bed of rice.

MINI BURGER BENTO

1/2 cup rice; sprinkling sakura denbu; 4 frozen mini burgers; 1 asparagus spear; 1 egg; pinch salt; pinch pepper; cooking oil; 2 broccoli florets; 1 cherry tomato. 1-tier bento box.

Cook rice; fill half of bento box with cooked rice. Make a heart-shaped stencil with tin foil, place on rice. Scatter sakura denbu onto stencil and rice, to make pink heart. Bake mini burgers in oven. Arrange cooked mini burgers in a row in bento box. Chop asparagus into bite-sized pieces. Beat eggs in small bowl and season with salt and pepper. Heat oil in a frying pan over medium high heat. Add asparagus to pan and stir-fry. Add egg and stir-fry until egg is just done. Fill a plastic cup with asparagus omelette.

Place cup of omelette into bento box. Cook broccoli in a pot of boiling water. Fill remaining gaps in bento box with broccoli and cherry tomato.

POTATO SALAD BENTO

2 potatoes; 1 onion; 1 carrot; 1 cucumber; 1 egg; pinch salt; pinch pepper; 1 1/2 tsp mayonnaise; 2 slices sandwich bread; 1 lettuce leaf; 1 chicken breast; 1 tsp honey; 2 tbsp lemon juice; 1 egg; 12 tbsp cereal; 1 golden cherry tomato; 3 green grapes. 1-tier bento box.

Boil potatoes. Finely dice cooked potatoes; allow to cool thoroughly. Finely chop onion, carrot, cucumber, and hard-boiled egg. Mix with potatoes. Season potato salad with salt, pepper, and mayonnaise. Make sandwiches with potato salad and lettuce as filling. Arrange sandwiches in bento box.

Preheat oven to a high heat. Cut chicken breast into bite-size pieces; marinate with honey and lemon juice. Coat chicken pieces with egg and crushed cereal. Bake chicken in baking tray for 20 minutes. Fill remaining space in bento box with chicken pieces, cherry tomato, and grapes.

MISO PORK BENTO

Handful green beans; 3 carrot slices; umeboshi; 1/2 cup rice; 1 serving zaru soba noodles; 1 sheet momi nori. For miso pork: 2 pieces pork loin; 2 tsp miso; 1 tsp mirin; 1 tsp sake; 1 tsp sugar. 2-tier bento box.

Trim pork. Combine miso, mirin, sake, sugar and add to pork.

Place in a bag and put in fridge to marinate for 20-30 minutes or overnight.

Scrape off reserve marinade and broil or grill pork, brushing with marinade as needed. Slice.

Cook rice. Add to bento box and gently push to one side in a triangular shape to make room for the pork.

Place pork slices into box one at a time, arranging neatly.

Steam green beans, cut diagonally and stack in corner of bento box, next to the meat and rice.

Using vegetable cutters, make three carrot flowers.

Press umeboshi into rice.

Cook zaru soba noodles according to package directions.

Allow noodles to cool and add to second tier of bento box.

Sprinkle with momi nori (flavored, shredded nori).

MISO PORK VARIATION

See ingredients list from Miso Pork Bento (left), remove 1/2 cup rice and umeboshi. 1-tier bento box.

Prepare bento as in Miso Pork Bento recipe, replace rice in first tier of bento with zaru soba noodles. Sprinkle with momi nori. This makes for a lighter lunch, and the noodles compliment the miso pork just as well as the rice.

NIGIRI SUSHI BENTO

1 cup sushi rice; 1 dab wasabi paste; 5 raw shrimp; 2 inarizushi wrappers; 1 tbsp mirin; 2 tbsp rice vinegar; 6 small broccoli florets. 1-tier bento box.

Prepare nigiri sushi. Cook sushi rice. Make a small ball of still warm rice, and form into an oblong shape. Butterfly the shrimp and then skewer along the back with a thin bamboo skewer.

This holds the shrimp so that they remain straight as they are cooked. Boil shrimp.

After they are cooked, flatten out on a board, cover with plastic wrap and pound with a flat mallet. Pack rice together into 5 tight balls. Add a small dab of wasabi paste to taste and then lay the shrimp on top. Squeeze together gently and pack into bento.

Make inarizushi. Cook rice in rice cooker. When cooked, add mirin and rice vinegar and mix to coat. Do not allow to cool too much.

Remove wrappers from their container and open very carefully. Cradle one Inarizushi no moto wrapper in your left hand and scoop a little rice at a time into the pocket. Press down gently with each small scoop of rice and then add more until pocket is full.

Steam broccoli. Pack one inarizushi at each end of bento box.

Arrange nigiri sushi in center of box and fill in gaps with broccoli florets.

TONKATSU PORK BENTO

1/2 cup short grain rice; handful mixed salad greens; 1 tbsp soy sauce; 1 tbsp lemon juice; 1/4 can mixed beans; 1 tsp red wine vinegar; 1 tsp olive oil; sprig parsley; 1 pork chop; 1 tbsp flour; 1 egg; 2 tbsp Panko (Japanese bread crumbs); frying oil; 1 tsp mayonnaise; 1 tsp tonkatsu sauce; pinch salt; pinch pepper. 1-tier bento box.

Cook rice. Place cooked rice into three quarters of bento box and leave space on the left for salad and beans. Fill top left corner of box with a handful of torn salad greens.

Sprinkle salt and pepper over salad.

Make salad dressing by mixing soy sauce and lemon juice.

Insert dressing into mini sauce container and place next to salad greens.

Rinse beans and cook in boiling water. Marinate cooked beans with red wine vinegar, olive oil, chopped parsley, salt and pepper.

Fill bottom left corner with small cup of marinated beans.

Lightly beat egg. Coat pork chop with flour, egg, and bread crumbs.

Heat frying oil in a small pan and fry breaded pork chop.

Remove pork chop when meat is cooked and coating is crispy. Allow to rest for five minutes.

Slice pork chop and arrange slices on the bed of rice, placing so it sits centrally in bento box. Drizzle mayonnaise and tonkatsu sauce over pork chop.

FISH FILLET BENTO

2 frozen fish fillets; 1 whole grain bread roll; 1 lettuce leaf; 1 tomato; 1 tsp mayonnaise; 1 sweet potato; frying oil; 1 dash sugar; pinch black sesame seeds; 1 Granny Smith apple. 1-tier bento box, 1 side container.

Cook frozen fish fillets according to instructions.

Divide bread roll in half. Slice tomato into thin slices.

Fill sandwich with a fillet, tomato slices, and lettuce. Cut into two pieces.

Drizzle mayonnaise over sandwiches. Place sandwiches into bento box.

Cut sweet potato into thin fries. Heat frying oil in a small pan and fry sweet potato.

Remove fries from heat when they turn golden. Remove excess oil from fries with paper towel. Sprinkle a dash of sugar and black sesame seeds over fries.

Place fries into a small container. Serve with Granny Smith apple.

BURGER VARIATION

2 frozen burgers; 1 whole grain bread roll; 1 lettuce leaf; 1 tomato; 1 tsp ketchup; 1 tsp mustard; 1 sweet potato; frying oil; 1 dash sugar; pinch black sesame seeds; 1 Granny Smith apple. 1-tier bento box, 1 side container.

Cook burgers. Make fries and sandwiches as in Fish Fillet Bento (left), layering burgers with tomato and lettuce.

Drizzle mustard and ketchup over sandwiches instead of mayonnaise.

PORK BENTO

BELOW RIGHT: 1/2 cup short grain rice; pinch toasted black sesame seeds; 3 oz ground pork; 2 cremini mushrooms; 1/2 medium carrot; 1/4 onion; 1 clove of garlic; 1 1/2 tbsp mirin; 1 tbsp miso paste; 1/2 tbsp sugar; 1/2 tbsp chili bean sauce; cooking oil; 2 lettuce leaves; 1 papaya. 1-tier bento box.

Cook rice in rice cooker. Fill two thirds of the bento box with cooked rice.

Sprinkle black sesame seeds over rice.

Mix 1/3 cup water, mirin, miso paste, sugar, and chili bean sauce in a small bowl.

Heat oil in a frying pan over medium heat.

Add minced garlic, finely chopped onion, and diced carrot to frying pan and cook for a minute.

Add ground pork and break pork into fine pieces with spatula.

Add diced mushrooms when pork is almost done. Add miso and mix.

Remove from heat when sauce has thickened.

Line leftover space in bento box with lettuce, forming a cup.

Spoon pork mixture into lettuce cup.

Slice papaya into bite-size pieces.

Fill remaining space with papaya pieces.

DOTS AND STRIPES BENTO

1/2 cup short grain rice; 1/4 cup green peas; 1 potato; 1/2 onion; 1/2 carrot; 1/2 cucumber; 1 egg; pinch salt; pinch pepper; 1 tbsp mayonnaise; 3 sausages; 1 cup red cabbage; 1 tbsp red wine vinegar; cooking oil; sprig parsley. 1-tier bento box.

Cook rice. Fill one section of bento box with cooked rice. Create polka-dot pattern on rice by adding cooked green peas. Boil potatoes until thoroughly cooked and softened. Finely dice potatoes and let cool thoroughly.

Finely chop onion, carrot, cucumber, and hard-boiled egg.

Mix potatoes, onion, carrot, cucumber, and egg. Season potato salad with salt, pepper, and mayonnaise. Place into a small cup and arrange on top of rice.

Heat cooking oil in frying pan over medium high heat. Stir-fry sausages until cooked. Finely slice red cabbage. Stir-fry red cabbage and season with vinegar, salt, and pepper. Line remaining section of bento box with red cabbage. Arrange sausages in a row over red cabbage. Sprinkle parsley over sausages.

PATTIES BENTO

RIGHT: 1/2 cup short grain rice; umeboshi; 2 lettuce leaves; 2 oz ground pork; 2 oz ground beef; 1/2 onion; 1 egg; 1/4 cup milk; 1/2 cup bread crumbs; dash salt; dash pepper; cooking oil; demi-glaze mix; apple jui e; 1 sweet potato; 1 tbsp honey; pinch sesame seeds. 1-tier bento box.

Cook rice. Place in half of bento box; garnish with umeboshi. Line other half of bento box with lettuce. Finely chop onion and caramelize. Mix pork, beef, onion, egg, milk, bread crumbs, salt, and pepper. Knead briefly and form large patties. Heat oil in a frying pan over medium high heat. Cook hamburger until thoroughly done. Place onto bed of lettuce. Cook demi-glaze according to instructions, substituting water with apple juice. Spoon over hamburger. Cut sweet potato into bite-size pieces. Bake for 35 minutes. Drizzle with honey; bake for ten more minutes. Sprinkle with sesame seeds, place in space.

HOLIDAYS AND SPECIAL OCCASIONS BENTO

BENTO FOR TWO

To prepare two bentos (halve to make one): 1 1/2 cups of rice; red bean paste; 6 oz lamb steak; 4 frozen shumai; 4 slices cheddar cheese; 1 egg; 2 small carrots; 1/4 cup edamame beans; 1/2 sweet potato; 4 slices green zucchini; 2 grapes; 4 strawberries; 10 blueberries; 2 sprigs parsley; pinch salt; pinch black sesame seeds; decorative nori shapes; 2 strips nori; 2 tbsp canola oil; 1 tbsp sesame oil. For lamb marinade: 1 tbsp olive oil; 1 tbsp lemon juice, chopped sprig parsley; 3 chopped fresh mint leaves; salt; pepper. 2 2-tier bento boxes.

Cut lamb into cubes, place in plastic bag with yellow pepper. Marinade in fridge overnight.

Cook rice. Hard boil egg. Rinse with cool water, peel shell and place in heart shaped egg mold. Cut sweet potato into flower shapes, boil for two minutes, then add edamame; boil for additional five minutes. Remove from heat and strain. Salt if desired. Fry lamb pieces in canola oil until cooked through. Fry shumai in canola oil, pressing down with a spatula each time they are flipped to form into patties. Fry julienned carrots in sesame oil until slightly crispy. Sprinkle with sesame seeds; place in two small oval containers.

Form onigiri with molds (five triangle shaped, two stars) while rice is still hot. Sprinkle with salt. Place nori strips and decorative nori shapes on some of the onigiri, sprinkle sesame seeds on the others.

Remove egg from mold and cut in half. Position onigiris in bottom tiers of the bentos as shown. Place sweet potato and edamame around the onigiri, with a single piece of edamame in the center of each of the stars.

In the top tier, position lamb pieces to far right. Place cheese slices next to the lamb, and set the carrots on top of the cheese. Place two shumai and one egg slice in each bento next to the carrots. Fill remaining space with zucchini slices, chopped strawberries, blueberries and grapes. Fill in any gaps around the lamb with parsley sprigs.

1/2 cup rice; 2 sheets colored mamenori (soy-paper); 2 sugar snap peas; 2 miniature corn croquettes; 1 slice apple. For sesame carrots: 5 large carrots; 2 tbsp sesame oil; 1 tbsp sugar; 2 tbsp soy sauce; 4 tbsp white sesame seeds. For lime cup noodles: 1 pack Zaru Soba noodles; 1 lime; pinch black sesame seeds; 2 tbsp soy sauce; 2 tbsp sesame oil; 2 tbsp brown sugar; 2 tbsp garlic powder; 2 tbsp teriyaki sauce; 2 tbsp lime juice. 1-tier bento box.

Boil thinly sliced carrots; sauté in sesame oil soy sauce and sesame seeds. Boil noodles; carve out lime. Mix sauce ingredients. Curl noodles into lime cup, sprinkle with sauce and black sesame seeds. Add to bento box.

Cook rice, make onigiri using mold; stick mamenori patterns on. Place in bento. Add sesame carrots, corn croquettes and steamed peas to gaps. Cut a white sheet of mamenori with a snowflake punch and place onto noodles. Add apple slice cut into bunny ears shape.

KISSES BENTO FOR TWO

To prepare two bentos (halve to make one): 1 1/2 cups short grain rice; 4 oz ground beef; 1 tbsp soy sauce; 2 eggs; 2 tsp sugar; 8 dumplings; 6 stalks of asparagus; handful snow peas; 4 tbsp shelled edamame; 4 cherry tomatoes; 2 small carrots; 2 slices cheddar cheese; 2 orange wedges; 3 strawberries; 10 blueberries; 2 small dessert cakes. 1 tbsp canola oil. 2 2-tier bento boxes.

Cook rice. Boil edamame for six minutes. Place in a small container; sprinkle with salt. Beat eggs, combine with sugar, and scramble into small pieces. Fry ground beef with soy sauce until cooked through. Drain well and pat with paper towel. Steam asparagus for two minutes. Add snow peas and steam for two more minutes. Fry dumplings in a little canola oil until brown on all sides.

Combine rice, egg and ground beef. Place plastic divider in bento box to divide off one third of the bottom tier. Add rice mixture to larger side of

bottom tier. Once cool, press down on rice to pack it in. Arrange snow peas decoratively. In the smaller section of the tier, arrange steamed asparagus diagonally with a cherry tomato in the opposite corners. Garnish with carrot sticks. Fill top tier starting at the right. Stack dumplings Place edamame next to the dumplings. Stack cheese slices above edamame. In the far left of the tier, stack orange slices. Fill remaining space with strawberries, blueberries and dessert.

BEEF ROLLS RECIPE

5 oz extra lean ground beef; 1/6 cup lime juice; 1/6 cup soy sauce; 1 tsp brown sugar; 1/2 tsp chili sauce; 1/2 tbsp sesame oil; 1 stem lemon grass (white part only); 1 1/2 tbsp chopped mint; 1 tsp hoisin sauce; 7 sheets rice paper; 1 scallion.

Mix the first five ingredients; sit for 20 mins. Fry until beef is cooked. Mix in lemon grass, mint, hoisin sauce. Wrap in rice paper, tie with scallion slices.

HEART BENTO

To prepare two bentos (halve to make one): 1 cup rice; 1 tbsp red bean paste; 5 beef rolls; 4 asparagus stalks; 6-8 snow peas; 1 sweet potato; 2 tbsp shelled edamame; 1 kiwi; 2 strawberries; 1/2 orange; 2 strawberries; 12 blueberries; 6 slices cheese; 2 truffles; 1 tsp brown sugar; 1 tsp butter; pinch salt; white sesame seeds; 1 tbsp canola oil. 2 1-tier bento boxes.

Cook rice. Heat 2 tsp canola oil. Fry beef rolls over medium heat until the rice paper starts to crisp. Cut sweet potato into flower shapes, boil for two minutes. Add edamame and boil for an additional five minutes. Sprinkle potatoes with brown sugar. Steam asparagus for two minutes. Add snow peas; steam for an additional minute.

Form onigiri with triangle molds, add bean paste filling inside. Place onigiri, beef rolls, asparagus strips, sweet potato, truffle in box Slice kiwi and cut into flowers with a veggie cutter. Fill gaps with remaining ingredients.

BIRTHDAY SAILOR BENTO

1 small tomato; serving minced pork; 1 sheet nori; 1 kani kama fish cake; 2 quails' eggs; 1 carrot; soy sauce; sake; 1 oz broccoli; 1 slice ham; 1 hampen fish cake; 1 boiled potato; mirin; 1 cup rice; 1 fish sausage; 2 lettuce leaves; 1 tsp mentsuyu; 1/2 eggplant; 1/2 egg; handful frozen soy beans; 1/2 cup bread crumbs; serving eggplant pickles; 1 tsp eggplant pickle syrup; 1 tsp ketchup; 1 kabocha squash; flour; pinch pepper; 1 cherry; pinch salt. 1-tier bento box.

Marinate a quail's egg with pickled eggplant syrup, covering only bottom half of egg. Mix water and starch (1 tbsp/1/2 tbsp). Put lettuce into bento box. Cook rice and make two onigiri. Create sailors by wrapping nori around onigiri, and cutting it to make face and hair details. Cut hampen with thick tapioca straw; add to onigiri as sailor caps. Cut eggplant pickles with a thick straw for top of cap. Add ribbon details with kani kama.

Make potato croquette. Shape mashed potato with salt and pepper into life ring shape. Dust with flour and dip in beaten egg, then bread crumbs. Fry in hot oil until browned. Add detail using ham slices and carrots. Make mini sailor. Add nori and kani kama for detail and a slice of eggplant pickle as his cap. Make present by tying quail's egg with kani kama ribbon. Stir-fry pork, add chopped eggplant; season with soy sauce, sugar, sake and mirin. Add soy beans. Cook chopped kabocha squash with diluted mentsuyu for seven mins. Assemble in bento box with steamed broccoli, carrot flowers, tomato and fish sausage flower.

BIRTHDAY CROWN BENTO

Pancake mix for 2 1/2 pancakes; 1 tsp silver nonpareils; 2 tbsp marshmallow fluff; handful blueberries; 1 sausage; 2 mini hash browns; 3 glace cherries; 1 satsuma. 1-tier bento box

Make two pancakes, stack. Pipe pancake mix onto a griddle in a decorative strip; curve around pancakes, using marshmallow fluff to attach to stack. Decorate with silver nonpareils. Make '13' from blueberries attached with marshmallow fluff. Add hash browns, sausage and fresh fruit.

CROQUETTE VARIATION

Replace hash browns with croquettes: 1 can sweet corn; 1/2 pack of silken tofu; 1/2 cup flour; 1 tsp salt; Panko bread crumbs; vegetable oil.

Mix silken tofu, water and flour, adding the flour gradually. Add salt. Drain corn, add and stir well. Take a tablespoon of mix and form into a ball, roll in panko bread crumbs until fully covered. Flatten into coin shape, repeat. Freeze croquettes. Cook in hot oil until golden brown and microwave for 30 seconds. Pack into bento.

HALLOWEEN BENTO

2 red sausages; 1 slice cheddar cheese; 1 tsp mentsuyu; curry power; 1 boiled quail's egg; 1 chicken leg; soy sauce; corn starch; pinch salt; pinch pepper; 1 broccoli floret; 1 slice pumpkin; 2 maitake mushrooms; 2 lettuce leaves; 1 cup rice; 1 slice ham; 1 sheet nori; 1 tsp mayonnaise. 1 hampen fish cake; 1 tsp ketchup; 1 bouillon cube. 1-tier bento box.

Line bento box with lettuce. Divide broccoli into small pieces, boil. Peel carrot, slice and boil. Cut into crescent and star shapes with cookie cutters. Slice sausages at ends, into four pieces. Boil for 20-30 seconds. Cook boiled quail's egg with curry powder and bouillon cube and hot water until it is colored yellow. Add nori eyes and mouth to quail's egg, using mayo as glue. Cut chicken leg into bite-size pieces. Sprinkle chicken with salt and pepper, coat with corn starch.

Deep-fry the pumpkin and maitake mushroom, then fry chicken. Marinade pumpkin, maitake mushroom and chicken in diluted mentsuyu for 20 mins. Cut hampen fish cake into ghost shape with cookie cutter. Stir-fry with one side resting in soy sauce. Add nori eyes and mouth and ham cheeks, using mayo to stick. Stir-fry rice with ketchup, salt and pepper. Shape rice into Jack-O'-Lantern. Place eyes and mouth, made with nori seaweed sheet and cheddar cheese. Add to bento box as shown in picture.

CURRIED RICE VARIATION

Replace onigiri with curried rice: 1 cup steamed basmati rice; 1 cup frozen peas; 2-3 tbsp curry powder; 1 tsp garam masala; 6 tbsp butter.

Cook rice. Boil peas. Drain, add two tbsp butter, melt, then add curry powder. Cook and place in casserole dish with cooked rice. Heat oven to medium high. Top dish with butter and garam masala. Cook for 10 minutes.

SPOOKY BENTO

2 red sausages; soy sauce; pinch pepper; 1 sheet nori; pinch salt; 1 broccoli floret; 1 slice cheddar cheese; 1 tsp margarine; 1 portion squid; 1 quail's egg; pancake mix for 4 small pancakes; sake; 1 tsp potato starch. 1-tier bento box.

Line bento box with lettuce. Divide broccoli into small pieces and boil. Slice sausages at ends, into four pieces. Boil for 20-30 seconds. Mix pancake mix, fry four small pancakes. Cut pancakes into flower shapes with large cookie cutter. Put into bento box.

Make squid dumplings. Mince squid and add potato starch, sake, salt and pepper. Knead the dough well and make small round dumplings. Stir-fry with margarine and soy sauce. Make bat and Jack-O'-Lantern using cheese and nori seaweed sheet. Put onto pancakes. Make scull with boiled quail's egg and nori details, stuck on with mayo. Place remaining ingredients into bento box.

PUMPKIN BENTO

1 cup Chinese cabbage; 1 tomato; 3 mini bell peppers; 1 cup rice; 1 chicken breast; teriyaki sauce; 1/4 sheet nori. 2-tier bento box.

Cook rice. Marinate chicken breasts in teriyaki sauce for 30 mins. Grill chicken.

Chop tomato into wedges, place at bottom side of one tier of bento box.

Layer Chinese cabbage in rest of tier to form a bowl shape. Fill with sliced bell peppers, putting pepper tops to one side.

Fill half of other tier with rice. Slice chicken and arrange to look like a brick wall. Using a pairing knife, cut out small faces in the bell pepper tops.

Cut a small piece of nori to place inside each pepper top. This gives the pumpkin faces more contrast.

Cut out a mini nori moon and place it on the rice.

TOFU BITES VARIATION

Replace chicken with tofu bites: 3/4 cup flour; 4 oz tofu; 1 carrot; 1/4 onion; 1 tbsp garlic powder; 1 tsp cumin; 2 tsp cilantro; Panko bread crumbs; vegetable oil.

Crumble tofu, 2 tbsp water, grated carrot, chopped onion; stir in the spices. Mix in the flour. Shape a pinch of mix into a ball, roll in bread crumbs. Repeat until used up; deep fry in oil.

To prepare two bentos (halve to make one): 1 cup rice; 2 tsp red bean paste; 5 beef rolls; 4 stalks asparagus; 8 snow peas; 1 sweet potato; 2 tbsp shelled edamame; 1 kiwi; 2 gooseberries; 1/2 an orange; 2 strawberries; handful blueberries; 6 small slices cheese; 2 truffles; 1 tsp brown sugar; 1 tsp butter; pinch salt; 1 tsp white sesame seeds; 1 tbsp canola oil. 2 1-tier bento boxes.

Cook rice. Chop asparagus and snow peas in half. Cut kiwi into flower shapes. Fry beef rolls in canola oil until the rice paper starts to crisp up. Cut sweet potato into flower shapes, boil for two minutes, then add edamame; boil for additional five minutes.

Steam asparagus for two minutes. Add snow pieces and steam for an additional minute. Make two onigiri adding bean paste as filling. Sprinkle with salt and sesame seeds. Place onigiri and beef rolls in box. Stack beef rolls if the bento is deep enough, to save space. Place remaining ingredients into bento box as shown below.

FRUITY BENTO FOR TWO

To prepare two bentos (halve to make one): 1 cup rice; 3 frozen pork dumplings; 3 strips cooked chicken breast; 1 quail's egg; 3 strips green pepper; 2 chives; 3 slices lotus root; 1 red pepper; 2 stalks asparagus; 3 broccoli florets; 8 snow peas; 4 grapes; 1/2 blood orange; 3 strawberries; 8 blueberries; 2 small cakes; 1 sheet nori; 1 tbsp sesame seeds; 2 tbsp sushi vinegar; 1 tbsp white vinegar; 1 1/2 tsp teriyaki sauce; 1 tbsp canola oil; small container wasabi; small bottle soy sauce. 1-tier bento box (to share).

Cook rice. Pan fry dumplings in canola oil until wrapper browns. Steam broccoli and asparagus together for two minutes. Add snow peas, cut in half; steam for an additional minute. Bring two tbsp water and white vinegar to a boil. Add lotus root and red pepper. Cover and cook five minutes. Make sushi using pepper, chicken, chives and teriyaki sauce as filling. Sprinkle with sesame seeds. Add to bento. Boil quail's egg and pack in box with other ingredients.

LION BENTO

1 1/2 cup of rice; 2 tbsp daikon; 1 tbsp scallion; 1 tbsp bonito flakes; 3 oz beef; 2 slices cheddar; 1 egg; 3 frozen gyoza; 4 slices each green and yellow zucchini; 1/2 plum; 1 mini kiwi; 2 slices cucumber; 2 tbsp teriyaki sauce; 2 tbsp soy sauce; 1 tbsp canola oil; 1 sheet nori; 1 small chocolate. 2-tier bento box.

Mix soy sauce and daikon; marinade in fridge overnight. Cook rice. Mix with daikon and soy, chives and bonito flakes. Boil edamame. Fry dumplings. Fry beef with teriyaki. Make a thin omelette, cut and add nori to make lion. Cut cheese into letter shapes. Place on rice with edamame. Fit beef next to rice. Steam zucchini. Chop other ingredients and add to top tier.

LION VARIATION

Use omelette to create two smaller lion cubs, facing towards each other on rice. Cut cheese into sun shape.

1 cup rice; 1 tsp red bean paste; 4 slices cooked chicken; 2 frozen gyoza; 1 egg; 1 1/2 cups spinach; 2 stalks asparagus; 2 broccoli florets; 2 snow peas; 2 tbsp shelled edamame; 1 sweet potato; 1 cherry tomato; 4 grapes; 1 strawberry; 2 blackberries; 1 sheet nori; 1 tbsp canola oil. 1-tier bento box.

Make spinach heart as in Faces Bento recipe (left). Form eight onigiri 'capsules' using a mold. Write message on a sheet of paper using letter stencils. Staple paper to nori and cut out letters with an exacto style knife. Prepare remaining ingredients as in bentos on left, place in box.

CHECKER BOARD RECIPE

Cut four horizontal and four vertical shallow slices across the apple slice, cutting through the peel but not the flesh. Slide a knife under every other square to remove the peel. Rub with lemon juice to keep from browning.

FACES BENTO FOR TWO

To prepare two bentos (halve to make one): 2 cups rice; 2 tsp red bean paste; 1/2 chorizo sausage; 5 frozen dumplings; 2 eggs; 3 slices each green and yellow zucchini; 3 stalks asparagus; 8 snow peas; 4 broccoli florets; 3 cups spinach; 9 pieces persimmon; 3 strawberries; handful blueberries; 2 small date squares; pinch salt; 1 sheet nori; 1 tbsp canola oil. 2 1-tier bento boxes.

Cook rice. Heat canola oil. Fry dumplings until wrapper is browned. Fry sausage and slice. Steam spinach, drain and form into a six inch long oval shaped strip. Pour 2 tbsp beaten egg in pan on medium heat. Place spinach on too. When egg is cooked on the bottom, roll spinach to layer omelette around it. Pour another tbsp of egg in the pan. Repeat until it is about an inch wide. Make onigiri, add red bean paste filling inside and decorate with nori. Steam asparagus, zucchini, broccoli and snow peas. Cut omelette and arrange in heart shape. Pack bento with ingredients as shown above.

FROWN BENTO FOR TWO

To prepare two bentos (halve to make one): 1 1/2 cups rice; 2 tsp red bean paste; 6 oz lamb steak; 1 cup shredded sweet potato; 2 tbsp minced white onion; 1/4 Chinese cabbage; 2 tsp beaten egg; 4 frozen gyoza; 1 bunch baby bok choy; 2 stalks asparagus; 4 broccoli florets; 6 snow peas; 4 cherry tomatoes; 8 grapes; 1 plum; 3 strawberries; handful blueberries; 2 small date squares; 1 sheet nori; pinch salt; pinch pepper; pinch nutmeg; 1/2 tsp Italian seasoning; 2 tbsp canola oil; 1 tbsp sesame oil. 2 2-tier bento boxes.

Cook rice. Mix sweet potato, onions, egg and a dash of salt, pepper and nutmeg. Form into six patties; fry in sesame oil until browned. Fry lamb strips in canola oil and Italian seasoning until cooked through. Add chopped Chinese cabbage, cook until soft. Fry dumplings in canola oil. Fry bok choy in sesame oil. Steam asparagus, broccoli and snow peas. Make two onigiris. Position in bottom tiers of bentos. Place remaining ingredients in boxes as shown above.

HOLIDAY FUN BENTO

1 tofu bite; 1 Yves meatless hot dog; 1 cup rice; Mrs. T's Potato and Cheddar mini pierogies; 3 broccoli florets; 1/2 lemon; 1 slice mozzarella cheese; 1 cherry tomato; 3 red grapes; 5 sugar snap peas; 1/4 red bell pepper; 1 sheet nori. 2-tier bento box.

Cook rice, pack into both tiers. Place mini pierogies at one end of top tier. Place a tofu bite in the center, decorate with nori. Cut a red pepper hat, place on top of tofu bite, add mozzarella for hat detail and scarf. Cook the hot dog. Cut off one end and make horizontal cuts along sliced end. Add nori and mozzarella eyes and nori mouth. Steam sugar snap peas and cut diagonally. Layer on top of rice in a tree shape. Cut out a mozzarella star with a tiny fondant cutter and place at the tip of the tree. Sprinkle sugar dots along the branches. Slot grapes, broccoli and tomato into gaps, add one slice and one wedge of lemon.

KIDICHI VARIATION

8 oz. dry yellow lentils, soaked; 2 cups basmati rice; 1 cup vegetable stock; 2 tbsp butter; 2 tsp ground cumin; 2 tbsp garlic powder; pinch salt; pinch pepper; 1 tsp cayenne powder; 1 tsp ground cilantro; pinch garam masala. 2-tier bento box.

Cook rice. Melt butter, add cumin. Add lentils and sauté for three minutes. Add garlic, salt, pepper, cayenne and cilantro. Pour in stock, simmer until reduced. Add garam masala and rice. Add to bento.

SANTA BENTO

1 croissant; 1 slice soy bologna; 1 lettuce leaf; 1 slice cheese; 1/2 tsp hot mustard; 4 baby tomatoes; handful blueberries; 1/2 cup radiatore pomodoro pasta; 4 cubes sage infused cheese. For Santa Claus Treats: 2 Ice cream cones; 2 sugar cookies; icing; red food color gel; sugar dots; m&ms; cashews; sultanas. 1-tier bento box.

Cook pasta, add cheese cubes. Make croissant sandwich using ham cheese, lettuce and mustard. Make Santa Claus Treats. Microwave store-bought icing just until melted. Mix in a generous amount of red food color gel and stir. Dip tips of ice cream cones into red icing; allow to dry. Spoon a generous amount of icing onto a sugar cookie. Spoon mixed m&ms, cashews and sultanas into an ice cream cone. Pick up the sugar cookie and upend it onto the cone. Turn over and place onto wax paper to set. Repeat. Once cones have set pipe on white icing for the hat, eyes, coat, buttons and beard. Use sugar dots for eyes and buttons. Pack the bento as shown below.

XMAS WREATH BENTO

1 Tofu bite; 1 Yves meatless hot dog; 1 serving kidichi (see Kidichi Variation left); Mrs. T's potato and cheddar mini pierogies; 3 spears steamed broccoli; 1 lemon slice; 1 slice mozzarella cheese; 3 cherry tomatoes on the vine; 4 sugar snap peas; 1 slice lemon peel; 1/2 red bell pepper. 2-tier bento box.

Arrange four mini pierogies in a slight fan shape against the side of the top tier. Add cherry tomatoes, broccoli spears and tofu bite. Make mozzarella and nori eyes for the mouse, adding a sliver of red pepper for the nose, and nori whiskers. Cook veggie hot dog and cut into slices. Place two on the tomatoes, touching the tofu bite to make mouse ears. Add a mozzarella star and lemon wedge.

Fill bottom tier 3/4 full with kidichi. Cut snap peas diagonally to make rhomboid pieces. Arrange on top of the kidichi in a circle, turning some inward and some outward. Cut a piece of red bell pepper into a bow shape, place at top of the circle. Cut lemon peel into three circles, place on the snap pea pieces. Three round slices of hot dog finish the wreath.

BOO! BENTO

1 slice ham; 1 sausage; 1 lettuce leaf; pinch salt; 2 broccoli florets; 1 /2 cup rice; 1 sheet nori; 1 tbsp ketchup; 2 cheese slices; 1 tbsp carrot flavoring; 1 slice carrot; 1 tsp mayonnaise; 1 egg. 1-tier bento box.

Layer ham slice and cheese slices, roll up and refrigerate for one hour.

Line bento box with lettuce.

Divide broccoli into small pieces. Boil with carrot slice.

Cut top of sausage into six pieces at top, boil for 20-30 seconds.

Cook rice and gently stir with carrot flavoring.

Make pumpkin shaped onigiri.

Place into bento box.

Take sliced cheese and ham from refrigerator and cut in half.

Cut sliced cheese into ghost shape with cookie cutter.

Make ears, nose and mouth with nori seaweed sheet.

Put them onto ghost.

Cut boiled carrot with straw and use for ghost's tongue.

Cut eyes, "BOO!" letters and web for Jack-O'-Lantern with nori seaweed sheet and cheese slice.

Add to Jack-O'-Lantern.

In a mixing bowl, put some salt, beaten egg and rest of cheese.

Pour the egg into pan and stir-fry egg on low heat.

Roll the egg in the pan, make tamagoyaki.

Cut tamagoyaki in half.

Put ghost shaped cheese into bento box.

Make cheeks with ketchup.

Add sausage, broccoli and other ingredients to bento box, placing as shown.

BOO! VARIATION

See ingredients list from Boo! Bento (above).

Prepare bento as in Boo! Bento recipe.

Take sliced cheese and ham from refrigerator and cut in half.

Cut sliced cheese into skull shape.

Cut skull features (eyes, nose and teeth) from nori seaweed sheet.

Put them onto skull.

Cut boiled carrot with straw and use for blood detail.

LOVE BENTO

1 slice white bread; 1 slice wheat bread; 1 tbsp peanut butter; 1 tbsp jelly; 1 mini Babybel cheese; 1 egg; 1 cup rice; 1 tsp red food coloring; 1 sheet nori; 1/2 strawberry; 1 mini cheesecake. 2-tier bento box.

Make peanut butter and jelly sandwiches in white and wheat. Cut with penguin and heart-shaped cookie cutters, replace hearts with alternating color heart. Place mini heart sandwich above penguins. Add Babybel cheese to box. Cook rice, with food coloring. Use mold to make heart-shaped onigiri. Hard boil egg and mold into heart shape. Place in top tier. Add nori decoration, strawberry, and mini cheesecake cut into heart shape.

LOVE VARIATION

See ingredients list from Love Bento (above). Replace 1 tbsp peanut butter; 1 tbsp jelly with 1 slice salmon; 1 tbsp cream cheese. Prepare as above.

VALENTINE BENTO

2 baked chicken wings; 1/2 cup rice; 2 drops red food coloring; 1 stalk asparagus; 1 slice dashimaki tamago (egg omelette); 1 imitation crab stick; pinch roasted sesame seeds; 1 kiwi fruit; 1/2 red bell pepper; handful raspberries; 1 lettuce leaf. 1-tier bento box.

Line bento box with lettuce leaf, making sure the leaf is visible around the edges. Place the baked chicken wings into the box, laying them slightly on top of each other.

Cook rice with 1 drop red food coloring. Mold into onigiri, place next to chicken wings. Cut bell pepper into hearts and tuck into onigiri. Sprinkle with roasted sesame seeds. Steam asparagus. Slice diagonally. Lay the stalks onto the chicken wings. Slice tamago (add red food coloring to recipe) and cut into flower shape with vegetable cutters. Slice the imitation crab stick diagonally. Cut the kiwi fruit. Add ingredients to box, fill gap with raspberries.

FESTIVE GYOZA BENTO

1/2 cup rice; 1 slice ham; 1 slice cheese; 2 chipolata sausages; 2 slices streaky bacon; handful rocket leaves; 2 stuffing balls; 2 cherry tomatoes; 1 tbsp cranberry sauce. For festive gyozas: 1 small box sage and onion stuffing; 2 onions; 1 1/2 oz butter; 1 tsp sugar; pinch salt; olive oil; 5 oz turkey breast; 1/2 tsp salt; 1 tsp soy sauce; 26 gyoza skins; oil. 1-tier bento box.

Make festive gyozas.

Mix sage and onion stuffing.

Use 2 1/2 oz for the gyozas, the rest can be made into stuffing balls.

Finely chop onions, cook on a very low heat with butter and sugar until they turn golden brown.

This could take an hour or more.

Shred the turkey breast with a knife.

You will end up with meat that's finely cut but has a bit more texture than mince.

Mix the caramelized onion, the raw turkey breast, 2 1/2 oz of stuffing and the salt and soy sauce together.

Fill gyozas. Place a small amount in the middle of a dumpling skin.

Wet the edges and fold it in half, pleating the edges, using a gyoza press or by hand.

Heat some oil in a pan and add six gyozas.

Pour water into the pan to cover 3/4 of the gyozas.

Cover and cook until the water has evaporated.

Remove the lid and fry until the bases are crispy.

Cook rice and make star shaped onigiri.

Top with star shaped ham and cheese.

Add pigs in blankets (chipolata sausages wrapped in streaky bacon and baked in the oven).

Fill spaces in bento with rocket leaves, stuffing balls, tomatoes and cranberry sauce for a dip.

Add two gyozas, freeze the others for future bentos.

FESTIVE GYOZA VARIATION

Make Bedam Burfi as dessert: 1 cup finely ground almonds; 3/4 cup sugar; 1/2 cup whole milk; 3 tbsp butter; 1 1/2 tsp ground cardamom.

Mix ground almonds, sugar, cardamom and milk in a sauté pan for five minutes. Add butter.

Stir vigorously.

When thickened, turn down heat; cook and stir for a few more minutes.

Grease casserole dish, spread in mixture.

Cool and cut into pieces.

TWO HEARTS BENTO

1 cup rice; 3 oz thinly cut pork; 4 frozen gyoza; 1 crepe; 1 stalk asparagus; 4 broccoli florets; 10 snow peas; 2 slices carrot; 7 pieces pineapple; 1 gooseberry; 1 cherry tomato; 2 strawberries; 5 blueberries; 1 small chocolate; 1 tbsp cream cheese; 1 tsp raspberry jam; pinch salt; 1 tsp sesame seeds; 1 strip nori hearts; 2 tbsp canola oil. 1-tier bento box.

Cook rice. Fry pork in canola oil. Steam broccoli, asparagus and snow peas. Pan fry gyoza. Spread cream cheese and jam on crepe. Roll and slice. Cook rice, use mold to make two heart-shaped onigiri. Position in bento with nori and carrot hearts. Place remaining ingredients as shown above.

TWO HEARTS VARIATION

Add: 1 drop red food coloring.

Add food coloring to rice when cooking to make red heart onigiri.

CHICKY BENTO FOR TWO

To prepare two bentos (halve to make one): 2 cups rice; 6 oz lean ground chicken; 4 tsp corn starch; 4 tsp flour; 2 tsp egg; 1/4 cup scallions; 11 sheet nori; 2 eggs; 1 baby bok choy; 6 slices each green and yellow zucchini; 6 asparagus stalks; 2 cherry tomatoes; 2 small carrots; 2 small slices iceberg lettuce; 1 chunk Gouda cheese; 4 strawberries; 10 blueberries; 2 small prepackaged dessert items; 1 tsp sesame seeds; 1 tbsp canola oil; 1 tbsp sesame oil. 2 2-tier bento boxes.

Cook rice, shape into triangles using mold. Combine chicken, corn starch, flour, beaten egg and minced scallions. Split mixture into eighths and shape into patties. Wrap nori strip around each patty; fry in canola oil. Boil eggs. Sauté bok choy in sesame oil. Steam zucchini and asparagus. Create egg chick by gently cutting a zig zag circle around the top of the egg so that the top of the egg white can be removed. Chop remaining vegetables and fruit and assemble bento box as shown in image below.

NOODLE BENTO FOR TWO

To prepare two bentos (halve to make one): 3 baby carrots; 1 inch each green and yellow zucchini; 4 half inch strips green pepper; 7 oz package shirataki (yam) noodles; 6 broccoli florets; 6 oz chicken; 1 tsp chicken seasoning; 1 orange; 1 kiwi; 2 inches cucumber; 2 pieces Gouda cheese; 4 cherry tomatoes; 2 strawberries; handful blueberries; 2 pieces prepackaged cake; 2 tbsp canola oil; 1 tbsp soy sauce; 2 sprigs parsley. 2 2-tier bento boxes.

Stir-fry slices of carrot, green zucchini, yellow zucchini, and green pepper in 1 tbsp canola oil, and soy sauce until cooked. Cook and drain shirataki. Add to stir-fry, fry for an additional two minutes. Steam broccoli. Fry chicken in 1 tbsp canola oil. Place chicken, broccoli and shirataki stir-fry in bottom tier. Slice cucumber and orange. Place cucumber slices on the far left and orange wedges on the right. Add kiwi slices, cheese, small cake, strawberries, blueberries and cherry tomatoes. Fill gaps with parsley.

To prepare two bentos (halve to make one): 1 1/2 cup of rice; 2 tsp red bean paste; 1 breaded chicken breast; 2 quails' eggs; 2 cherry tomatoes; 4 small pieces havarti; 1/3 cup chopped Chinese cabbage; 1/2 can mandarin oranges; 8 stalks asparagus; 8 snow peas; 6 slices cucumber; 1 kiwi; 10 blueberries; 2 strawberries; 2 mini corn bread muffins; 2 truffles; 1 tsp rice vinegar; 1 sheet nori; pinch black sesame seeds; 3 tsp canola oil; pinch pepper. 2 2-tier bento boxes.

Cook rice. Fry chicken in canola oil, slice into strips. Mix cabbage, mandarin oranges, canola oil, rice vinegar, pepper and mix well. Rest for 20 mins, drain and pack. Steam asparagus and snow peas for an additional minute. Boil quails' eggs, place on skewer with tomato. Mold rice into twelve onigiri, adding red bean paste filling. Decorate with nori strips and sesame seeds. Slice kiwi and make into hearts with a cookie cutter. Assemble bento as shown below, placing onigiri and chicken in bottom tier.

CHICKEN BENTO FOR TWO

To prepare two bentos (halve to make one): 2 cups rice; 2 tsp red bean (adzuki) paste; 6 frozen pork dumplings; 6 oz pre-cooked chicken; 3 avocado strips; 3 cucumber strips; 4 cherry tomatoes; 4 asparagus stalks; 6 broccoli florets; 6 raspberries; 3 strawberries; 10 blueberries; 10 slices cheddar cheese; 2 small marzipan fruits; 1 sheet nori; 1 tsp sesame seeds; 2 tbsp sushi vinegar; pinch salt; 1 tbsp canola oil. 2 2-tier bento boxes.

Pan fry dumplings, slice chicken into strips. Chop other vegetables. Steam broccoli and asparagus together for three minutes. Cook rice. Take 1 cup of rice and spread on a plate. Fold vinegar into rice and cover while the rice cools. Take remaining rice and shape into two onigiris using mold. Add red bean paste as a filling, sprinkle salt and sesame seeds on the outside. Press one nori strip on the edge of each onigiri. Make maki sushi using avocado and cucumber as filling. Pack bento as shown above. Cut cheese shapes and add to bottom tier.

HEART BENTO FOR TWO

To prepare two bentos (halve to make one): 1 cup rice; 2 tsp red bean paste; 6 oz chicken; 2 tbsp soy sauce; 1/2 tsp grated ginger; 1 cup peeled and grated lotus root; 3 tbsp corn starch; 1/4 cup chive; 1/4 cup basil; 2 eggs; 3 slices each green and yellow zucchini; 5 cherry tomatoes; 5 stalks asparagus; 3 cups spinach; 1/2 avocado; 2 tbsp honey; 2 tsp grated carrot; handful lettuce; 3 strawberries; 12 blueberries; 2 sprigs fresh parsley; 2 small dessert cakes; pinch sesame seeds; 2 nori flowers; 1 tbsp canola oil; 1 tbsp sesame oil. 2 2-tier bento boxes.

Cook rice. Heat canola oil, fry chicken with honey, ginger and soy sauce. Combine lotus root, corn starch, chives and basil. Form into six small patties and fry in sesame oil. Prepare sushi and egg hearts (see Faces Bento). Mold rice to make two onigiri; add red bean paste filling. Place nori strips and sesame seeds on onigiri. Mash avocado and mix with 1 tbsp honey. Place in two small containers with a nori heart on each. Assemble bento as shown above.

SNOWMAN BENTO

2 red sausage; 3/4 oz salmon; 1 cheese slice; 1/4 tbsp sugar; 1 slice thin salami; 1 quail's egg; 1/2 oz broccoli; 1/2 tsp mirin; 1/4 tbsp sake; 1 sheet nori; 1/2 oz sweet potato; 1 cup rice; 1 tsp soy sauce; sake; pinch salt; 1/2 egg; 1 simeji mushroom; 1 lettuce leaf; 1 tsp plum flavoring. 1-tier bento box.

Line bento box with lettuce. Boil broccoli. Slice sausage into six pieces at end, boil for 30 seconds. Cook rice and stir in plum flavorings. Make 2 onigiri, tie with nori belts. Add to bento box. Peel skin of sweet potato into checked pattern. Boil. Cut cheese into snowman using cookie cutter.

Make eyes and mouth with nori seaweed sheet. Make cheeks, muff and cap with salami. Make nori snowflakes on cheese circles. Stir-fry salmon. Add simeji mushroom and season with soy sauce, mirin, sake and sugar until it boils down. Pack bento as shown left.

SICK DAY BENTO

1 cup rice; 1 package plum-flavored rice seasoning powder; 2 eggs; 3 baby carrots; 2 drops black food coloring; 2 drops red food coloring; 1 small piece blue roll-up fruit snack; 1 small piece white rice paper; 2 strawberries; 1/4 cup deli bean salad; 1/4 cup melon pieces. 2-tier bento box.

Cook rice and mix in seasoning. Pack cooled rice in 2/3 bottom tier. In the final 1/3 of the tier, add a thin layer of rice to the bottom. Hard boil eggs. Dip a flexible toothpick in food color to draw face on one of the eggs. Prop the egg in the hollow. Cut a rectangle of the blue fruit roll snack to place as a compress. Use a paring knife to shave thin slices of carrot; arrange around the egg as hair. Cut thin slices of egg white from the remaining egg. Carve two slices into hands and use an aspic cutter to cut stars from the rest of the egg white. Scatter the stars over the blanket as decoration. Wad the rice paper in one hand to serve as a tissue.

Trim a piece from the end of a red wooden toothpick. Press into the mouth to serve as a thermometer. Place silicone cupcake cups in top tier and fill with the remaining ingredients.

VAMPIRE VARIATION

See ingredients list from Sick Day Bento (left), replace 1 package plum-flavored rice seasoning powder; 3 baby carrots; 1 small piece blue roll-up fruit snack; 1 small piece white rice paper with 1 strip nori; 1 drop red food coloring. 2-tier bento box.

Prepare bento as in Sick Day Bento, adding one drop food coloring to rice when cooking. Draw vampire face on egg using red and black food coloring. Cut nori into shapes for hair, cape collar and cape detail. Add egg hands.

EASTER BENTO

1/2 cups rice; 1 drop pink food color; 1 drop yellow food color; 1 tbsp Thai peanut sauce; 1 cup shredded iceberg lettuce; 3 hard egg-shaped candies; 2 carrots; assorted chunks of colorful fruit; handful chocolate chips. 1 divided food-storage box, letter-shaped fondant cutters.

Cook half of rice with pink and half with yellow food coloring. Mold rice in bunny and chick-shaped molds, using peanut sauce as filling. Scatter shredded lettuce in the larger portion of the divided container. Place onigiri on and candies on lettuce. Use a mandolin slicer to cut long ribbons from the length of the carrot. Drape strips like noodles into smaller portion of the container. Hard boil eggs. Use a paring knife to slice medium-thin, flat pieces of egg white. Cut out the letters "HAPPY EASTER" and arrange them on the carrot strips. Spear fruit on food picks. Arrange to one side of carrots. Microwave chocolate chips until melted. Use a flexible toothpick to add dots for eyes and nose.

PUMPKIN BENTO

TOP RIGHT: 1/4 cup leftover entree; 1 wrapped sweet-cake; 5 nuggets crystallized ginger; 1 serving leftover stir-fried vegetables; 1 idli, made from boxed mix, colored orange; 1 sprig cilantro; 1/2 cup frozen red seedless grapes; 8-10 baby carrots, well-washed; 2 pumpkin mini-muffins; 1/2 apple; 1 tbsp prepackaged caramel apple dip; 1 pinch crushed peanuts; black decorating gel. 2-tier bento box.

Paint a Jack-O'-Lantern face on the idli using decorating gel. Add leftover entree and stir-fried vegetables to two sections of the divided tier. Arrange wrapped sweet-cake and candied ginger to top right section. Transfer idli to lower right corner of the tier. Tuck in cilantro to act as pumpkin vine. Chop apple, place in silicone cup, garnish with caramel and chopped nuts. Place in center of undivided tier. Add pumpkin muffins and carrots. Grapes fill in the blank space between the carrots and the muffins.

EASTER BUNNY BENTO

1/2 cup shredded lettuce; 1/2 cup rice; 1 sheet nori; dab sakura denbu; 3 broccoli florets; 2 quails' eggs; assorted food coloring; 2 hot dogs. 1-tier bento box.

Line bottom of box with lettuce. Cook rice, shape into bunny using mold. Add nori face and sakura denbu accents. Cook hot dogs, slice into flower shapes. Hard boil eggs and dye with a few drops of food coloring.

ST. PATRICK'S DAY BENTO

2 mini steamed dumplings; 2 quails' eggs; 1 pepper; 2 scotch eggs; 2 broccoli florets; 2 cherry tomatoes; portion leftover tonkatsu chicken; 1/2 cup egg noodles; 3 carrot flowers. 2-tier bento box.

Fry eggs in 2 rings of sliced pepper. Cook noodles, steam broccoli. Add butter to noodles, garnish with pepper shamrock. Pack as shown on right.

WINTER SOBA BENTO

Make zaru soba noodles, onigiri and sesame carrots, from Snowflake Bento recipe; 3 sugar snap peas; 1 miniature corn croquette; 2 apple slices. 1-tier bento box with side dish.

Pack onigiri, a paper cup full with sesame carrots, a corn croquette, steamed peas and apple slices into the bento box. Twirl the soba noodles into a separate bowl. Pour in a little bit of sauce, add mamenori snowflakes.

APPLE BUNNY VARIATION

Replace apple slices with 1 apple.

Take an apple and slice off a side. Cut side into vertical strips about 1/2 inch to 2/3 inch wide. Carefully create a V with a knife into the peel of the apple in the middle of a strip. Cut off the peel from the edge to the inner angle of the V. Soak in a mixture of water and lemon juice for one minute. Tuck the apple bunnies into the bento box.

GOOD LUCK BENTO

3 Morningstar Farms Chik'n nuggets; handful snap pea snacks; 5 carrot sticks; 1 fruit roll; handful mixed dried fruit; 4 Graham crackers; 1 tbsp peanut butter; 1 portion leftover curried rice; 1/2 cup peas; Alphatots French fries. 2-tier bento box.

Cook Chik'n nuggets. Spread peanut butter on crackers to make sandwiches. Make a rose from fruit roll. Steam peas and cook fries. Pack curried rice into a measuring cup. Pack bento as shown below. Add three carrot stars, cut using a fondant cutter.

FALL COLOR BENTO

1 cup rice; Japanese gummy candy; 1 piece takuan; 2 carrot slices; 1/2 cucumber; 1 pea; 1 green seedless grape; 1 sheet nori. For udon noodles with fall sauce: 1 pack udon noodles; 1/2 cup vegetable stock; 1 tbsp soy sauce; 1 tbsp garlic powder; 1 tsp ground ginger; 1 tsp sesame oil; pinch black sesame seeds. 1-tier bento box.

Cook noodles. Heat sesame oil in a skillet, make up the vegetable stock.

Add noodles to hot sesame oil, stirring quickly.

Add the vegetable stock, soy sauce, garlic and ginger.

Keep stirring until the sauce is mostly absorbed.

Cook rice. Mold into large round onigiri, place in bento and fill space with udon noodles, sprinkling a few black sesame seeds over them.

Use a Japanese vegetable cutter to cut out one carrot ginkgo leaf and one takuan ginkgo leaf.

Shape two cucumber slices with a knife for hair.

Cut a carrot bow. Lay in place. Use a punch to make nori face.

Add steamed pea for nose.

Next, put in the green grape.

Prop wrapped candy beside it for color.

FALL FRUITS BENTO

3 miniature corn croquettes; 2 frozen vegetable gyoza; 1 cherry tomato 6 broccoli florets; 1 cup rice; 1 carrot; 1 sheet nori; 3 Japanese maple cakes; 6 blackberries. 2-tier bento box.

Cook rice, mold onigiri.

Steam broccoli, cook croquettes and gyoza.

Place onigiri into bottom tier, with gyoza broccoli and corn croquettes.

Wedge a cherry tomato into gap.

Cut a pumpkin shape from a carrot. Add nori face.

Place on top of the onigiri.

Layer three maple cakes into top tier with blackberries.

PICNIC BENTO

4 lettuce leaves; 2 cups rice; 1 drop pink food coloring; 1 drop blue food coloring; portion leftover meat; 1 sheet nori. 1-tier bento box.

Divide rice into two pots, add food coloring before cooking.

When cooked, using your hands or an onigiri mold, make 16 round onigiri, filled with leftover meat.

Add nori faces made with punches.

Line bento box with lettuce.

Add onigiri to box.

SPORTS VARIATION

4 lettuce leaves; 2 cups rice; 1 drop orange food coloring; portion leftover meat; 2 sheets nori. 1-tier bento box.

Divide rice into two pots.

Add orange food coloring to one before cooking.

When cooked, make 16 round onigiri, filled with leftover meat.

Add nori details to make orange onigiri basketballs and white onigiri baseballs.

Line bento box with lettuce. Pack.

PARTY BENTO

1 tin Spam; 1 tbsp soy sauce; 1 tbsp sugar; 3 cups rice; furikake; 4 lettuce leaves; 1 serving pipi kaula (smoked beef); 1 sheet nori; sprinkling shrimp flakes; 9 sprigs parsley. 2-tier bento box.

Cook rice. Simmer Spam slices in soy sauce and sugar, flavor with furikake.

Use special mold to make Spam musubi. Pan fry sliced pipi kaula, line top tier with lettuce; pack as shown. Make 16 round onigiri, filled with filling of your choice.

Add nori faces and place shrimp flakes for cheeks. Pack in bottom tier with parsley.

GLOSSARY

A

aburaage   deep-fried tofu, often used to wrap inarizushi

aduki   a red bean

ahi   Hawaiian name for yellowfin or bigeye tuna

B

bento   a single portion packed meal, created at home or readymade

bouillon   a broth

bumbu   Indonesian spice blend

C

cabbage bao   steamed bun, filled with cabbage

calamansi   small Filipino citrus fruit

cannellini   a small, white kidney-shaped bean

canola oil   variety of rapeseed oil

cha siu bao   Chinese pork buns

chai tea   spiced tea, sometimes milky

chicken inasal   Filipino chicken dish, marinated chicken grilled on a bamboo skewer

chicken parmigiana   Breaded chicken dish, fried breaded chicken in a marinara sauce, topped with mozzarella and baked

Chinese cabbage   Chinese leaf vegetable, also known as snow cabbage. Variations include bok choy and pak choi

cremini mushrooms   smaller, younger form of Portobello mushroom

D

daifuku   Japanese confection, rice cake filled with sweet filling (most often anko)

daikon   Japanese mild-flavored large white radish

dashi   Japanese soup or stock, forms the base for miso soup

dashimaki tamago   rolled egg omelette

denbu oboro   processed fish cake, also known as imitation crabmeat or seafood salad

donburi   a rice bowl dish

dragon fruit   sweet pitaya fruit, native to Central and South America

E

edamame   baby soybeans

eggplant   oval-shaped dark purple vegetable, also known as aubergine

F

forbidden rice   short-grained dark purple-colored rice

frittata   Italian omelette, often filled with meat or vegetables

furikake   Japanese flakes, used to sprinkle on rice. Often includes ground fish and seaweed

G

garbanzo beans   edible beans, also known as chickpeas

gingko   herb with distinctive shaped leaf

gochujang   Korean hot sauce

guava roll   fruit roll made from dried guava

gyoza   Chinese dumpling filled with ground meat or vegetable filling

H

harissa   spicy North African red paste made from chilis

hijiki   Japanese seaweed

I

idli   savory Indian cake

inarizushi   aburaage stuffed with sushi rice

K

kabocha   Japanese winter squash

kamaboko   Japanese processed semi cylindrical fish cakes, pink or white-colored

kichdi   South Asian lentil and rice dish

kim chee/kimchi   Korean fermented vegetable dish

kiwano   horned melon

kolrabi   spherically-shaped cultivated cabbage

koshihikari   popular Japanese variety of rice

M

maki sushi   rolled sushi, generally wrapped in nori

mentsuyu   Japanese soup base

mirin — rice wine, similar to sake
mochi — Japanese rice cake

mochi candy
Japanese rice cake with sweet filling

morcon — Filipino beef dish
musubi — Hawaiian onigiri-style snack, made of rice, spam and nori

N

nonpareils
tiny sugar balls, also known as sprinkles, or hundreds and thousands

nori — dried seaweed sheets

O

okonomiyaki sauce
Japanese sauce, similar to Worcestershire sauce

onigiri — rice ball

P

pad Thai sauce
sauce made from tamarind paste, fish sauce, chili sauce and sugar

Panko/Panko bread crumbs
Asian variety of packaged bread crumbs

perilla (shiso)
red or green herb, from the mint family

pierogy — Slavic stuffed dumplings
pipi kaula — Hawaiian-style beef jerky

Q

quinoa — green leaf vegetable

R

ramen noodles
wheat noodles, sometimes packaged dried with sauce

ratatouille
French stewed vegetable dish, made from eggplant, tomatoes, bell peppers and zucchini

S

sakura — Japanese flowering cherry trees

sakura denba/sakura denbu
ground sweetened codfish, colored pink

Sakura Noodles
brand of Japanese and Oriental style noodles

sanbaizuke
pickled daikon

scallion greens
green onion, also known as spring onion

shirataki — Japanese low-carbohydrate noodles

shiso furikake
furikake flavored with Japanese basil

shiso (perilla)
red or green herb, from the mint family

shumai — Chinese steamed dumpling
SPAM — brand of canned precooked meat, made from pork shoulder and ham by the Hormel Foods Corporation
star anise — star-shaped spice with a liquorice-like flavor

T

taco seasoning
blend of spices made to flavor tacos

tahini — sesame seed paste
takuan — Japanese daikon pickle

tamagoyaki
Japanese omelette made by rolling together layers of cooked egg

teriyaki sauce
Japanese sauce made from soy sauce, sake and sugar, can be used as a marinade for meat

tobiko — flying fish roe
tofu — soy milk curd, pressed into blocks
tuyo — dried salted fish

U

umeboshi — picked ume fruit

unagi sauce
eel sauce

usuyakitamgo
thin omelette

V

Vietnamese bean cake
mung bean cake from Vietnam

W

wakame — seaweed, used in miso soup
wasabi — Japanese horseradish, a hot green paste often served with sushi

wasabi peas
roasted green peas coated in wasabi paste

Y

yaki soba noodles
wheat flour noodles

Z

zucchini — small summer squash, also known as courgette

CONTRIBUTORS AND CREDITS

Graffito Books would like to thank all of the contributors who have conceptualized, designed, made, photographed and shared their unique bento recipes.

Special thanks to Amorette Dye for writing the Bento Basics introduction.

Mari Baker

Mari 'Natakiya' Baker is a bento fanatic, weaver, mom and belly dance teacher. She loves anime, manga and books, but her passion is textiles. She is a weaver and an embroiderer, making Japanese kumihimo cords and knits whenever possible. Studying Asian textiles opened up her interest in bentos and she has presented panels about Bento lunches at anime conventions.

bentoanarchy.blogspot.com

Images on 12-13, sequence photos on 15 Recipes and images: 28-29 Aargh Bento; 36-37 Balloon Bento; 42-43 Dragon Bento, Sweet Love Bento; 62-63 Savories Bento; 68-69 Veggie Curry Bento, Hearts Bento; 70-71 Smiley Face Bento; 72-73 Fun Hearts Bento, Lion Bento; 74-75 Caterpillar Bento; 76-77 Koala Bento; 98-99 Flat Pie Wedge Bento, Flat Pie Recipe; 110-111 Bun of Steel Bento, Teriyaki Tofu Recipe; 112-113 Bouquet Bento, Smiley Heart Bento; 116-117 Bratwurst Bento; 126-127 Airplane Bento; 130-131 Monkey Faces Bento; 132-133 Toddler Bento; 134-135 Pretty Rabbit Bento; 178-179 Autumn Bento, Fried Rice Bento, Sausage Roll Bento; 246-

247 Half Moon Bento, Tonkatsu Pork Bento; 250-251 Triangle Bento; 326-327 Snowflakes Bento; 336-337 Holiday Fun Bento, Kidichi Variation, Santa Bento, Xmas Wreath Bento; 350-351 Good Luck Bento, Fall Color Bento, Winter Soba Bento, Apple Bunny Variation, Fall Fruits Bento.

Francesca Bondy

flickr.com/photos/francescabondy

Image on 10-11

Recipes and images: 26-27 Two Flowers Bento; 114-115 Butterfly Bento, Hearts Bento, Radish Heart Bento, Scottie Dog Bento; 156-157 Orecchiette Bento, Little Stars Bento, Omelette Bento; 168-169 Couscous Bento, Chickpea Bento, Tofu Soba Bento; 170-171 Rocket Bento, Frittata Bento, Canellini Bento; 190-191 Hummus Bento; 192-193 Walnut Bento, Eggplant Bento; 196-197 Pasta Bento, Feta Bento, Lentils Bento, Rocket Bento, Romaine Bento; 198-199 Two Muffin Bento; 230-231 Maki Sushi Bento, Avocado Bento, Inside Out Bento, Carrot Sushi Bento; 266-267 Sushi Roll Bento, Simple Bento.

Arielle Brousse

flickr.com/photos/thewordunheard

Recipes and images: 82-83 Moth and Lamp Bento; 84-85 Pig and Star Bento, Angry Peach Bento; 160-161 Sunburst Bento, Pretzel Bento; 162-163 Midnight

Bento, Lentil Curry Bento; 166-167 Cow Bento; 172-173 Garden Bento; 202-203 Candy Bento, Bird's Nest Bento; 212-213 Vietnamese Bento, Star Bento; 214-215 Alien Bento; 216-217 Striped Bento; 220-221 Cute Egg Bento, Steam Chicken Bento, Liberty Bento; 222-223 Cobb Bento, Colors Bento.

Gemma Cox

Gemma is a Japanophile, Asian food lover, and the editor of NEO magazine, the UK's only anime, manga, Asian film and Japanese pop culture magazine. Her Bento Business website is a resource for bento fans and features a blog, picture galleries and a collection of recipes. She is constantly on the lookout for stockists of Japanese food and bento boxes in the UK, and is creating a resource directory for UK bento makers. Any feedback or contributions are gratefully received!

bentobusiness.co.uk

Recipes and images: 64-65 Garlic Prawn Bento; 66-67 Hamburger and Pepper Egg Bento; 68-69 Egg Chick Bento; 94-95 Teriyaki Salmon Bento; 96-97 Omelette Bento; 132-133 Meatballs Bento; 138-139 Indian Chicken Bento; 164-165 Pork Pie Bento; 226-227 Vegetarian Bento; 228-229 Chicken Wing Bento; 232-233 Teriyaki Chicken Bento; 236-237 Salted Salmon Bento; 240-241 Mayo Prawns Bento; 244-245 Inari Sushi Bento; 248-249 Hot Cucumber Bento; 238-239 Scattered Sushi Bento, Stuffed Chili Bento; 250-251 Balsamic Chicken Bento;

254-255 Pork and Egg Bento, Hijiki Bento; 256-257 Miso Chicken Bento; 258-259 Ginger Pork Bento, Golden Chicken Bento; 262-263 Thai Omelette Bento, Spicy Thai Bento; 264-265 Carrot Rice Bento, Nikujaga Bento; 266-267 Yaki Udon Bento; 268-269 Nikujaga Bento, Leftover Bento; 270-271 Tea Marbled Egg Bento, Yakitori Bento; 272-273 Chicken Wing Bento; 306-307 Spanish Omelette Bento; 342-343 Festive Gyoza Bento.

Amorette Dye

Amorette's work has appeared in numerous books and magazines. She currently resides with her family in the Midwestern United States and regards bento as both a creative outlet and a labor of love.

Images on 12 and 14; Bento Basics text Recipes and images: 18-19 Goose Bento, Guitar Bento; 22-23 Marie Antoinette Bento, Health Spa Bento; 24-25 Bento In Bento, Used Car Lot Bento; 30-31 Geisha Bento, Zucchini Bento; 32-33 Aquarium Bento; 34-35 Lobster Bento, Torii Gate Bento; 38-39 Tree Frog Bento, Giraffe Bento; 40-41 Orchid Bento, Hive Bento, Painter's Bento; 44-45 Heron Bento, Ladybug Bento, Garden Bento; 46-47 Sakura Girl Bento, Fake Kamaboko Recipe; 48-49 Frappuccino Bento, Mantis Bento; 50-51 Snow Globe Bento, Dessert Sushi Bento; 52-53 Green Eggs and Ham Bento; 54-55 Jaws Bento, Tour Eiffel Bento; 64-65 Daikon Sakura Bento; 66-67 Elephant Bento; 78-79 Almond Sakura Bento; 86-87 Grouchy Boy Bento, Scared Sarnie Bento, Monster Bento; 88-89 Happy Tomato Bento; 100-101 Small Packages Bento, Gyoza Girls Bento; 104-105 Mini Caramel Apples; 150-151 Banana Bento; 176-177 Taco Bento;188-189 Chick Berry Bento, Adventure Bento; 200-201 Pancakes Bento; 226-227 Heart Sushi Bento; 346-347 Sick Day Bento; 348-349 Easter Bento, Pumpkin Bento.

Ruthy Fraterman

Ruthy says that making bento boxes "is one of my ways to make daily life more fun and less predictable". She loves Japanese food, bought all her lunchboxes in Tokyo and loves packing them because they look so cute.

flickr.com/photos/puckduvinylle

Recipes and images: 58-59 Pacman Bento; 70-71 Ducky Bento, Crayfish Bento; 146-147 Green Tea Bento;150-151 Gyoza Pumpkin Bento; 166-167 Muffin Bento; 176-177 Sweet 'n' Sour Bento; 180-181 Spinach Bento; 198-199 Kim Chee Bento; 200-201 Veggie Bento; 204-205 Miso Stew Bento, Sakura Denba Bento; 206-207 Flowers Bento, Muffin Bento, Gyoza Bento; 210-211 Meatball Bento, Bun Bento; 234-235 Fig Bento, Seaweed Salad Bento, Yaki Onigiri Bento.

Jennifer King

Jennifer says that for her, bento is not as much about the box as it is the aesthetics, appeal, and balance of the food. She chooses natural colors or black boxes to compliment and protect the meal. Jennifer makes bento most days, but doesn't always photograph them. "If there is a new technique or something special I want to share, I will, but sometimes it is just a secret for me".

Photography by Michael Beasley.

mbeasleyphotography.com

michael@mbeasleyphotography.com

Recipes and images (photography by Michael Beasley): 278-279 Pink Noodle Bento; 282-283 Marbled Egg Bento, Divided Bento; 288-289 Seaweed Salad Bento; 284-285 Kitsune Soba Bento; 286-287 Inarizushi Bento; 290-291 Soup Bento, Tree Bento; 292-293 Beef Roll Bento, Painted Bento, Sardine Bento; 300-301 Daikon Bento, BBQ Chicken Bento; 302-303 Three Onigiri Bento, Soup and Tofu Bento; 318-319 Nigiri Sushi Bento.

Myria Kutchravy

Myria is from Yokosuka, Japan. She is the mother of two kids, age thirteen and one and a half. Her website is:

MyBentoLunch.com

Recipes and images: 20-21 Fishies Bento; 38-39 Cherry Blossom Bento; 78-79 Fox in the Henhouse Bento; 108-109 Star Pancake Bento; 116-227 Rabbit Bento; 132-133 Wrap Sandwich Bento; 134-135 Red Sandwich Bento; 146-147 Two Bear Bento, Sugarbunnies Bento, Egg Daisy Bento; 166-167 Daikon Bento; 328-329 Birthday Crown Bento; 340-341 Love Bento; 348-349 Easter Bunny Bento, St. Patrick's Day Bento.

Chrissie Mata

Chrissie, or kaoko as she's known online, is an advertising copywriter by profession. She likes preparing bento because it's delicious, economical, challenging, artistic and the closest she can get to playing with her food.

kitchencow.com

Recipes and images: 26-27 Starry Night Bento; 58-59 Peeping Mice Bento; 60-61 Under the Sea Bento; 90-91 Chicken Fingers Bento, Hambearger Bento, Cute Bento, Skeleton Bento; 92-93 Nest Bento, Salad Monster Bento; 126-127 Korean BBQ Chicken Bento; 140-141 Seamonster Bento; 156-157 Morcon Bento; 164-165 Visayan Bento; 194-195 Chicken Popcorn Bento; 202-203 Spam Bento; 210-211 Salmon Bento; 216-217 Fried Rice Bento; 218-219 Quails' Eggs Bento; 246-247 Tsukune Bento.

Joyce Ng

Freshly out of college, Joyce is currently working as a news reporter in Vancouver. She enjoys planning dinner parties for friends and sampling new recipes. Her bentos can be found on her blog:

franktastes.wordpress.com

Recipes and images: 94-95 Breakfast Bunny Bento; 98-99 Moustache Bento; 242-243 Golden Rice Bento, Rice Ball Bento, Seaweed Strip Bento, Pattern Bento; 260-261 Prawn Ball Bento, Salmon Fillet Bento; 276-277 Polka Dot Bento, Asparagus Bento; 294-295 Shrimp and Egg Bento, Korean Beef Bento, Checked Bento; 298-299 Seaweed Square Bento, Message Bento, Chili Bean Bento; 304-305 Chive Pancake Bento, Ginger Pork Bento, Ground Pork Bento; 306-307 Omelette Bento, Spaghettini Bento, Sausages Bento; 316-317 Salmon Avocado Bento, Mini Burger Bento, Potato Salad Bento; 320-321 Tonkatsu Pork Bento, Fish Fillet Bento; 322-323 Dots and Stripes Bento, Pork Bento, Patties Bento.

Maki Ogawa

Maki is a bento designer and mother of two sons. She has created bento recipes for Japanese companies and some of her bentos appear in Face Food, published by Mark Batty.

Images on 13
Recipes and images: 80-81 Three Piggies Bento, Chicken and Egg Bento, Panda Bento; 88-89 Three Chicks Bento; 102-103 Penguin Bento; 108-109 Burger Bear Bento; 118-119 Piggy Onigiri Bento; 120-121 Clock Bento, Russian Doll Bento; 122-123 Piggy Bento, Pink Pigs Bento, Bunny Bento, Funny Man Bento, Chestnut Bento; 128-129 Whale Bento, Mini Cooper Bento, Flat Pigs Bento;

130-131 Little Cows Bento; 136-137 Three Piggies Bento, Panda Sundae Bento; 138-139 Ladybug Bento; 140-141 Two Lions Bento; 142-143 Pig and Monkey Bento, Smiley Cloud Bento; 144-145 Kitty Bento, Fried Noodle Bento; 314-315 Shisho Bento, Sandwich Bento; 328-329 Birthday Sailor Bento; 330-331 Halloween Bento, Spooky Bento; 338-339 Boo! Bento; 346-347 Snowman Bento.

Amanda Quintana-Bowles

Amanda's Bento-licious project was born in January 2007 as "part of a personal journey to incorporate beauty and enjoyment into all aspects of life". Her bentos are all about portion, proportion and presentation.

bento-licious.com

Recipes and images: 62-63 Cucumber Tail Bento, Fishtank Bento, Circles Bento; 82-83 Peek-a-Boo Bento; 152-153 Stripes Bento, Tequila Bento, Santa Fe Bento; 154-155 Trail Mix Bento, Pastoral Bento, Atomic Bento; 174-175 Not Just Fruit Bento, Miss Muffet Bento, Short Sweet Bento, Happy Garden Bento; 184-185 Breakfast Bento, Sweet Chili Bento, Summer Grill Bento; 186-187 Hyacinth Bento, Yaki Onigiri Bento; 198-199 Tofu Scramble Bento; 208-209 Antipasti Bento, Red Potato Bento; 212-213 Harvest Bento; 214-215 Edamame Bento; 252-253 Modern Art Bento, Haiku Bento, Takeaway Bento, Hefty Miso Bento; 260-261 Furikake Bento.

Jacki W

jackiw.blogspot.com

Crystal Watanabe

Crystal is a 29-year-old Japanese American woman born and raised on the Big Island of Hawaii. Crystal turned her creativity to food in April 2007, when she began the Weight Watchers Core program. By combining the program with bentos she lost 22 pounds in four months. Wife to Randall and mother to two toddlers, she is currently in the process of writing a bento book and writes about life and foodie adventures on her blog Adventures in Bentomaking.

aibento.net

Jennifer Wolpoff

Jen has always been fascinated with Japanese culture. When she first discovered the art of bento she was enthralled by the obnoxiously cute containers. As time progressed she "learned that making cute food isn't as daunting as is seems. There's nothing better than sitting down with a super cute lunch".

flickr.com/photos/mothhunter

jenwolpoff@gmail.com

All remaining recipes and variations by Graffito Books.